FROM IDEA
TO FUNDED PROJECT

FROM IDEA
TO FUNDED PROJECT

GRANT PROPOSALS FOR
THE DIGITAL AGE,
5th EDITION

JULIA M. JACOBSEN
AND JAN FAY KRESS

PRAEGER

Westport, Connecticut
London

Library of Congress Cataloging-in-Publication Data

Jacobsen, Julia M.

　　From idea to funded project : grant proposals for the digital age.—5th ed. / Julia M. Jacobsen and Jan Fay Kress.
　　　p.　cm.
　　Rev. ed. of: From idea to funded project / by Jane C. Belcher and Julia M. Jacobsen. 4th ed.
　　Includes bibliographical references and index.
　　ISBN-13: 978–0–275–99087–9 (alk. paper)
　　1. Endowments—United States—Handbooks, manuals, etc.　2. Education—United States—Finance—Handbooks, manuals, etc. I. Kress, Jan Fay, 1955–　II. Belcher, Jane C. (Jane Colburn), 1910– From idea to funded project.　III. Title.
　　LB2336.B43　2008
　　379.1′2140973—dc22　　　2007036157

British Library Cataloguing in Publication Data is available.

Library of Congress Catalog Card Number: 2007036157
ISBN-13: 978–0–275–99087–9

First published in 2008

Praeger Publishers, 88 Post Road West, Westport, CT 06881
An imprint of Greenwood Publishing Group, Inc.
www.praeger.com

Printed in the United States of America

The paper used in this book complies with the Permanent Paper Standard issued by the National Information Standards Organization (Z39.48–1984).

10　9　8　7　6　5　4　3　2　1

To my good friend and coauthor, the late Jane C. Belcher, PhD, Professor of Biology and DuBerg Chair of Ecology at Sweet Briar College. Dr. Belcher was the coauthor with me (Julia Mills Jacobsen) for the first four editions of this book. She was noted for her precise use of words, subtle sense of humor, and a "never give up" attitude. After writing her first successful proposal to the National Science Foundation, she continued developing proposals that added up to several million dollars for Sweet Briar College.

Contents

Preface

Ideas are products of individual human minds. Some of the ideas that emerge in educational, cultural, health-related, community, service, and faith-based organizations are potentially as important to the institutions as their endowments. These ideas are the concern of this guidebook: how to encourage their articulation, how to muster the cooperation necessary to turn them into formal blueprints, and how to secure whatever support is needed to see them materialize as projects serving the interests of the originators and their institutions.

Today's Christopher Columbus must find a different kind of patron, usually a foundation or government agency known to have an interest in the area of the quest. Once a possible sponsor has been identified, a proposal must be written, a proposal so well prepared and so convincing that it will receive serious consideration for support in competition with numerous other proposals. This guidebook will assist you in conducting your research for appropriate funding sources, in writing a proposal, and in all the preliminaries leading to a funded project. It will also include developing the idea into a detailed outline and securing support of others in your organization that will be affected by the project.

This new and expanded edition of *IDEAS*, now titled *From Idea to Funded Project: Grant Proposals for the Digital Age, 5th Edition*, contains listings of useful resources and the most recent data on forms and required information for conventional and electronic submission of proposals. This fifth edition provides new information for locating funding sources. The fourth edition relied heavily on telephone numbers and addresses; this new edition relies on Web-based resources. Because of the ever-increasing emphasis that grant-making agencies place on accountability and evaluation of funded projects, we have expanded sections on the administration of grants and the evaluation of projects.

All names and addresses of agencies and organizations and all required documents included in this book were current in 2007. We urge you to double check with your funding source to be certain you have the most current requirements for submission and administration.

Acknowledgments

The authors wish to express appreciation to their families for their love and unconditional support during the revision of this fifth edition and Martha Mansfield Clement and Flora Harper for proofing and objective comments.

A special note of thanks must go to two students John Emmanuel Domingo and Persis Piaget for scanning copy from the previous edition.

PART I: A PROCESS FOR DEVELOPMENT OF IDEAS

Introduction

PURPOSE

This book discusses how institutions, and the individuals, who make up those institutions, create and develop ideas. Though reference may be made more frequently to institutions than to individuals, the reader must never forget that it is the people who count, and it is the ideas they produce that are the heartbeats of the institutions.

The people within an institution can be classified as either those who actually perform the institution's primary function, the faculty, professional staff, nurses, therapists, etc., and those who play a supporting role, the administrators. The partnership between these two groups can and must create an atmosphere that eliminates whatever reluctance people feel in expressing ideas and stimulates the germination of ideas. Although, in general, it is the role of the administrative staff to welcome the ideas produced by members of the institution and assure moral, institutional, and financial support for those ideas worth adopting, sometimes the roles are reversed; that is, an individual in either position may at one time be a creator and at another time a supporter of developing ideas. In spite of shifting roles, the ideal partnership maintained in a healthy institution guarantees the production and nurturing of ideas. This book provides suggestions that will help maintain this partnership.

Ideas range over a spectrum from good to bad, and this year's bad idea may become next year's good idea. How can ideas be selected, put into motion, doctored, trimmed, embellished, fitted to other ideas, and attuned with institutional goals? How can they be judged feasible in terms of resources both within and outside the institution?

The life of an idea, from the moment of its conception to the time of fruition, particularly when it needs help from outside the organization, can be long and often risky. The object of this guidebook is to provide a pattern or method for directing an idea through its entire existence. We, leaning on our own and others' experience, believe this method is adaptable to varied institutions, varied demands within the institution, and varied stages of developing ideas—from those within a small organization to those affecting the entire institution and from those involving purchase of equipment to those involving radical alterations in the tasks of many people. This process ensures the continuous involvement of all individuals who will be affected by the idea or who can influence its development and provides a continuous, step-by-step evaluative process. By minimizing or eliminating risks through constant evaluation, the pattern *or* method will lead to a mature, refined proposal and a significant and successful project.

The purpose of this book will have been achieved if it aids educational, cultural, health-related, community, service, and faith-based organizations in ensuring cultivation of ideas and then turning those ideas into realities by finding and applying the needed human, material, facility, and financial resources.

INSTITUTIONS AND IDEAS

Every organization is the result of a person's idea; the idea then persists as the organization's founding principle. Throughout its life, the organization stimulates people to produce new ideas which, in turn, determine change, all within the bounds of the founding principle. Ideas and organizations thus work together to produce not only change, but orderly change, improvement, correction of flaws, and adjustment to changing environments.

A history of the organization reveals ideas that were exemplary and ones that were duds, ideas that met long-term needs and those that met short-term ones, the modest ideas and the ones with wide ramifications, and those with glowing potential but ended in disaster and the ones with dubious promises but ended successfully. And finally, every organization has its reserve of ideas that are waiting for their time to come.

The method described in this guidebook stimulates the generation of new ideas and ensures development of ideas to the point where they will be put to work in serving the institution and the individual who produced them.

A COOPERATIVE APPROACH TO DEVELOPING IDEAS

In working with large and small educational, cultural, health-related, community, service, and faith-based organizations, we have had many years of experience with the entire process of developing ideas: planning projects, preparing proposals, administering grants, and achieving goals. We have also gained first-hand familiarity with the process as it operates in larger educational institutions and in community service organizations. Along with success, we have known failure.

We have seen a wide range of reference materials, attended conferences with representatives from funding agencies, and taken part in workshops on proposal writing. All of these were concerned with just one or maybe a few aspects of the process of development of ideas—and this, perhaps, is the clue to, the rationale of this publication.

The process of developing ideas into a funded project is all too often segmented instead of being dealt with as an entire process. A great majority of "how to" guides or "how to" workshops focus only on one or two of the segments of the proposal development process (e.g., preparation of a proposal, sources of funds, or administration of grants), and many institutions fall into the same trap and parcel out these segments in the same fashion when developing an idea.

The practice of parceling out does permit several functions of the process to go on simultaneously, an attractive method if time is of the essence. There are, however, serious weaknesses to be weighed against this one advantage. When segments of work are done independently, most of the benefits resulting from integrated, comprehensive planning are sacrificed, such as the sharing of ideas and experiences.

A working partnership among participants is the best way to avoid pitfalls and to produce a good proposal. If a working partnership is not established, those in charge of the different segments may forget or misinterpret the original idea and be ignorant of changes as the idea develops; they forfeit the opportunity of guiding the growth of the idea during its formative stages and educating each other in the creative and supportive activities applied during all stages and hence lose the opportunity to provide their own insights during the constant evaluative process.

How often, for instance, have development officers misrepresented an idea when conferring with funding agencies? How often has a faculty member muddled the budget when preparing a proposal? How often has a site visit been a disaster because an administrative officer has been ignorant of the project?

We will propose a constant evaluative system to avoid such pitfalls.

The idea that develops most successfully is not fragmented but, like a developing organism, retains its integrity throughout an orderly developmental process that has well-marked stages and critical points.

Our process helps reduce or eliminate obstructionist attitudes and procedures and accentuates cooperative ones, secures not only the involvement but also the commitment of all participants, and stimulates each participant to contribute at every stage of development. The process is thus educational for all and encourages the articulation and implementation of more ideas.

The most fertile ground for the emergence of ideas is in that part of the organization most directly concerned with the mission of the organization. For example, the faculty in an educational institution, the health care providers in a home health organization, the artists in a community art center, and the parishioners and church leaders know the problems best and are most likely to find the best solutions. The process described in this guidebook will ensure that all the participants in a given project will not be lost or shunted aside as the idea develops. This process will ensure continued contribution in all stages of development within an environment that encourages their inventiveness and imagination.

WHO NEEDS THIS GUIDE?

Any individual affiliated with a nonprofit, educational, health-related, service, or faith-based organization and needing assistance in finding additional human, material, facility, and financial resources, whether within or from outside the institution, should benefit from the process described in Part I of this guide and will find updated, varied, and useful "yellow page"-like resources in Part II. Successful projects are a "win-win" situation for the individual and the institution it represents.

The type of nonprofit institution we refer to in this guidebook is best described by the Internal Revenue Service in a digest of the IRS code prepared by the Lutheran Resources Commission, Washington, DC, during the seventies. The quote follows:

> The Internal Revenue Service requires that an organization seeking to qualify for exemption from Federal income taxes under section 5O1(c)(3) must file information which will show, among other things, that:
>
> 1. The organization is organized exclusively for, and will be operated exclusively for, one or more of the following purposes: Charitable, Testing for public safety, Religious, Literary, Scientific, Education or Prevention of cruelty to children or animals.
> 2. No part of its net earnings will inure to the benefit of private shareholders or individual's; and
> 3. It will not, as a substantial part of its activities, attempt to influence legislation, or participate to any extent in a political campaign for or against any candidate for public office.

We could have legitimately used any nonprofit organization, such as the local historical society, the visiting nurse agency, or a food bank to demonstrate our process of developing the idea. Because of our experience, we will use the small liberal arts college as our example of an institution. Small colleges have traditionally proven to be producers of ideas, innovators, and experimenters, particularly in periods of social turbulence. Unlike the large, prestigious institutions, small colleges were slow to discover ways of securing the assistance that was made so abundantly available during World War II to the present. Today small colleges have found ways of securing aid but the springs are being wrung dry by competing societal interests and needs. They must learn to meet stiff competition for assistance, which ranges all the way from advice on better ways to use the already available human, material, facility, and financial resources to the securing of grants to establish new programs.

This guide, we hope, will bring together institutions needing help and agencies whose function it is to supply help, never forgetting that the essential element in the process is showing the imaginative individual what to do to turn dreams into reality.

Origin and Early Development of an Idea

ROLE AND RESPONSIBILITY OF THE INSTITUTION

Institutions of all kinds must recognize that ideas are its lifeblood and that although there is no way of predicting where ideas will emerge, the most rewarding ones are most likely to arise from that group most closely associated with the mission of the institution. While we can provide no prescription guaranteeing idea production, our general observations suggest that the most favorable milieu is the one marked by freedom, informality, open doors, a strong commitment to the institutional goals, and lack of barriers among parts of the institution. Each institution must find its own "yeast" and make it clear that ideas are valued whether or not they are adopted or developed.

HOW TO DEVELOP AN IDEA

The *Originator of the idea* is the key person in the process discussed in this book. Without an idea, nothing will happen. We quote some views on "how to develop an idea" from a paper written by Dr. St. Elmo Naumann, which was given at a workshop at Lynchburg College, in Lynchburg, Virginia. Dr. St. Elmo Naumann has written several books on philosophy, and was a professor of philosophy at Christopher Newport College of the College of William and Mary and has served in the U.S. Navy.

We think it is the most succinct description of an "idea" that we have found. The following is quoted with his permission:

> *An idea is an invention.*
> *It must be related to a problem which it solves (this may be an intellectual problem).*
> *The more important the problem,*
> *The more important the idea.*

Ways of Developing an Idea:

1. Read the most authoritative sources until you come to the point where the sources disagree! At that point, you are in a position to make a discovery of your own.

2. Talk with the leading figures in your field. Attend their lectures and ask them careful (and difficult) questions. Ask what their next project is going to be. This may tell you what direction research is going to take.
3. Write the most significant thinkers, if they are too far removed for you to see. If you ask them (courteously) a knowledgeable question, the reply will indicate the direction their thought is taking on the problem at issue.
4. Translate a significant article or book not generally known in this country. The interaction between a new perspective and more familiar ways of thinking may suggest a new path for research. Even administrators can make use of the method of translation.
5. Contemplate your own experience. If there is a frustration blocking your way to fulfillment, you may be able to invent a solution with wider application. "To believe that what is true for you, in your private heart, is true for all mankind: that is the essence of genius." Trust your own instincts.
6. Hurry! If you don't want that new idea, someone else does. The discovery will be made by someone. "Live life as though it were a cavalry charge!"

Dr. Naumann's philosophy is simple: No one will force you to have an idea or to express your idea to others. Read about your subject and talk to others about it. Don't work in secrecy. Again in his words, "Your aim should be to know more about your subject than anyone else in the world."

This last line of Naumann's quote is important to remember and should be emphasized. Do your research and know more about your subject than anyone else!

ROLE AND RESPONSIBILITIES OF THE ORIGINATOR OF THE IDEA

After coming up with an idea, the Originator will instinctively imagine steps in the idea's development:

1. The extent to which the idea will solve the basic problem.
2. The extent to which it will create new problems.
3. The extent to which those affected by the idea will respond to it.

Exhibit 1. Titles of People Involved in the Development of Ideas.

Higher Education Agency	Faith-Based, Service, Community Agencies	Health Care
Department Chair Department Members	Division Director Staff Members	Division Director Physicians, Nurses, Therapists (OT, PT, SLP)
Academic Dean Chief Fiscal Officer	Organization Director Chief Fiscal Officer	Executive Director/Administrator Chief Fiscal Officer
Chancellor/President Grants/Sponsored Programs Officer	Board Chair Fund Raiser/Development Officer	Board Chair Fund Raiser/Development Officer

If the idea stands up to this period of self-evaluation, it is ready to be described to others.

Up to this point, the Originator has sole control of the idea and of how far details should be worked out before the idea is shared. Sharing of the idea is really important. Consider what your reaction would be if you were the Department Chairman or lab assistant.... Everybody else knew about this idea, and you have not been informed. You as the Department Chairman would be taken aback knowing you are the one who would have to approve of this and convince the President this idea should go forth. If you were the lab assistant, this idea would double your work.

The Originator should recognize, however, that the idea, once shared, will affect the thoughts and lives of others. The Originator must anticipate who will be affected if the idea develops, how they will be affected, and what role each person will play in the process.

The Originator should compose a list of those most likely to be affected and, at the most propitious moment, share the idea with one of them, probably the department head or supervisor, and seek advice for the next steps. The people to be affected would probably include those described in Exhibit 1.

Let's assume the proposal has been fully developed, internally approved, and submitted to one or more appropriate funding agencies. At least one agency has approved it for funding. The Originator then notifies all concerned in the project, making sure that all the participants understand their roles; the goals, freedoms, and limitations in each role; and the manner in which separate goals will ultimately fit to make an integrated whole.

The Originator must then supervise all portions of the project while keeping the overall goal in clear focus. He or she must also see that all records are kept, particularly that meticulous, day-by-day financial records are available at all times, and that expenditures are consistent with line items in the budget section of the proposal.

As the project develops, changes in the original plans are almost inevitable, for an idea doesn't stop growing or changing just because it has been detailed and its implementation has been funded. Participants discover new possibilities or find unexpected pitfalls; personnel may change and the resulting changes in areas of expertise call for adjustments; and even inflated costs of equipment prohibit some procedures. It is the Originator's responsibility to weigh alternatives and, if necessary, request that the funding agency allow certain changes to be made.

The Originator will be responsible for the momentum of the project, for setting and meeting deadlines, and for maintaining morale among the group. In other words, the Originator becomes the Project Director.

SPECIFIC PEOPLE AND THEIR TASKS

Who are the people the Originator/Project Director needs to notify? They probably would be those listed in Exhibit 1, depending upon which of the five types of organization applies for funding. As we proceed, you can adjust this chart to fit the titles in your organization. It should be recognized at the outset that institutional projects require change, and change inevitably entails major and minor adjustments, compromises, and realignments of priorities. In other words, change affects all the people involved. Though one person articulates the idea that grows into a project, the full development of the project requires aid from those who will be affected by it, those trained to deal with special facets of its development, and those responsible for making change an orderly and constructive process.

Ideally, the various people assisting in a project provide support and enthusiasm, and understand each other's roles and views so well that success is assured. This group is the single most potent factor serving the harmony, effectiveness, and ultimate success of the developing project. The most severe threat to a project's success is failure to communicate within the group.

To avoid failure, therefore, all affected people should meet regularly throughout the life of the project, not only during the preliminary stages. Much communication can be carried on through e-mail conferencing. One of the advantages of electronic communication is creation of a written record. Live meetings can be reserved for the most important issues. Providing refreshments can encourage attendance of these meetings.

Originator of the Idea/Project Director

The Originator/Project Director must share the idea, probably, first with the person who she/he reports to. This could be the department chair, supervisor, minister, manager, and/or head nurse.

The person responsible for "coordinating" plans is called the Grants/Sponsored Programs Officer. The Chair and Grants Officer, assuming they express approval and willingness to cooperate, will advise the Project Director on procedures. Some of the procedures will undoubtedly relate to the academic or professional aspects of the project, others to the logistical or managerial aspects. Procedural failure in either category, may result in poor communication, delays, and unexpected *snafu* and can often kill a plan almost before it has seen the light of day.

The next duty of the Originator/Project Director will be to describe the idea to appropriate colleagues and administrative officers. Together, all of these people will become the group that will aid the Project Director in guiding the plan throughout its life. Project Directors may have many unexpected tasks to perform, but one thing is certain—they will have to stay with their projects from start to finish and be responsible for making or approving all substantive changes as the plans evolve.

Department Chair

The Department Chair is in the best position to judge the merits of a plan in terms of feasibility, desirability, and possible ramifications within the department. In examining the plan, this person must also consider the kinds of encouragement and constructive contributions to be counted on from other members of the department. It goes without saying that if a Department Head wishes to encourage the professional development of all department members, when a plan proposed by one of these members is approved, he or she will take whatever steps are necessary to see the project through to completion with the Project Director.

The first steps would include planning time and resources if the project calls for changes in schedules and staffing and balancing the new plan with other ongoing departmental projects.

The Department Chair, whether a member of the group guiding the new project or not, must be familiar enough with the project to

1. solve problems of time and personnel,
2. present it effectively with representatives of funding agencies on site visits, and
3. interpret the significance of the new project to those outside the department.

Once the proposed idea is approved, the Chair will combine whatever talents of diplomacy, persuasion, and understanding she/he may have in securing positive responses from those who will be directly or indirectly related to the success of the project.

Department Members

Members or staff, depending on areas of specialization, talents, general interests, and available time in their schedules, may be called on to fill major or minor roles in a developing project as one of their departmental tasks. Such responsibilities are a normal part of life within a department and the Chair usually will make suitable adjustments if new duties jeopardize their other responsibilities.

Academic Dean

The Academic Dean, or the person responsible for leadership in planning the academic program, is the officer with the most comprehensive understanding of the entire instructional program. The Dean will be inevitably intimately involved with any new idea affecting the curriculum and teaching faculty. Insights gained as Academic Dean enables that person to judge not only the feasibility and desirability of a new academic venture in the context of institutional goals, but also to provide expert advice on procedure, timing, human resources, and economy of effort during the entire period of development. The Dean will also help describe the plan to the representatives of funding agencies when they make site visits and to interested faculty, students, and visiting graduates and parents.

Chief Fiscal Officer

The Chief Fiscal Officer is one person completely familiar with all details of the institution's finances. A new project requires resources, including financial resources. The money, whether found within the institution or sought from outside donors, contracts, or grants, must be considered in reference to the institutional budget. The Fiscal Officer is responsible for considering all financial facets of the new proposed project, including matching money, cost-sharing, indirect costs, social security payments, and record keeping for audit. Schedules for outlay of funds and requests for payment must also be made by the finance office.

President/Chancellor

The President reinforces some of the contributions of the Fiscal Officer and Dean, and is the person who speaks officially for the institution, bearing the overall responsibility for its vigor and the success of new *ideas*. If funds are sought from an outside source, it is the President, or in some cases the Vice President or Provost, who signs the proposal and, if the proposal is accepted, the final contract. The President may deputize a representative to the group guiding the idea's growth but ultimately should be familiar with the final proposal.

Grants/Sponsored Programs Officer

The Grants Officer decides which agencies would be appropriate sources of funding if financial assistance is sought from outside the institution. It will be this officer who will undoubtedly assist in preparing a proposal and often, before submitting a proposal, will visit or make contact with selected agencies to discover whether or

not they would be interested in the project. It is important, therefore, that this officer should understand not only the nature of the project but also the ways in which the realization of the project's goals would benefit the institution. The Grants Officer can prepare for the tasks of composing and presenting a proposal only by participating in the whole process of planning.

If the institution has no grants officer on its staff to coordinate the kind of planning being described, it should designate such a person. In most of the institutions with which we are familiar, it is the Grants Officer, Director of Development, or Vice President for Advancement who is responsible for seeking outside support (sponsored or externally funded) for new projects. This person is the logical coordinator, because his/her work with externally funded, i.e., sponsored, programs and research requires coordination of academic, development, and administrative issues.

The Grants Officer, a catalyst, should have a talent for making things happen. The responsibilities may include convening an appropriate mix of participants, timing, establishing momentum and maintaining pace, setting deadlines, facilitating mechanics of the planning procedure, taking initiative, ensuring communication among participants, and avoiding pitfalls. In short, the Grants Officer should be a "gear greaser," diplomat, politician, source of information, and gadfly all in one. Without someone to coordinate the effort, the plans will get bogged down, deadlines will be missed, serendipitous opportunities will pass unnoticed, frictions will develop, and participants will fail to appreciate their own and other's roles.

The Grants Officer will probably be the first person after the Department Chair to discuss the plan with the Project Director and to assess its feasibility. From the moment of approval, the Grants Officer will be the chief agent in guiding development of the idea and guarding its integrity, in assisting the Project Director/Originator in every way, and in helping to prepare a proposal. If a grant is received, the Grants Officer will guide the Originator/Project Director and all the participants in administering the grant and proceeding to the desired goals.

The most pressing responsibilities of the Grants Officer are in the process of proposal development, planning and scheduling work, preparing the proposal so that it will be ready for internal approval in time to meet the deadline for submission to the selected funding agency. Early in the process, the Grants Officer should prepare a timetable to cover the entire period (Exhibit 2).

Exhibit 2. Six-Month Timetable.

JUNE	JULY	AUGUST	SEPTEMBER	OCTOBER	NOVEMBER	DECEMBER
15th Meeting to discuss idea with those affected						
	15th Develop details of plan for internal comment Draft 1					
		15th Revise to reflect comments received Draft 2				
			Circulate Draft 2			
				15th Revise to reflect comments Final Draft 3		
					Circulate Final Draft 3 for approval	
						Dec. 1 Submit Proposal Prior to deadline

THE PROCESS OF DEVELOPING AN IDEA BEGINS

The Originator/Project Director, having been encouraged by the Chair and the Grants Officer, puts the idea on paper together with a brief abstract of the plan, its cost, the resources required, and a list of those whose help will be needed. The Grants Officer arranges a meeting of those identified by the Originator/Project Director (the same people identified in Exhibit 1). It is important that there be an actual meeting rather than sending a concept paper, notes, and/or memos by e-mail or fax. For the good of the project, the group needs to interact, to hear the comments and criticisms of others.

This meeting becomes the first general exercise in evaluation and determines whether or not plans should proceed. Assuming the idea is judged worth pursuing, the group considers details of the plan, what further information is needed, and what steps should be taken.

Important questions to consider:

- Does the idea affect the academic program that the academic policy committee should be notified?

- Does the plan require approval from some committee or office?

- Does it commit the institution to such a fundamental change in concept of the institution's mission that the President should notify the Board of Trustees?

- Does it infer a financial commitment or obligation, either additional funds or ongoing costs?

- Does it require cost-sharing or matching funds? "Cost-sharing," depending on the agency, may mean contributions in kind, in time, space, materials, or the contribution of indirect costs. "Matching funds" usually means finding a dollar-for-dollar match in hard cash. Both are financial commitments. Are there others outside the group whose help will be needed? If so, their willingness to assist must be determined and permission to use their names must be secured.

The first order of business in the meeting will be to block out a realistic schedule to serve as a basis for the Grants Officer's timetable. This timetable will detail all deadlines up to and including the date of submission of the proposal. See Exhibit 2 for an example six-month timetable.

The first item on the timetable will be the securing of approvals and willingness to help from all parties. The timetable will include allowance for delays, and ideally will provide a comfortable interval between the date set for completion of the proposal and the deadline date for its submission to a funding agency. Even though

the Grants Officer has checked the availability of those people whose signature is required on the completed document (President, Chief Fiscal Officer, or Department Head), accumulated delays and unforeseen exigencies can turn this interval into a critical or even hectic period. An important point to remember is one should never expect the funding agency to extend its deadline for the receipt of the proposal.

At the close of the first meeting, immediate tasks will have been assigned to members of the group, roles of members will have begun to take shape, and chief target dates will be clear. The Grants Officer should prepare timetables starting with a six-month timetable for the distribution of drafts to meet the submission deadline and follow up with a more detailed timetable for each month prior to the submission deadline. (Exhibits 2 and 3) Today, much of the burden of communication and distribution of documents can be handled through e-mail and conference calls. These serve as planning and reminding documents.

Exhibit 3. Activity Schedule/Status Report.

Date	Activity	Status
June 1	meet with Department Head to discuss idea	
June 6	meet with Coordinator to get logistical help and get idea on paper	Abstract on paper
June 15	meet with all those affected by idea to discuss idea and seek encouragement	
June 15-July 15	develop detailed plan for circulation to those who met June 15	Draft #1
July 15	circulate draft for committee by August 1, enlist campus participants	
Aug. 1-Sept. 1	respond to comments and prepare Draft #2 for comments--those who will participate will revise draft	Draft #2
Sept. 1-15	circulate Draft #2 to those affected and those enlisted; comment by October 1	
Oct. 2-15	revise and work out changes with those affected	Revision Draft #2
Oct. 15-Nov. 1	prepare final draft for approval, in form for duplicating	Final Draft
Nov. 1-15	circulate final revisions	Circulate Final Draft
Nov. 15-20	final approvals, assurances; submission papers collected and required number of copies duplicated and assembled	
Nov. 20	signature of Chief Fiscal Officer	
Nov. 21	signature of President	
Nov. 22	finished proposal packaged and mailed or delivered to meet deadline	Submission

The Proposal: A Design for Putting an Idea to Work

WHAT IS IN A SOUND PROPOSAL?

General Considerations

Plans for implementing the initial idea inevitably lead to step 1, i.e., preparation of an outline, then to a rough draft of a proposal. The individual or individuals composing successive drafts should constantly strive for a thoroughly detailed and clearly articulated description of the needs that must be satisfied for fulfillment of the initial idea. The needs must be clearly consistent with institutional and departmental goals, not contrived to match areas of interest specified by a potential funding source that have nothing to do with the purpose of your organization. For example, if a foundation is interested in funding projects related to the arts, and your project is for teacher training, do not warp your teacher-training program to match the foundations interests by calling it the "art of teaching!"

Remember that the role of the Grants Officer is to discover a funding source whose interests include those described in the proposal. (This is not to say that an online newsletter from a funding source might not trigger a good idea, which, of course, would then be described with that particular source in mind.)

Step 2 is to turn the rough draft into a sound proposal, realizing that before the proposal is submitted, it will gradually undergo major and minor changes as the idea grows and as the participating group examines it critically. Preparation of a formal proposal is a valuable exercise whether or not the proposal is to be submitted to a funding agency. The process helps to clarify ideas, calls attention to weaknesses, and helps nonparticipating colleagues understand the idea and the contemplated project. Furthermore, those who authorize internal support and make official commitments to support the project should be as demanding as an outside funding agency in requiring detailed plans. A proposal should, therefore, be prepared whether or not it is to be sent outside the institution.

Assuming that outside support is to be sought and an appropriate agency has been selected, Step 3 would be to adjust the proposal to conform to the agency's guidelines.

All funding sources ask for basically the same information (Exhibit 4) and it is exactly the kind of information already gathered if preliminary planning has been properly carried out. We mention this because one misunderstanding is the notion that no two funding sources ask for the same information. Though the general format of a proposal varies *little* among agencies, descriptive terms may vary and the order in which information is requested may differ. We reviewed guidelines from a wide variety of agencies and foundations and collected terms used for the various components of a proposal. Topics were the same, regardless of the terminology.

Exhibit 4 lists various parallel terms used for the contents of a proposal. You may find an agency that uses alternate terms listed in Exhibit 4, but remember that you should always use the terminology, order, and format the funding agency requests. This makes it easier for anyone reviewing the proposal.

Keep in mind that preparation of a formal and final proposal is one part of a process; it must follow the initial identification of need (problem statement) and description of an idea, formulation of plans to implement it, and establishment of priorities (schedule/timetable).

A successful proposal is the culminating event of an orderly, thorough, and thoughtful developmental process. In fact, the principal fault we find with most of the literature and seminars on proposal writing is that the total process in developing the project is not considered within the total context of the developing idea. People jump to a conclusion before developing the process from inception to completion/conclusion.

Much has been written on proposal writing from a management standpoint. People tend not to think of the process of developing an idea as a "management system,"

Exhibit 4. Components of a Typical Proposal with Variations in Terminology.

Most Common Headings	Variations
Cover Sheet	Application Form, Title Page
Table of Contents	
Abstract	Summary, Executive Summary
Problem Statement	Statement of Need, Needs Assessment, Description of Need, Questions to be Addressed
Goals	General Objectives, Solutions
Measurable Objectives	Specific Objectives, Expected Outcomes Activities, Narrative, Operating Plan
Procedures	Action Plan, Research Design, Strategies Formative and Summative Evaluation, Instrumentation for Assessment
Evaluation	Assessment of Outcomes
Dissemination	Transferability, Distribution of Results, Utilization Plan, Replicability
Facilities	Space and Equipment Requirements
Personnel	Capability of Staff, Special Competencies
Budget	Fiscal Requirements, Project Cost, Financial Resources
Appendices	Background Material, Supporting Documents

but the process—including motivation, design, implementation, assessment, administration, reporting, and final audit—is, in fact, a management system.

Another helpful source comes from the internal policy manuals developed and shared by administrators in other institutions. These internal policy manuals often contain methods of motivating those with ideas and systems for matching faculty capability with sources of support for their research. These have been developed by institutions in ways we found particularly useful and applicable to small institutions. We found helpful information in guidelines provided by the National Science Foundation and the Department of Education's "Fund for improvement for Post Secondary Education."

Developing the final proposal should still be preceded by outlines and a series of drafts that have been gradually improved and refined, satisfying the critical judgment of all participants. The drafts may also serve as the clearest exposition of the developing plan for those directly or indirectly affected by the plan at various times during the process of development. Greater coherence and orderliness in the proposal may be achieved if you think of it as a set of instructions for someone to carry out; you must realize that a final, polished version may be many drafts away. Never underestimate the value of the drafts, for they will be the means of securing internal support, which, of course, must precede the seeking of external support.

Step 4 is to prepare an abstract or summary of the proposal, whether or not it is specified in guidelines. It is a useful document, particularly for grants officers as they seek suitable funding agencies. The abstract, a distillation of the entire proposal, should occupy no more than two pages; it must be carefully and concisely constructed and must include all of the major features of the project, especially how it will satisfy needs and the anticipated cost. A "preliminary proposal," sometimes requested by a funding agency, should provide the same kind of information as an abstract but can include more details and descriptive material. We emphasize again that however brief the abstract or preliminary proposal, all major elements must be included.

Step 5 is to get approval from the person in charge of approving the proposal.

Step 6 is to send the proposal out to the funding agencies.

The Specific Parts of a Proposal

The headings given below, and the appropriate information that goes with them, should be used even during your earliest preparation, because they will correspond in major respects to most funding agency guideline instructions. This procedure will spare you from making extensive revisions when you write the proposal in its final form. These are typical headings used by most funding agencies, but in actuality, it is best to use the headings that your funding agency requires. It also makes it easier for the proposal reviewers to follow your plan.

Cover Sheet

Title   The title should be brief but should include the most important words describing the project, preferably the words likely to be picked up by a computer preparing bibliographies, e.g., *Improving Competency of Women in*

Securing Support for Research. Then, on the same page, give the following information:

Submitted by: Name and Degree

      Address

      Rank

      Insitition

      Address & e-mail

Date: (Date of submission)

NB: If an agency provides a cover sheet form, use it. This will then serve as your title page and must therefore be the first item in the proposal. Plan on sending a letter of transmittal and endorsement, unless otherwise stated. This is discussed in the chapter on submission.

Table of Contents

This should follow the cover sheet and should include section headings and subheadings with the page where each one starts. Be sure that the headings in contents match those in the body of your proposal. One of the worst things is to have headings and subheadings in your table of contents that differ from the headings in the body of the proposal. For example, writing Abstract in the table of contents and Summary in the body of the proposal.

Abstract

We put the sample abstract first because that is where it should be placed. However, write the Abstract last! We suggest this because you never know what will evolve as you develop the proposal. This may be your most important and most difficult effort, as its quality will determine whether or not the reader examines the rest of the proposal. Write a simple summary of what is to be accomplished, how it will be accomplished, how the project will be evaluated, who will benefit from it and how, and what it will cost. This should fill no more than two pages. We emphasize, tell all, but be concise.

Exhibit 5 is an abstract for a hypothetical proposal to the National Endowment for the Humanities.

Problem Statement

The idea worth developing is the one answering a recognized need. State the need or problem clearly. Don't exaggerate it or give it dimensions beyond the scope of the proposal or the competence of those involved. Take to heart a warning that appeared in an article published

Exhibit 5. Abstract.

Institution: Northwest State University, Taxville, WA
Type of institution: State University
No. of students: 15,000
Type of grant: Planning
Inclusive dates of grant: 1/1/07–3/31/07
Project Title: Northwest Coast Studies Program
Project Director: Arthur Foresight
Amt. requested: $27,532

OBJECTIVES: Through NEH funds the departments of Anthropology, Art, History, and English, in cooperation with the staff of the Fells Museum, will develop an undergraduate concentration in Northwest Coast Studies. This program will offer an intellectual focus to departments that presently offer a large but fragmented set of courses and suffer declining enrollments. We propose, therefore, to offer one new course in each department, an interdisciplinary junior–senior seminar on culture change in Northwest, an undergraduate internship at the Fells Museum, and a research colloquium for students and staff concerned with Northwest Coast Studies. This program will build on the research interests of 5 of 14 members of these combined departments, expand the use of the Fells collection and summer archaeology program, and promote a more meaningful interaction between the departments cited. Our goals are to strengthen the quality of instruction, increase student sensitivity to the interrelationship of disciplines, and to increase enrollment in upper-level history and anthropology courses.

TIMETABLE: Anthropology will offer a sophomore level course "Indians of the Northwest" in the fall of 1976; in the spring of 1977, History will offer "Northwest from 1750" and English will offer "Literature of the Northwest." A select group of 6 sophomores will begin 10 hr/wk museum internships in this semester. The summer program will be a continuation of the museum archaeological program. We will continue the sophomore sequence in the fall. In addition, Art will offer "Art and Architecture of the Northwest." Four teachers will offer a junior–senior interdisciplinary seminar on "Culture Change in the Northwest" and the Humanities Program will sponsor the research symposium "Recent Scholarship on the Northwest." In 1977 two courses will be dropped from the curriculum: "History of Latin America" and "Ethnography of Appalachia."

TEACHING STRATEGIES: Departmental offerings will be taught as lectures. The seminar will be taught by two members each of History and Anthropology with occasional assistance from Music, English, and Art. Interns at the museum will be assigned to the curator or the assistant curator who will supervise their project in cooperation with a faculty advisor. The seminar, symposium, and museum programs will draw on faculty and students from the departments of Linguistics, Religion, Botany, and Geology.

FACULTY: Dean Foresight, Project Director; H. Herodotus, Ch., Dept. of Hist., & B. Boas, Ch., Dept. of Anthro.; Project Cochair, Prf. Fulcrum, Dept. of Hist. & Anthro; S. Potter, Curator; P. Wissler, Asst Curator; Prof. Baal, Hist; A. Jenson, Art; W. Shakespeare, Engl.

EVALUATION: Four kinds of evaluation will be used: enrollment data, use of interdisciplinary facilities and number of interdisciplinary projects undertaken by faculty and students, faculty evaluation by a committee not involved in the program, and outside evaluation by Franz Salmon and J. Totem, leading Northwest Coast scholars.

by the American Association of State Colleges and Universities (AASCU), "Don't take on the problems of the universe." Focus *sharply* on the problem in such a way that the limits of the problem and its solution become clear. Following the example for the title of the project used earlier under cover sheet, the need could be stated as follows: *Women have not had equal opportunity and assistance necessary to secure grant support.*

Goals and Objectives

An examination of various guidelines indicates that two kinds of objectives usually need to be stated.

The first objective, often called a "goal," is more general, inclusive, and describable in qualitative terms.

The second objective is a series of specific expectations describable in quantitative or measurable terms and serving the first general objective or goal.

The following is an example of a title, problem statement, goals, and objectives. This will help you translate your idea into proposal language.

The Title (under cover sheet): *Improving Competency of Women in Securing Support for Research*. It would then be followed by:

Problem Statement (need): *Women have not had equal opportunity and assistance necessary to secure grant support.*

Goal: *To improve the competency of women in securing financial support for research projects in their particular fields.*

Objectives: *To enroll 25 women with Ph.D.'s and with no experience in applying for grants in a workshop and train them to the point where each can plan and design a project and describe it in the form of a proposal that would be judged competitive in terms of Office of Education review criteria, and to accomplish the objective in a three-week summer training program.*

The greatest weakness in proposals probably appears in the statement of objectives. Grandiose ideas whose expected outcomes are not measurable in quantitative or qualitative terms are too often the rule. When you set forth your objectives, list them, and consider carefully how you would measure or judge the success of each objective.

Procedures

Restrictions for this section are less severe than on others; the *first rule* is to write simply and clearly and according to a logical outline. Strive for a maximum of "protein" in your writing and a minimum of "carbohydrate" and "fat." Avoid esoteric and technical terms unless you are assured that readers and reviewers will be familiar with them. Avoid "buzz" or "in" words—by the time your proposal is read, they will probably be "out." Avoid flowery prose. Strive at all times for clarity in your writing!

The following are examples of "what not to do" in proposal writing. This *Newsweek* excerpt dates back three decades and is a type of writing that is still offensive today:

> Nowhere has the art of obfuscation been more refined than in the drawing up of administrative proposals. Lloyd Kaplan, former information officer of the New York City Planning Commission, made a hobby of analyzing the technique. "Proposals," he reports, "are habitually placed in frameworks so that they can be viewed from the proper perspective. Looking through the framework, it is easy to chart appropriate guidelines. Such guidelines are flexible and handy for making bold thrusts, dramatic approaches and pioneering break-throughs. "Money" continues Kaplan "is never mentioned." "Resources is the prime substitute, although expenditures, allocations, appropriations and funds are also popular. Resources is also aesthetically pleasing because it brings to mind the act of digging up and forms a truly Miltonic phrase when preceded by "overburdened municipal."

Another example of "what not to do" actually happened at a recent review panel. The author of a proposal when responding to the question in the guidelines asking him to describe his capability for carrying out this project related to improving math and science stated:

> I live in an ivy covered cottage just outside of the city where XXX college is located. My residence is shared with my wife of 25 years, two noisy and active children and my dog, Bosco. Bosco is noted for his shaggy coat and friendly disposition. He wants to play with his favorite toy when I am working. He barks at everyone when they come into the room.

This has absolutely nothing to do with the plan to develop a new comprehensive introductory course in math and science!

The *second rule* is to not to fluff up a proposal with the sort of euphemisms that bestow an aura of importance without revealing anything specific. An application for a federal grant from a small southern California college illustrates the technique. Describing a proposed project, the applicant states: "It is not simply a cross-disciplinary venture or an inter-disciplinary venture; it is a pan-disciplinary venture and this, of course, is in the nature of all real experience." We read a proposal a short time ago that literally copied that language and we had no idea of what they were trying to do.

The ultimate in "sure-fire-how-to-write-a-loser" proposal is set forth in the following game. This game has been copied and passed around agencies and foundations for over 40 years and continues to cause laughter and elicit stories about bad proposal writing.

How to Win at Wordsmanship

After hacking for years through etymological thickets at the U.S. Public Health Service, a 63-year-old official named Philip Broughton hit upon a sure-fire method for converting frustration into fulfillment (jargon-wise). Euphemistically called the Systematic Buzz Phrase Projector, Broughton's system employs a lexicon of 30 carefully chosen "buzzwords":

Column 1	Column 2	Column 3
0. integrated	0. management	0. options
1. total	1. organizational	1. flexibility
2. systematized	2. monitored	2. capability
3. parallel	3. reciprocal	3. mobility
4. functional	4. digital	4. programming
5. responsive	5. logistical	5. concept
6. optional	6. transitional	6. time-phase
7. synchronized	7. incremental	7. projection
8. compatible	8. third-generation	8. hardware
9. balanced	9. policy	9. contingency

The procedure is simple. Think of any three-digit number, then select the corresponding buzzword from each column. For instance, number 257 produced "systematized logistical projection," a phrase that can be dropped into virtually any report with that ring of decisive, knowledgeable authority. "No one will have the remotest idea of what you're talking about," says Broughton, "but the important thing is that they're not about to admit it."

Clear writing is important because the procedures section is where you explain how you plan to do the things set forth in your objectives, when you plan to do the work, how long it will take, who else will be working on the project, exactly what they will be doing and where they will be doing it, and what will be needed in facilities, equipment, supplies, time, and personnel. Be specific.

Describe your institution and the competence of both the institution and the people involved in the project to carry out the objectives. Explain what will happen to the project when the funds are all expended, and the extent to which this project may dovetail with other ongoing projects, or pave the way for future plans. Continuing with the example suggested in the cover sheet and objectives sections, we will now illustrate the kind of detailed plan that should appear in your procedures.

The first thing to do is list the steps you will take, when you will start each activity, who will do the work, where it will be done, when it will be completed, and what it will cost in time and materials (Exhibit 6).

Continue this procedure to include the entire project. Once you have completed such a schedule of activities, describe each activity in detail with appropriate charts and references. For example, if we turn to the June 15 activity (Exhibit 2 and 3) we should find:

> The initial activity in the training program will be a one-day workshop designed to illustrate the roles and relationships of the various persons affected by an idea. A Dean, Business Officer, Development Officer, Grant Manager, and Faculty Member with experience as a department head and success in securing grants will be teamed with representatives of government, private, and corporate funding sources to address the topics outlined for the workshop. These persons will be recruited from outside the faculty of the training program.

The method prescribed in this book for the development of the idea is the basis for the workshop and the training program detailed in this sample proposal. An outline for the first session of the workshop is shown in Exhibit 7.

The design for this workshop on proposal development is such that it can be readily adapted to different settings and interest groups. It is important that at least two of the instructors have a thorough understanding of the process we are describing. Through role playing, persons recruited to represent the roles of the Originator, Department Head, Administrator, and Grants Officer can interpolate the views represented in the group into the roles mentioned in the panel portion of the workshop at 9:45AM (Exhibit 7).

We suggest that this workshop serves as a training session for the representatives of the colleges, universities, and community agencies and as an example of an exercise that can be performed at their home institutions when projects are being developed.

Evaluation

An essential inclusion in any proposal is a statement on evaluation: how the developing idea and proposal and, finally, the completed project will be assessed. Funding agencies often ask how the evaluative process will be conducted and require reports on the process itself and on the conclusions drawn by those administering the project. Even if an agency doesn't ask for an evaluation, you should have an evaluation system for your own and your institution's benefit. (Two actual evaluations are given in the chapter on evaluation.)

We deal with evaluation more fully in "Tests for Soundness of a Proposal" rather than here because the topic includes more than just the description of the evaluation process needed for developing the proposal. Evaluation of a project is increasingly important to the grantor. It is so important that we have included a separate chapter with an example evaluation following the chapter on grant administration.

Dissemination

Proposals often state that the project is a "pilot study," or that the results would be useful to other institutions.

Exhibit 6. Detailed List of Activities.

January 5	Develop an application form for the training program
February 1	Distribute application to 200 institutions; set Feb. 20 as deadline for receiving applications
March 1–15	Screen applications and select 30 who will provide range in type of institution, interests, and geographic location
April–May	Produce in final form the list of materials to be used in the program (outlines, topical papers, bibliographies, etc.), and the budget; (this will help you in drafting a final budget.) 4 working-weeks $4,000 Secretarial help $500 Postage $500 Publications $150
June 15	Opening of workshop, directors $400 Consultants, 5 @ $100/day + travel @$100 $1,000 Materials $300

If the latter is the case, how will the results, materials, and projects or plans be made available to others, and how will the transfer be implemented? These questions should be carefully considered before answers are given. Be realistic and practical in anticipating what can and will be done. Funding sources may press for answers to the transferability questions in such a way that the proposer is tempted to contrive an answer. Don't be tempted! If a dissemination plan is required by a funding source and such a plan is not appropriate for your proposal, it is wiser not to apply to this source.

Your project, on the other hand, may have some very clear implications in terms of its applicability elsewhere, or it may already be adapted to dissemination with no difficulty. If you consider a project plan adaptable to another setting, state this in your proposal, explain the means of dissemination and make any necessary provisions in your budget.

Dissemination can be taken care of through a series of workshops, through a publication, or posted on a Web site. The workshop on proposal development, which was described earlier, illustrates a replicable device because the role-playing approach is open to a new set of characters as long as the principle is understood and applied.

Publications and materials produced by many good projects, however, fill shelves and gather dust because there was no plan to advertise and make these materials available. For example, it is reasonable to argue that a new method involving computerized instruction and/or distance learning may be transferred by making the programs available or by devising or using a system permitting access to your computer. Nevertheless, it is still necessary to explain in your proposal how you will make this known and how you will pay for, handle production and distribution, or accessibility of the material requested.

We have often written to project directors whose proposals claimed that reports would be made readily available to other institutions only to discover that dissemination ended with 10–25 copies because no provision for distribution had been made in the grant budget or through internal resources. An actual example is of the *Women in Chemistry Project*. Descriptions of the laboratory modules developed with the National Science

Exhibit 7. Workshop Outline.

The purpose of this workshop is to expose the audience and the participants to the interrelatedness of the roles of the many persons affected by an idea and will demonstrate how effective use of the process will lead to a sound proposal.

Workshop on Proposal Development and Grant Opportunities for Individuals, Departmental, and Institutional Projects

8:30	REGISTRATION, COFFEE, AND DANISH	
9:15	WELCOME & INTRODUCTION OF PARTICIPANTS	
9:30	OUTLINE OF DAY'S ACTIVITIES	Workshop Director
	Presentation on Process of the Development of an Idea	
9:45	PANEL: FROM IDEA TO THE WRITTEN PROPOSAL	
	The Idea Originator	Professor Green
	The Head of the Department	Professor Smith
	The Administration	Dean Jones
	The Grants Officer	Ms. Reed
	The Funding Organization	Dr. Black

5-minute presentation by each participant to describe his role in developing an idea and 35 minutes for questions.

10:45	COFFEE BREAK	
11:00	FUNDING ORGANIZATIONS	
	Private Foundations	Dr. Black
	Corporation Foundations	Mr. Davis
	Government Agencies	Dr. Bird

Three 15-minute presentations covering:

a) what each foundation, corporation, or agency funds,

b) what each expects in a proposal, and

c) how each judges a proposal?

An open discussion will follow on the similarities and differences among the 3 groups.

12:15	BREAK FOR LUNCH	
1:15	THE INGREDIENTS OF A PROPOSAL	Workshop Director

The Director will address the subject in outline form. A panel is made up of one grants officer, one funding agency representative, and a third person from among the outside participants (Dr. Black, Dr. Bird, Ms. Reed).

3:00	PEER-PANEL REVIEW

A submitted proposal will be reviewed by a panel convened for this purpose. Copies of this proposal will now be distributed to all participants. One funding source representative will serve as convener. Panel will include three outside participants and three trainees. (Dr. Black, Dr. Bird, Professors Smith & Green, 3 trainees).

3:45	CONCLUSIONS OF THE PANEL WILL BE DISCUSSED	Dr. Black
4:00	ACTUAL REVIEW OF THE PROPOSAL	Workshop Director
4:30	ADJOURN	

Foundation (NSF) grant are still being distributed at cost plus shipping through advertising and descriptions on the Learn-4-Success-Inc. Web site. Over a thousand institutions, colleges, and high schools have ordered one or more or full sets of these modules to date. The cost of advertising them would have been prohibitive without a Web address. This project is still active and self-supporting.

Today the Internet, Web sites, and the present and future electronic devices make dissemination readily available and inexpensive. Just be sure to explain your plan and method and include it in your budget.

Facilities

The proposal should include a statement indicating the availability of needed facilities. If, for instance, large audiences are expected for a lecture series or continuing education activities, give information on the space available for the group you expect. Be certain classrooms, auditoriums, and other places are free for use. See to it that those who are responsible for assigning space and seeing that the buildings are open know and agree to your requirements. If technical facilities such as LCD or DLP or traditional audiovisual equipment are not available, be sure to make allowances for these needs in your budget. A proposal describing plans for large community audiences of 500 or more stands no chance of support when the description of facilities indicates that the largest available auditorium holds only 250 people. Be meticulous and thorough in anticipating your needs. The prospective funding source appreciates and respects thorough planning.

Personnel

Give an honest assessment of the extent to which the capabilities of personnel to be involved satisfy requirements of the project. Does the project demand competency in a subject not taught at your institution? If so, explain how you will fill the gap and make any budget allowances necessary. Explain special areas of expertise represented among involved personnel. We are reminded of a proposal submitted by a young instructor in a small institution, requesting a rather sophisticated and complex configuration of apparatus. His proposal would have been turned down because a reviewer questioned whether anyone in such an institution would have enough experience to use such equipment. It was discovered by pure chance that the proposer had been responsible for setting up and maintaining similar equipment as a graduate student. This should have been made

clear in the proposal as granting agencies are naturally unwilling to approve investments in equipment that no one knows how to use. When listing the competencies required in the project do not overlook those needed for some special task. If outsiders must be brought in, explain where you will find the people you want. We suggest that you list by name several such specialists, even though you have no commitment from them. If certain distinguished experts are sought, explain what makes you think you can secure them. Have similar institutions had their services? Are they personal friends, related to a trustee, or known to be willing to come for a particular fee?

The qualifications of your personnel are best supported by the *curriculum vitae* of each, particularly those with key roles in the project. The list would include, of course, the Project Director (PD), or the Principal Investigator (PI), in a research project, and those with some important specializations spelled out in the proposal. We suggest using a uniform, standard format for the *curriculum vitae,* and we have provided a sample form with instructions in Section V (Forms and Required Information) of Part II (Exhibit 40). If some agency asks for specific information not included in the suggested form, simply add the required information.

Budget

Every item in the budget should be described in the narrative part of the procedures. It is helpful to the reader if the section of the narrative devoted to these brief descriptions lists them in the same sequence in which they appear in the budget. One can also add very brief descriptions to the individual budget items. Every anticipated cost should be listed, adjusted to projected price increases. Do not inflate the budget—too often proposal writers equate an inflated budget with a complete and adequate budget; this is a false assumption. Prepare a reasonable backup budget for a less costly approach to the project, but do not agree to changes that would jeopardize the success and quality of the project.

The business officer of any organization must approve the budget and sign financial reports. It is this individual who will be most helpful in preparing the budget, particularly in including such items as social security withholding figures, which are often overlooked by writers of proposals. The business officer will also know the institution's current indirect cost rate, or, if one has not been recently negotiated with the appropriate federal agency, will develop this figure. The following Web addresses will provide a basis for calculating indirect costs and institutional contributions until a final rate is negotiated.

Current indirect cost instructions are described in the *National Science Foundation's Grant Administration Manual,* which can be found at http://www.nsf.gov/bfa/dias/caar/docs/npicp.pdf, and *A Guide for Colleges and Universities. Cost Principles and Procedures for Establishing Indirect Cost and Other Rates for Grant and Contracts with the Department of Education, ED119596,* which can be found at http://eric.ed.gov/ERICWebPortal/Home.portal?_nfpb=true&_pageLabel=RecordDetails&ERICExtSearch_SearchValue_0=ED119596&ERICExtSearch_SearchType_0=eric_accno&objectId=0900000b800f1a54.

Other such documents explaining indirect costs or budgets can be found on the Internet by the agency name plus.gov. For example: IRS.gov. The indirect cost rate is usually based on salaries and wages (S + W) but some have separate rates for off-campus or overseas activities. Large universities and other nonprofit agencies use a formula involving total cost to calculate the indirect rate. Few private foundations recognize indirect costs or overhead figures. Ask the sponsor, if it is not a government agency, what direct and indirect costs will be allowed before finalizing your budget.

For those unfamiliar with the term "indirect cost" or "indirect expenses," we quote from the Combined Glossary, Terms and Definitions from the *Handbooks of the State Educational Records and Reports Series, U.S. Department of Health Education and Welfare, Educational Division,* 1974. Variations of this statement show up in current publications. This particular wording seemed to be most helpful to the neophyte.

> Those elements of cost necessary in the provision of a service which are of such nature that they cannot be readily or accurately identified with the specific service. For example, the custodial staff may clean corridors in a school building, which is used jointly by administrative, instructional, maintenance and attendance personnel. In this case, a part of the custodial salaries is an indirect expense of each service using the corridors. However, it is impossible to determine readily or accurately the amount of salary to charge each of these services.

The indirect cost figure is important because the claimed indirect costs on a grant may provide your most important, if not the only, means of sharing costs with a funding source. Demonstration of the institution's support of a project is often sought through a requirement to "cost share." If you can share the cost of a project by using indirect cost money for project expenses and by making contributions "in kind," such as support devices, facilities, and supplies. The terms "cost sharing" and "matching" are not to be confused. "Matching" money is a cash outlay made by the institution according to whatever ratio the funding source sets. Many federal agencies suggest formats and items to be included in the budget. Examining a sample budget used for a funding agency requiring cost sharing is perhaps the best way for a beginner to learn how to develop a budget. Exhibit 8 is a sample budget that provides a thumbnail sketch of the times and activities that would be described in the proposal narrative.

Appendix

At the top of our list of items to be included in the appendix is a description of the institution. The introduction undoubtedly contains an abbreviated description, such as "XYZ College, located in the state of ABC, offers a four-year program leading to a B.A. degree to approximately 700 women selected from the fifty states and several foreign countries." A more extensive statement, covering about one page and providing additional descriptive material, should be given in the appendix. This statement should contain solid, demonstrable facts, e.g., "The Susan and Emma Cash Library contains 500,000 volumes and subscribes to 1,200 periodicals, this does not include information on microfiche." Nebulous or extravagant claims, such as those that often appear in catalogue statements or in promotional brochures, are out of place in this description.

The appendix should also contain other relevant documentary material that, owing to subject matter, length, or format, would be inappropriate or would disturb the continuity of the narrative. The *curriculum vitae* should definitely be in the appendix unless otherwise specified. Required letters of endorsement, such as those from cooperating agencies, may be put in the appendix, unless you are instructed to place them elsewhere. Other documentary material might well include maps, graphs, charts, detailed listings, reports of consultants, special studies related to the project, reading lists, and bibliographies. A decision as to which of these items belong in the body of the proposal and which in the appendix should be made after you have examined the final draft.

One of the most useful appendices we have seen contained, in proper sequence, some chart, graph, or fact sheets to reinforce or illustrate each major point in the proposal. The appendix thus became a coherent map of the material described in the body of the proposal.

Exhibit 8. Sample Grant Budget.

	SPONSOR	APPLICANT	TOTAL
A. Personnel			
1. Professor Jones, P.D.			
1/2 released time for acad. yr.;			
salary $60,000	$15,000	$15,000	$30,000
2. Professor Smith			
1/2 released time fall semester;			
salary $40,000	$10,000	$10,000	$20,000
3. Professor Brown			
1/2 released time fall semester;			
salary $30,000	$7,500	$7,500	$15,000
4. Professor Green			
1/2 released time spring semester;			
salary $30,000	$7,500	$7,500	$15,000
5. Secretary			
1/2 time; salary $20,000	$5,000	$5,000	$10,000
SUBTOTAL—Salaries & Wages	$45,000	$45,000	$90,000
B. Fringe Benefits (22% of S&W)	$10,800	$9,000	$19,800
C. Consultants			
1. Consultants (2 @ $250/day for 2 days)	$1,000		$1,000
2. Consultant Travel (2 @ $350 + 2 days			
x $75 per diem)	$1,000		$1,000
SUBTOTAL—C	$2,000		$2,000
D. Staff Travel			
1. Professor Jones: 1 trip to U.S College			
to observe similar program, 500 miles x			
$40 per mile = $200, per diem $75 for			
3 days = $225.	$425		$425
2. Professors Smith & Green: 1 trip to			
National University for (purpose).			
Plane fare est. $340 for each = $680. + $75			
per diem for 2 days each = $300.	$980		$980
SUBTOTAL—D	$1,310		$1,310
E. Supplies			
1. Institutional materials (slides, tapes)	$600	$200	$800
2. Office supplies (paper, ink, etc.)	$500	$100	$600
SUBTOTAL—E	$1,100	$300	$1,400
F. Other			
1. Communications (Tel, text/e-mail, etc.)			
@ 200/mo for 12 months	$1,468	$932	$2,400
2. Equipment rental: camcorder @ $200, LCD			
Player @ $200	$400		$400
3. Library acquisitions: books, tapes, CD			
(attach breakdown)	$1,200	$800	$2,000
SUBTOTAL—F	$3,068	$1,732	$4,800
G. Total Direct Costs	**$63,278**	**$56,032**	**$119,310**
H. Indirect Costs x 65% of S & W (subtotal A)			
predetermined HHS	$29,250	$29,250	$58,500
I. TOTAL COSTS	**$92,528**	**$85,282**	**$177,810**

TESTS FOR SOUNDNESS
OF A PROPOSAL

General

An underlying, secondary theme in our philosophy of idea development is the importance of evaluative procedures. One of the values inherent in the method described in this guidebook is the almost automatic presence of evaluation from start to finish. The first time an idea is shared, it is evaluated by the second party. From conception to fruition, the idea is exposed to the judgment of others, and the reactions of this constant evaluation foster the idea's growth and development.

In the proposal itself, the details of this continuous or "formative" evaluation should be described as background, as evidence of your sound planning process to date, and as an integral part of the procedures of your project. Projects, once started, seldom proceed exactly according to expectations and therefore a plan for constant, continuous assessment should be outlined. Such a plan, devised in the expectation of change, permits change at the most propitious juncture. Anticipation of the circumstances that would lead to change is almost impossible; an assistant with special abilities may have to leave the project, new developments in the field may obviate the need for some of your preparatory work, the sequences of stages in a training program may need amending because the trainees advance faster than expected. A program of continuous evaluation will result in speedy, effective, and often advantageous adjustment to unexpected contingencies.

The process of "summative evaluation" follows the completion of the project. What devices or instruments will be used, what will be done with the results, who will assist, to what extent have objectives been satisfied? It is not sufficient to say, "Outside consultants will be retained with expertise in the field of Training Programs for Women to conduct an impartial evaluation." Such generalities are inadequate for internal planning, as well as for proposals.

Referring back to our example, *Improving Competency of Women in Securing Support for Research*, there is an obvious built-in device for evaluating this project. First, the sample proposal already suggests a peer review of the trainees' work as the course proceeds. Instructors, reacting to these reviews, can increase the emphasis on certain points that aren't getting across to the trainees. Second, receiving the help of an outside group of reviewers who can judge the trainees' work objectively will ensure a measure of success for the programs. There

is at this time no way to measure trainees' improvement in proposal writing since, presumably, they have never before attempted such an exercise. It would be necessary to plan a review of proposals prepared at future times and compare them with the first efforts made in the workshop to determine the effectiveness of the workshop in training participants. Such a review would show not only the extent of continuing interest and motivation but improvements, if any, in the facility of preparing proposals and in the quality of the proposals.

In fact, the idea of writing the original edition of this guide was precipitated by the expressed interest of the Virginia State Agency for Title I, HEA, Continuing Education and Community Service, for improving the quality of evaluation.

Review Process Criteria

Criteria used by representative funding agencies in judging proposals, together with the processes used in applying the criteria, screening proposals, and reaching decisions are given in Exhibits 9–13. (We have cited several examples, but we call your attention to Exhibits 9 and 10 not because the criteria differ greatly from those used elsewhere, but because they are simply stated and can be easily applied to a variety of proposals.) This sphere of activity is obviously external to the institution and beyond its control. This is not to say, however, that the common criteria and processes of selection are not relevant to the preparation of a proposal. The constant revision of drafts of a proposal results from constant criticism and evaluation on the part of all concerned with the project. An effective way for these internal evaluators to view the proposal objectively is to apply the criteria and simulate the process used by external evaluators.

Among funding agencies there is more variety in the mechanics of selection than in the criteria for selection. The process of selection reflects the size of the funding agency or organization, its goals, the amount of money it has to disburse, the annual volume of proposals received, and whether it is tax-supported or privately supported. The decision-making process may be the responsibility of a permanent board, large or small, whose membership represents broad, general backgrounds or very limited, specialized fields. The decision makers, on the other hand, may be groups of peers in your own field invited to serve on a panel for the express purpose of screening. The so called peer panel is an example of the latter, where members of the panel are specialists in the field represented by a collection of proposals; the panel

Exhibit 9. A Private Foundation's (Bank's) Helpful Hints for Proposal Reviewers.

HELPFUL HINTS IN ANALYZING A PROPOSAL			
ELEMENTS TO CONSIDER	*QUESTIONS TO ASK*	*IN-HOUSE KNOWLEDGE*	*OUTSIDE KNOWLEDGE*
NEED	Who is assessing the need? Comparative figures In program really charitable? (IRS tax-determination imperative; make sure proposals meet WCT guidelines)	Minority employment served, Training needs, Geographic area (brand banks) Consumer relationships	Metropolitan Cultural Alliance United Community Planning Council Associated Foundation of Greater Boston, Governmental Agencies Other Foundations (Permanent Charities)
OBJECTIVES	Is there a goal? What is it? Is it realistic?	Experience with other similar proposals Experience in bank with similar objectives (training, recruiting, etc.)	
PROGRAM	Has it been tried before? What was the result? What specific methods are being used to take advantage of the other resources?	What other similar programs is bank involved in? (direct or indirect, i.e., United Way)	
BUDGET	(In reviewing the proposal budget, we should carefully screen to see if sound accounting practices are employed)		
MANAGEMENT	What is the role of the organization's Board of Directors? Is group visible (i.e., do they supervise policy-check internal operation, etc.)? How are staff and clients recruited? Does staff member have job definitions? Are local people in neighborhood employed? Do they have adequate insurance, licensing, etc.?	Experience with corporate or Bank staff serving on organization's Board of Directors Compare B and C with Bank experience	
BUILDING	(Refer to Organization's Guidelines)	Use bank /management expertise in evaluation process (i.e., is this a good investment?)	
EVALUATION	Criteria for evaluation should be pre-established What is being measured? Is progress being made? On-site visits Reports from Organizations		
FUNDING	Where is funding coming from? Is funding objective realistic? Is it capital vs. operating funds? Will funds be needed for continuation of project in future years (i.e, will new facility create greater future budget needs?)	What are alternative to assisting project vs. direct financial aid Examples: A. Mce CA-Bank matching contributions/ memberships B. Loan vs. Grant C. Volunteer activity staff help	AFGB computer list re: current funding to similar organizations. Is this funded through the United Way? Are other corporations supporting this project? Local contracts, "Givens Group" support?

Exhibit 10. The U.S. Department of Education's Criteria for Evaluation Provided to Reviewers.

EVALUATION CRITERIA	YES	NO	COMMENTS	WEIGHT FACTOR
MANAGEMENT--Identify the applicant's organizational elements, and describe how they function internally, including subcontracts, to insure the project is accomplished within the time limits and resources available.				
1. Is the proposed plan of operation sound? Consideration of soundness should include the following points: Are the objects of the project capable of being attained by the proposed procedures and capable of being measured?				
Are provisions made for adequate evaluation of the effectiveness of the project and for determining the extent to which the objectives are accomplished?				
Where appropriate, are provisions made for satisfactory inservice training connected with project services? and,				
Are provisions made for disseminating the results of the project and for making materials, techniques, and other output resulting therefrom, available to the general public and specifically to all those concerned with the area of education with which the project is itself concerned?				
2. Published Application Review Criteria				
FINANCE & ACCOUNTING --Provide adequate project cost details to support the proposed budget in relation to the anticipated end results.				
1. Is the estimated cost reasonable to the anticipated results?				
COMMENTS: (use extra sheets)				

Exhibit 10. (*Continued*)

EVALUATION CRITERIA	YES	NO	COMMENTS	WEIGHT FACTOR
ORGANIZATION--Describe the applicant's background, facilities and personnel expertise as it relates to performing the proposed project. 1. Are the qualifications and experience of applicant's personnel adequate to carry out the proposed project?				
2. Are applicant's facilities and other resources adequate?				
3. Published Application Review Criteria				
PROGRAMMATIC--Define all the work and related resources required to perform the applicant's proposed project pursuant to the applicable regulations.				
1. Is the proposed activity needed in the area served or to be served by the applicant?				
2. Is the proposal relevant to priority areas of concern as reflected in provisions contained in the applicable Federal statutes and regulations?				
3. Is there potential for utilizing the results of the proposed project in other projects or programs for similar educational purposes?				
4. Are the size, scope and duration of the project sufficient in order to secure productive results?				
5. Are the objectives of the proposed project sharply defined and clearly stated?				
6. Published Application Review Criteria				
COMMENTS: (use extra sheets)				

Exhibit 11. A Foundation Official's Advice for Reviewing a Proposal Budget.

REVIEWING A PROPOSAL'S BUDGET

The proposal should provide:

1. A projected income and expense statement for the year for which funding is being sought, as well as a statement of actual income and expenses for the previous year.

2. If the request is for a special program or capital project, budgets for the program or project should be included in addition to the agency's overall budget.

3. The income statement should itemize by category amounts received from:

   fees
   donations
   fund-raising events
   government contracts or grants
   United Way allocations
   foundation grants
   individual contributions
   other

4. The expense statement should itemize expenditures within the the following categories:

   salaries
   fringe benefits
   social security
   rent
   utilities
   materials and supplies
   other (consultant fees, transportation costs, etc.)
   equipment needs

5. Provide an audited financial statement if available.

Exhibit 12. A Corporate Foundation Proposal Review Sheet.

```
               A CORPORATION'S REVIEW SHEET
                     Proposal Review
ORGANIZATION_____

      FOUNDATION_____TURNDOWN_____DATE OF REVIEW_____

 1.   Quick evaluation of purpose and amount requested:_____

      _____

      _____

      _____

      _____

      _____

      _____

      Total Budget_____Area to be served_____

      Project  Administrator_____

      Business Address_____

      Indication of ability to raise funds from other sources for this

      purpose:_____

      _____

 2.   Amount, Date and purpose of previous grants:  _____

      _____

      _____

      Acknowledgement Card_____Date_____Additional Comments_____

      _____

      _____

      on file  requested              on file  requested
      _____  _____  IRS Letter  _____  _____  Income statement
      _____  _____  Budget per  _____  _____  Audited report
                            req. purpose _____  _____  Staff background
      _____  _____  Overall budget_____  _____  Board list
```

Exhibit 13. A List of Shortcomings from the National Institutes of Health.

NATIONAL INSTITUTES OF HEALTH

SHORTCOMINGS FOUND IN STUDY-SECTION* REVIEW OF 605 DISAPPROVED
RESEARCH GRANT APPLICATIONS

No.	Shortcoming

Class I: Problem

1. The problem is of insufficient importance or is unlikely to produce any new or useful information.

2. The proposed research is based on a hypothesis that rests on insufficient evidence, is doubtful, or is unsound.

3. The problem is more complex than the investigator appears to realize.

4. The problem has only local significance, or is one of production or control, or otherwise fails to fall sufficiently clearly within the general field of health-related research.

5. The problem is scientifically premature and warrants, at most, only a pilot study.

6. The research as proposed is overly involved, with too many elements under simultaneous investigation.

7. The description of the nature of the research and of its significance leave the proposal nebulous and diffuse and without clear research aim.

Class II: Approach

8. The proposed tests, or methods, or scientific procedures are unsuited to the stated objectives.

9. The description of the approach is too nebulous, diffuse, and lacking in clarity to permit adequate evaluation.

10. The overall design of the study has not been carefully thought out.

11. The statistical aspects of the approach have not been given sufficient consideration.

12. The approach lacks scientific imagination.

13. Controls are either inadequately conceived or inadequately described.

14. The material the investigator proposes to use is unsuited to the objectives of the study or is difficult to obtain.

15. The number of observations is unsuitable.

16. The equipment contemplated is outmoded or otherwise unsuitable.

Exhibit 13. (*Continued*)

NATIONAL INSTITUTES OF HEALTH

No.	Shortcoming

Class III: Personnel

17. The investigator does not have adequate experience or training, or both, for this research

18. The investigator appears to be unfamiliar with pertinent literature or methods, or both.

19. The investigator's previously published work in this field does not inspire confidence.

20. The investigator proposes to rely too heavily on insufficiently experienced associates.

21. The investigator is spreading himself too thin; he will be more productive if he concentrates on fewer projects.

22. The investigator needs more liaison with colleagues in this field or in collateral fields.

Class IV: Other

23. The requirements for equipment or personnel, or both are unrealistic.

24. It appears that other responsibilities would prevent devotion of sufficient time and attention to the research.

25. The institutional setting is unfavorable.

26. Research grants to the investigator, now in force, are adequate in scope and amount to cover the proposed research.

---

* Study-sections are advisory boards organized according to fields of study and composed of research scientists nation-wide.

meets together at the same time and place, each member rates each proposal, and the final decision rests on this collective rating. A peer panel may also discuss the most promising proposals before reaching a decision. A proposal may also be mailed to selected peers for their independent reviews, and their ratings are then assessed by the agency.

In preparing a particular proposal, when a decision has been made on which agencies might be interested in it, it is not out of order—in fact it is advisable—to correspond with or visit the agencies. The agency, after all, has the responsibility of investing money in the wisest ways consistent with its stated goals. A representative of the agency thus often welcomes the opportunity to discuss a preliminary proposal or abstract with a representative of the institution, to describe the agency's goals and standards of selection, and to explain ways in which the proposal does or does not meet the particular requirements and criteria of the agency. This representative frequently encourages the proposal writer to rewrite a proposal, and often will make an estimate of the revised document's chances of receiving a grant.

One of the *most successful devices for assessing the quality of a proposal* is to present it to a group of your colleagues who will judge it by criteria used by the federal government, or in terms of the standards of the particular foundation to which it will be submitted. A group of eight or ten faculty members representing a variety of disciplines, some of whom have experience in presentation and review of proposals, can be asked to serve as internal reviewers. The flaws, vagueness, and presumptions will be found. Final revisions would then be made on the basis of the collective judgment of this group, and individual criticisms and suggestions of the members. This exercise of internal review is educational, and time spent in this process is worthwhile and should result in improving the quality of proposals.

The following pages give samples of the kinds of guidelines given to reviewers. Read these various requirements for review and the questions that must be answered. The order and the wording of the forms may vary but the questions do not. Ask several of your colleagues to apply the Department of Education's review questions to your proposal. Would they reject it? Fund it? Or suggest changes to clarify and strengthen it?

Following the samples of review criteria is a list of shortcomings in proposals to the *National Institutes of Health* (Exhibit 13). The problems with weak proposals haven't changed since these data were compiled.

Finding a Source of Support

Go first to the institution's Grants Officer. If there is no Grants Officer or Office of Development, go to the head of the institution to make sure that certain sources of funds are not already being approached to support other institutional programs. Never, under any circumstances, approach an outside agency without clearance from the Development or Grants Office or the head of the institution; such independent action could not only jeopardize an institution's prior request but often results in neither request being granted because the credibility of the institution appears in a dubious light to the agency. Most individuals in an institution are ignorant of the various institutional projects contemplated and the kind of orchestration that must be devised by those responsible for setting institutional priorities in seeking supporting funds.

Assuming advice in this guide has been followed, the Originator has already described the idea, project, and dimensions of the project to the Grants Officer. This officer or his/her deputy has readily at hand the *Catalogue of Federal Domestic Assistance* (CFDA), Web site reference is: http://12.46.245.173/cfda/cfda.html. There are many other source materials to aid the Originator in selecting potential sources of funds. Together they will prepare a list of prospects, but the major responsibility for this task belongs, naturally, to the Grants Officer.

Experienced and capable Grants Officers do their homework thoroughly before a final list is compiled, certainly before any funding agency is approached. The officer will first study the stated purpose and recent grants record of each prospective source of funds and will eliminate those not compatible with the project under consideration. We are aware that institutions may not have a grants officer available to specific departments and therefore you will be on your own to search for appropriate sources of funding. The CFDA is useful for selecting government grants and the Web site of *The Foundation Center*, http://foundationcenter.org, is an extensive resource for private sources of funding. The Foundation Center has regional and local libraries staffed by experienced personnel to guide you through their vast resources. A list of sources of information regarding the process of grant seeking and grant administration can be found in Section V.

Suppose, for instance, a foundation is interested in problems of the aging people. What sort of work does it favor in attacking these problems? Basic research? Teacher training? Direct services in the areas of health, continuing education, etc.? Much time will be saved if the prospective donor's objectives are thoroughly understood. This understanding also indicates to the donor the degree of accountability and seriousness of purpose of the applicant. If some funding sources fail to state what they will support, write or call to ask for their guidelines. Following preceding advice should ultimately yield a final list of potential donors.

The next step for the Originator and Grants Officer is to prepare a letter of inquiry and a description of the plan to send to each agency on the final list. It is essential, whether dealing with donors in person or in writing, that the Originator and Grants Officer work together. The latter brings experience to the job, but this experience without full understanding of the project may produce a presentation that at best is superficial, at worst phony. Integrity and understanding of the project must mark the initial and all later contacts with donors, and these qualities can be achieved only *if* the Originator and Grants Officer work together.

Considerable advice is available on methods of approaching prospective donors, but in the end, sensitivity, good judgment, and luck may play equal parts in winning their confidence. An experienced Grants Officer already has a fairly good idea of how to approach various private sources. How important, for instance, is direct contact through a member of the institution's board of trustees or some other friend of the institution? Should an interview be requested and, if so, who should make the call? The Grants Officer? The Originator? The Board Member? The President? Or some combination of these individuals? There is no one answer to these questions except to do what the foundation or corporation tells applicants to do. Some welcome a personal call, some suffer it, and some refuse to discuss a plan until it is deemed appropriate to their own interests on the basis of a written abstract or draft. An influential trustee with contacts on a foundation's board may reinforce a statement of competency and open doors for the applicant. Experience proves, of course, that some foundations make decisions on a personal basis, but, in general, the best advice to applicants is to place their trust in the quality of their effort and the professionalism of the foundation not in personal contacts.

Follow the same advice when you apply to a government agency, except that you can assume that every grant program has a professional staff. Whatever you have heard of using congressional help in securing favorable action on a proposal, our best advice is to inform your senators and representatives of your intentions but do not ask them to exert influence on your behalf. An even better procedure would be for the official in your organization responsible for government relations to inform the representatives and for them to make the decision as to just what should be reported and how. There are a few instances where congressional intercession has helped, but more instances where such intrusion has so antagonized the agency staff that its forced approval of a project may be its last positive response to your proposals. Agency tenure tends to outlast congressional tenure.

The same planning and attention to details should mark the applicant's approach to foundations as has marked other parts of the process of growth and development of an idea. Follow the advice and instruction of each of the foundations on the final list. An abstract of twenty pages may be acceptable to one, five pages to another, one page to still another. The preparation of each is an exercise in combining degrees of brevity and precision while preserving the chief ideas and information needed by the donors.

Government programs may have very sharply focused interests, such as those described in the guidelines of the National Science Foundation's Research in Undergraduate Institutions Program or the Department of Education's International Educational Program (http://www.ed.gov/about/offices/list/ope/iegps/index.html).

Secure guidelines from these agencies and be sure that the application follows all directions regarding content, format, and order. Remember that an agency's guidelines not only reflect the many voices which aided in their preparation but also have had to be cleared by the agency's legal counsel, finance officers, and legislative liaison officer, and in final form may seem to contain ambiguities. It is strongly recommended that you visit or at least make a phone call to the agency's Program Officer before submitting a proposal or preliminary proposal, to discover whether you have correctly interpreted all directions.

Most of the preceding advice is based on the assumption that the institution provides competent professional help in finding outside support; details have been included, however, that will make the advice equally or even more useful to those lacking such help. The following additional tips will help those in such a situation. Most large city libraries carry the *Federal Register* along with other publications. The Federal Register online can be found at http://www.archives.gov/federal-register/the-federal-register/ or http://www.archives.gov/federal-register/the-federal-register/. Headquarters of the United Way and other large charitable institutions or development offices of colleges and universities subscribe to and hold many publications of sources. The Foundation Library has many branches and its staff, as we have said before, is notably competent and helpful. The local telephone book usually lists local foundations. More information about these local foundations can be found via their Web address or online at the Foundation Directory (http://fconline.fdncenter.org). You may wish to purchase or subscribe to some of the basic sources of general information to become familiar with the kinds of sources and the level of sophistication grant seeking has reached.

In short, do the homework and give no less attention to answering the questions and following the specifications of a funding source than to other phases of guiding a developing project to completion.

To clarify the viewpoint of the prospective supporter or donor we quote part of a paper given by Dr. Nils Y. Wessell, former President of the Alfred P. Sloan Foundation. The full text of his paper appeared in the *Society of Research Administrators Journal,* Spring 1975. The comments apply to his foundation's position and probably reflect the position of an increasing number of foundations.

> I could not believe *my* eyes and ears one bright morning when the three individuals who represented *my* ten o'clock appointment walked in carrying an easel and colored flipcharts. One of the three served only as a flipper of the charts on cue. The second must have been a former Florida underwater land salesman. The third was the president of the institution who simply sat in the background, grinned, and nodded his head. The faculty members who conceived the project and were to carry it

out, given support, and who were the only ones who really understood what it was all about, were hundreds of miles away back home. That is what I call the Madison Avenue brand of sophistication. Making the whole thing even more unbelievable was the fact that if any one of them had bothered to read our last annual report, he would have known that the proposed program was specifically one which did not meet our program guidelines.

Don't start your funding search with a "ceremonial" visit. Do your homework to learn what the funding source is interested in or how it wishes to be approached.

Submission of a Proposal

Although every agency or funding source has its own peculiar requirements that should be met to the letter, it is safe to say that the total body of material, ready to be submitted for consideration, will consist of (1) a cover sheet, (2) letters of endorsement, and (3) the proposal proper, in exactly this order. This material represents everything you wish to have considered by a reviewer. These pages should be secured by a single staple or grommet in the upper left hand corner. Do not add protective or decorative covers and bindings, for these will be promptly torn off to expose the official cover sheet as well as to lighten the load and to facilitate filing. A letter of transmittal should accompany the proposal but should not be permanently attached to it.

Today electronic submission of proposals is encouraged by most government agencies and an increasing number of private foundations. One example of a foundation using electronic submission can be found on the Lowe's Foundation Web site: http://apps.bridgetree.com/funding/default3.asp?sid=200458743052.

Again, follow the instructions listed on each individual Web site and print or save all (if the Web site allows) information before submission. An increasing number of foundations, corporations, and government agencies are requiring electronic submissions. There is always a contact person listed if you run into technical problems.

The contents of the proposal have already been described in "Specific Parts of a Proposal" section within the chapter on proposal, but more should be said concerning the cover sheet and letters of endorsement and transmittal.

Dr. Robert Lichter, who was the head of a major foundation based in New York, frequently spoke at workshops on grant seeking and proposal development. He had 10 points of advice for the experienced and the newcomer.

1. Get the guidelines.
2. Read the guidelines.
3. Follow the guidelines.
4. Follow the guidelines.
5. Follow the guidelines.
6. Follow the guidelines.
7. Follow the guidelines.
8. Follow the guidelines.
9. Follow the guidelines.
10. Follow the guidelines.

COVER SHEET

The cover sheet is always the top page and carries all of the information that identifies your organization and proposal. Federal agencies usually provide their own forms for a cover sheet: the forms vary from program to program but the same kinds of data are sought and probably include the following two:

Employer identification number (EIN), which is the same number assigned to an employer in connection with Federal Withholding Tax.

State Clearing House Number. Certain programs require clearance with the State Planning Commission before action can be taken on a proposal. In other cases, state institutions must secure clearance from the planning authorities and their state education commissions. The agency you are applying to can tell you whether its program requires state clearance. Your regional office, state commission on education, or state planning commission can provide you with the needed information and appropriate forms to file.

These may seem like trivial points, but your proposal can be rejected on technicalities such as omission of pieces of required information.

Cover sheets or your own title page should also contain certain other information:

1. The title of the project
2. Name and address of institution
3. Project Director's name, address, telephone/fax numbers, and e-mail address
4. Dollar amount of grant requested
5. Signature of authorizing official at your institution, usually the president

Exhibit 14. Example Letter of Transmittal.

_____, 19___

Dr. William Black, Executive Director
The Susan and Emma Cash Foundation
1000 East Bay Street
Boston, MA 02101
Dear Dr. Black: (title)

The enclosed proposal _____ has been addressed to the Susan and Emma Cash Foundation in response to your stated interest in projects that will improve the ability of women to compete in professional activities. We have noted that your upper limit of support for administration training programs is $50,000. Our proposed training program will require $31,280 for implementation.

I am personally familiar with the thorough study and detailed plans that Professor Edna Driver has carried out to prepare this proposal. Since _____ College is committed to the education of women and has a faculty with an excellent record in research and project design we heartily endorse this project as an appropriate mission for this institution. Should you have any further questions concerning the institution's commitment or Professor Driver's plan, please feel free to call me or to call Professor Driver directly.

        Sincerely yours,

        (signed)

        Title: President; Executive Director, etc.

---

6. Chief Fiscal Officer's name, title, address, telephone/ fax number, and e-mail address; Grants Officer's name, title, address, telephone/fax number, and e-mail address
7. Proposed date for starting project
8. Submission date

LETTERS OF ENDORSEMENT

If you wish reviewers to read letters of endorsement, place them following the cover sheet or in the first appendix. The letter of transmittal accompanies the proposal but is not permanently attached to it and is presumably filed separately by the official to whom it is addressed. A letter of endorsement signed by the officer empowered to speak for your institution is an appropriate or even very desirable part of your proposal because it assures the reviewer of the institution's confidence in and commitment to your project. In the case of a cooperative venture, the endorsement of each of the heads of the cooperating institutions should be included. The letter of endorsement should contain (a) a brief statement endorsing the idea of the proposal, (b) an explanation of why the particular agency was selected (i.e., the philosophy and objectives expressed in its literature and policy statement make it appropriate for the envisioned project), and (c) a request that the accompanying request for XYZ foundation to support the project over a period of___years be given serious consideration. The letter of endorsement can also contain other points that the signer believes will reinforce the potential significance of the project to the institution.

LETTER OF TRANSMITTAL

Every proposal to a private funding source should be accompanied by a transmittal letter. State which program you are applying to, what sum of money you need, and what you want the reader of your letter to do, i.e., do you want that person to read it, file it, or respond to it?

It is wise to enclose a letter of transmittal with your proposal even though a letter of endorsement is already an inclusion. The letter of transmittal, signed by the person authorized to speak for the institution, asks the receiver to do whatever is necessary to have your proposal considered. This letter may be all that is required as an endorsement, or the letter of endorsement may be an exact copy of the letter of transmittal (Exhibit 14).

WAIT! PROFESSOR, YOUR SIGNATURE

FORMATTING REQUIREMENTS

Note the formatting requirements, if any. If there are few or no specifications, we suggest the following:

1. Use a blank white $8^1/_2$ 11 paper.
2. Set your word processing program to use a standard typeface, no smaller than 12 point such as Times New Roman, double space between lines, and leave a $1^1/_2$-inch margin on the sides and bottom and a 1-inch margin at the top.
3. Place page numbers at top right corner, center top, or bottom, but be consistent.
4. Put the organization's or Project Director's name at lower left corner of each page or block of pages that might be extracted from the full proposal for purposes of handling and circulation, e.g., cover sheet, budget page, abstract, vita.
5. Use capital letters for main headings, write subheadings in uppercase and lowercase letters.
6. Consider the advantages of outlining your proposal, using a conventional system of numbers and letters to designate sections and subsections; some word processing programs have outline formats.
7. Beside each budget item, note the page where this item is described in the narrative portion of your proposal.
8. Provide a table of contents, include the page number where each section or subsection begins, and provide appropriate outline numbers and letters if this system has been used in your proposal.
9. Be sure that section headings and subheadings and outline designations in the table of contents correspond exactly to those in the body of the proposal and that all references to these items correspond similarly.
10. Some agencies specify margins and type size; follow their instructions.

FINALLY AND FIRST: FOLLOW INSTRUCTIONS, FOLLOW INSTRUCTIONS

1. Check the following to be certain of the deadline:

   date for receipt of proposal;
   date for mailing (send by Certified Mail to ensure safety and also to guarantee having evidence of date of sending, keep the receipt; Express Mail and commercial carrierreceipts are not always acceptable proof to the agency); or
   date for hand-delivery.

2. Do not ask for extensions unless there is some real and urgent reason. Do not expect to receive an extension.

THE FINAL CHECK

Before submission, make one final check. Have you included

1. required assurances and certification—for example, Civil Rights Act, Treatment of Human Subjects, Animal Subjects, Drug-Free Work Place, Lobbying, Debarment and Suspension, etc.? (See Section V (Forms and Required Information) of Part II)
2. correct number of copies, including extras of any section requested?
3. Internal Revenue statement on tax exemption and private foundation status?
4. a *curriculum vitae* for the Project Director and each person with a key post in the project?
5. all official forms filled out as per instructions of the funding agency?
6. required signatures of officials in your institution?

Submit your proposal and patiently wait for a response from the funding agency.

Grant Administration

Accountability and capacity to account for funds and the activities in a funded project are increasingly important in awarding a grant. Your track record in doing what you proposed as supported by sound evaluative practice and good fiscal accounting puts you in a stronger position for future grants. The following pages provide an administrative process designed to accommodate small organizations and institutions where there may be only one or two people responsible for management of grant funds.

First we will go through some of the typical responses you might receive from a sponsor and how to respond.

We then provide some general advice and checklists to prepare you for securing and spending awarded funds.

Following that general advice is a section to help you negotiate an agreement if you are not offered full funding for your project.

Next, we offer suggestions for action if your proposal is rejected.

Finally, we will lead you through the process starting with a sample budget, typical communication with the grantor, award letters, forms for justifying and authorizing payments, and a simple spread sheet for record keeping.

COMMUNICATION FROM AND WITH THE SPONSOR

The day eventually comes when you hear from the outside agency whose support you sought for your project. Below are the kinds of replies you may receive and some of the possible ensuing actions you can take:

1. A form or personalized letter rejecting your proposal—respond politely and ask for more explicit comments as to why you were turned down. Explain that you would value constructive criticism to guide you in considering resubmission.
2. Request for additional information—provide what is requested promptly.

3. Letter suggesting that you (a) review your proposal, (b) limit your project activities, or (c) decrease the dollar amount of your request—a conference should be sought. Following such a meeting, revise your proposal if this can be done without jeopardizing your mission or the quality of the anticipated results.
4. Official letter stating that a grant or contract is going to be awarded to you. Some agencies require an official acceptance signed by (a) the official authorized to obligate the institution and (b) the Project Director. Others assume you have accepted unless you tell them otherwise. If your grant comes from a federal agency, your congressional representative is always notified first. The good news thus usually comes from your elected representative.

PREPARATION FOR SECURING AND EXPENDING THE GRANT FUNDS

Don't count on spending the first dollar until you have the funds in hand. Before you arrange to draw down the funds from the grantor (the federal government usually makes payments upon submission of quarterly request vouchers while some private foundations will remit the entire grant amount in one check in advance), we suggest the following preparation:

1. Discuss your grant and the institution's procedures for handling grant funds with the Fiscal Officer. Learn what steps you must follow to secure payment of expenses. We assume some person, probably the Grants or Sponsored Programs Officer again, is responsible for overseeing the official accounting for grants and contracts. You should learn from that person and the agency what latitude you have in spending funds without seeking written permission, i.e., "change order" from the grantor, and what kinds of expenditures are not allowed. Re-read your agency guidelines and your proposal with care.
2. Keep complete records for yourself as a double check. It is wise to assume there will be an audit and, thus, to

maintain not only official records but work paper to refresh your memory after the work has been completed. All correspondence with the grantor and a record of all expenditures should be kept in the files so that you can tell what has been spent and what funds remain at any given time.

3. For the purposes of making payments on grant activities, a special voucher form is recommended that has spaces for the internal account number, the grant number, the grantor or agency, identification of expenditure by line item, the Project Director's signature, and the signature of that person in the business office who authorizes payments.

The following is a summary *checklist* to assist you in anticipating and solving the major administrative problems:

- Acknowledge the award and secure the grantor's guide or requirements for accounting and reporting.

- Meet your Fiscal Officer and have an account established for your grant so that it will be included in the regular accounting of the institution.

- Learn what you should do to secure payments from the grant-making agency.

- Prepare an estimate of your expected costs for the next three months, and ask the Fiscal Officer to request these funds from the grantor (assuming the money has not been paid in advance).

- Discuss and review expected expenses with Project Director before spending the money.

- Revise budget accordingly if expenses are at variance with those projected in the original proposal, and secure permission to make the changes if such permission is required by the grantor. Usually there is a limit on changes allowed without permission. Permission is usually required for additions or deletions of line items.

- Forward approved requests for expenditures to Fiscal Officer for review and payment.

- Copy and maintain a file of all vouchers submitted for payment.

- Compile statements of services performed and appended to vouchers. The name, time spent, and budget items authorizing the activity should be on the voucher.

- Gather all airline stubs, hotel bills, and other receipts to request travel reimbursement according to institutional policy.

- Arrange for compensation of temporary personnel. Work with the Fiscal Officer to be certain that Social Security and benefits are covered. The round figure in the proposal budget should cover all costs, not just the gross salary.

- Be alert to requirements for competitive bids or acceptable justification for dealing with a particular supplier.

- Review with your Fiscal Officers all extra compensation for regular employees. An institution is subject to Social Security and income tax withholding based on the employee's total compensation from that institution.

- Contact awarding agency to determine classification for grants made to individuals. Certain grants for study made to particular individuals are considered fellowships and are not subject to income tax. The awarding agency should be consulted to determine the classification. However the IRS Code makes it clear that the term "fellowship" is not synonymous with "tax exempt." Most compensation under grants and contracts is treated as taxable income.

- Find out the allowed current rate for per day plus expenses for fees for consultants. Most federal grants set a limit of per diem plus expenses for fees for consultants. Find out what the current rate is and be certain of the fees allowed by your grant-making agency before paying consultant fees.

- Obtain approval in advance from federal agency for foreign travel. Foreign travel, although approved as a line item in a grant budget, must have specific approval before the trip is taken.

- *Prepare and file your required reports on time.*

NEGOTIATION AND ACCEPTANCE

Your award letter or a telephone call from the sponsor has come! Ideally, they will say they desire to provide assistance in the amount you requested in the proposal. If this is the case, there is little problem and your most important task is to review any accompanying terms, conditions, or stipulations to be sure that

1. your institution is prepared to comply and
2. the terms conform to the policies and practices of your institution.

For example, if the project involves human subjects, there are federal regulations covering their use and treatment, the same applies for animal subjects. Or, the sponsor may request certain restrictions on publishing material derived from the project. You should make sure that any such restrictions are in concert with your own institutional policies before accepting the award.

BUT, THEY SAID THE POPULATION TO BE STUDIED SHOULD BE REPRESENTED ON THE RESEARCH COMMITTEE!

Unfortunately, total funding of the amount requested in your proposal is a rare occurrence. Usually you will receive a letter or telephone call suggesting that you revise your proposal by

- limiting your project activity or

- decreasing the dollar amount of your request.

It is important at this point to review the sponsor's request with the Grants Officer as that person usually accepts the award on behalf of the institution and is therefore familiar with institutional policy and negotiations. The Project Director and Grants Officer, either by letter or telephone, must seek a resolution with the sponsor. When a general agreement is reached, prepare a revised proposal that does not jeopardize the mission of the project or quality of the anticipated results. The next step is usually the receipt of an official award letter stating a grant or contract has been awarded to your institution to perform the project you proposed. Some agencies require official acceptance signed by the person authorized to obligate the institution. Others will assume that you accept the award unless you tell them otherwise. You are now at liberty to begin work and expect the sponsor to pay for the costs.

REJECTION/SELF-APPRAISAL/ RESUBMISSION

If the communication you receive from the outside agency is a form or personalized letter rejecting your proposal, do not despair.

The competition for funding of academic and other proposals for research and/or curriculum, instruction, and training programs is very keen. In fact, the number of requests for funding from federal and foundation sources has shown a significant increase over the past decade. The rejection of a proposal for funding is a common occurrence, particularly in the case of a first submission.

One of the most important steps to be taken after a rejection is to learn why the submission was unsuccessful. All federal agencies are obligated to provide you with

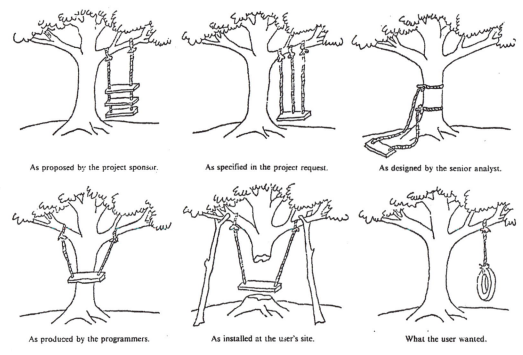

As proposed by the project sponsor.   As specified in the project request.   As designed by the senior analyst.

As produced by the programmers.   As installed at the user's site.   What the user wanted.

Source: The drawings above are reprinted, with permission, from *Front Lines*, a publication of the U.S. Agency for International Development.

either a written or oral debriefing on the reasons for the denial. In the case of federal agencies, which use "peer review" or "study-section review" in proposal evaluations, copies of the reviews are available to the Project Director upon request. You should always request the written evaluation or an oral debriefing.

The situation for unsuccessful foundation proposals is quite different. There is no obligation to furnish the grant applicant with any reasons for denial. Nevertheless, one should always pursue any agency directly or indirectly as to the reasons for rejection. Some foundations will not provide any information. Still others are very helpful and constructive in discussing the rejection.

It is generally a good idea to conduct a self-appraisal to complement the sponsor's comments on denial by asking questions of the following nature:

1. How pressing a need does the project fill?
2. Does the proposal demonstrate a clear anticipation of problems that are likely to occur, and an awareness of relevant scholarship and available resources?
3. How does the applicant's background (education, publications, professional standing) clearly qualify him/her to carry out this project successfully?
4. Is the budget sound?
5. In general, does the proposal have promise of making a significant contribution?

For the self-appraisal to be worthwhile, one must be objective and brutally frank.

The only purpose of the internal critique and solicitation of the reasons the proposal was not funded is to secure information to guide you in considering resubmission. Through the information you have gathered, there should be strong possibilities of improving the quality of the blueprint for carrying out your ideas.

Don't get discouraged by rejection. Consider and weigh the reviewers' comments and strengthen your proposal for resubmission. The chances of funding are much greater for proposals that have been improved and re-submitted as opposed to starting fresh with a new idea.

A CASE STUDY FOR ADMINISTRATION OF A GRANT

Anyville College Receives an Award

Anyville College has submitted a proposal to the Department of Education to develop a new program in Latin American Studies. Faculty need released time during the academic year to participate in a course developed over the summer. A consultant will be brought in to meet with faculty during their summer working sessions for assistance with evaluation after courses are tested. The narrative description of costs is a reflection of the detailed description of activities in the narrative. The original budget submitted requested $42,000. $5,000 was for part-time secretarial support. Seven months have passed since the submission deadline. The person listed on the cover sheet of the proposal in Exhibit 18, contact person, receives a phone call from a person in the agency grants/contracts office to discuss some budget changes. The Grants or Sponsored Program Officer's name is not on the cover sheet, just the Project Director' name: In this case study Jane Doe is the Project Director and since there is no place for the Grants Officers' name on the cover sheet, Jane Doe receives the phone call from the Education Department to discuss the budget. Anne Perking is the Education Department contact specialist. Ms. Perking asks Jane Doe to reduce her submitted budget by $5000, and eliminate the secretary since Anyville's overhead includes secretarial support. Professor Doe recognizes that she does not have authority to make a change of this sort without consulting with the Anyville Grants Officer, George Smith. George Smith calls Ms. Perking and agrees to the reduction in the budget. Ms. Perking asks for a revised "budget" to be submitted in one week, revising the new grant total to $37,000. In addition to the reduction, Ms. Perking asks the Grants Officer, George Smith, for an explanation of the basis for Professor Rich's salary and for assurance that the college will support his released time.

The Cast of People Involved

Before we move on to the example budgets, letters, and forms, let us list below the cast of people involved in the awarding and administering of this grant.

First Actions to Be Taken

The first thing to be done is the preparation of a written response to the Education Department's Grants Specialist, Ms. Perking. This requires a letter from George Smith answering her questions and a revised budget and revised coversheet (Exhibit 16, 18, & 19). Anyville's President, Dr. Bartholomew Pressley, needs to write a letter to the Program Officer, approving Smith's revised budget (Exhibit 17). This documentation is important for records. At last, an official award letter arrives addressed to the

Exhibit 15. A List of People Involved.

• Anyville Project Director	Dr. Jane Doe—It's her proposal and project to carry out
• President of Anyville College	Dr. Bartholomew Pressley—He is the person with authority to commit the resources of Anyville
• Education Department Program Officer	Dr. Edna Green—Government Official for Program Decisions
• Education Department Grants/Contract	Ms. Anne Perking—Government Official for Fiscal Decisions
• Anyville Sponsored Program Officer	George Smith-College Official for Fiscal Decisions
• Anyville Business Officer	Susan S. Jones—College Official who issues checks

President and/or the Project Director. This letter will be accompanied by an official award document citing the award number, authorized funding, the budget period, the project period, and the method of payment (Exhibit 21). Review this document carefully to be certain it contains the information you agreed to. This document is the official authorization telling you the granted money is available.

Spending the Grant Funds

The following postaward process for administration of sponsored programs (grants) was designed for a small college or organization. It defines a sponsored program for the purpose of determining who is responsible for accounting, approving expenditures, and reporting. It also calls for three signatures on each voucher in order to have a check written. This procedure protects everyone from making unallowable expenditures, incorrect calculations, and overexpenditure of funds. This procedure provides documentation, for each expenditure, sufficient to meet audit requirements.

Anyville College—Postaward Policy

All projects funded from external sources—government, foundation, corporation, or individuals—with multiple line item budgets, time limitations for expenditure of grant funds, and/or requirements for fiscal reports are defined as "sponsored programs" and are subject to these procedures for administration of grants.

1. **Awards Notification** may come to the President or the Principal Investigator/Project Director (PI/PD).

Upon receipt of notification of award, copies of the award documents or letter should be sent to the Fiscal Officer and the Director of Sponsored Programs. The latter will forward the information to the Dean and the Director of Development.

Any changes in the budget for obligation of time and college facilities must be approved by the person(s) authorized to obligate the college—the President or the Chief Fiscal Officer.

When required, an acceptance of the award should be sent to the funding source in accordance with its instructions. The grantor may require an acknowledgment from the President or the Chief Fiscal Officer. The Director of Sponsored Programs must review the award to make certain there are no unexpected terms and conditions in the award document (Exhibit 21).

2. **Administration of Grants—The Anyville College Prior Approval System.** The Director of Sponsored Programs has the responsibility for this organizational prior approval system (OPAS).

Have the Fiscal Officer assign an account number to the grant (Exhibit 22). Provide the PI/PD with a supply of vouchers (Exhibit 23), time and effort report sheets, and secretarial log sheets.

Maintain expenditure records on an accrual basis (Exhibit 24).

Provide the PI/PD with guidance on allowable changes and assistance in securing approval of modifications.

3. **Expenditures (Procedures and Policy Information).** PI/PD initiates request for expenditures.

The Director of Sponsored Programs reviews request to see that there are funds in the grant account and that the expenditure is allowable under the grant/contract terms and conditions.

The Fiscal Officer checks the voucher after it is signed by PI/PD and Director of Sponsored Programs and signs to authorize payment.

All vouchers must be supported by internal purchase orders with supplier's invoices, Anyville travel vouchers and documentation, and time and effort reports as appropriate.

Purchase orders must be initiated by the Director of Sponsored Programs to obligate funds. This is important since the monthly expenditure reports provided to the PI/PD are on an accrual basis and federal fiscal reports are also made on an accrual basis.

No changes can be made in salary and wage items or items specifically limited by the grantor without prior approval of the Director of Sponsored Programs because these changes may reflect additional costs to the college.

Anyville employment policy applies to all grants and contracts unless prior approval for deviation in policy is approved by the President/Dean/Chief Fiscal Officer.

4. **Reports**. Final fiscal reports will be prepared by the PI/PD and Sponsored Programs Officer for signature and transmittal by the Chief Fiscal Officer (Exhibit 25).

PI/PD is responsible for preparing nonfiscal project reports in time to meet the grantor's schedule.

5. **General Information**. Current fringe benefit and indirect cost rates are available from the Sponsored Programs Officer. The rates are revised annually under a formula set by the government by OMB Ruling A-21 (Exhibit 16).

The Department of Health and Human Services (HHS) is the cognizant agency and has the responsibility for audit of all federal funds. Anyville College is required to conduct an annual audit of federal funds.

Summer salaries for faculty are calculated at one-ninth of the academic year base salary unless some other terms are negotiated and agreed to by the grantee and grantor.

Specific information related to federal regulations for compliance with civil rights, sex and age discrimination, privacy, animal care, safety standards, accessibility for the handicapped, drug-free workplace, and accounting requirements are kept on file. Anyville College policy requires compliance with such regulations.

Here's my final report, Dean! I'm finished!

Exhibit 16. Letter of Transmittal for Revised Cover Sheet/Budget. Ms. Anne Perking.

Department of Education   January 16, 2007
Contracts Office
7th & D Streets SW
Washington, DC 20202

Dear Ms. Perking:

Enclosed is a revised budget for Grant #000000375.

Anyville College will provide the released time required for Professor Rich to serve as the group leader specified on line item A-2. This figure is based on 1/7 base salary per course per term.

The remaining adjustments in the budget reflect actual salaries for Anyville College's next academic year commencing on July 1, 1985, and revised estimates in the other line items based on current costs.

The total of this revised budget is $37,000 from the Department of Education with an additional $15,276 in cost sharing from Anyville College.

I appreciate your assistance in making this revision. Please let me know if you have any further questions.

Sincerely yours,

George Smith
Director Sponsored Programs

GS/prc
Enclosure

Exhibit 17. Letter of Transmittal Signed by President of Anyville College.

Dr. Edna Green
Department of Education
International Studies Branch
7th & D Streets, SW, ROB3
Washington, DC: 20202

Dear Dr. Green:

Enclosed is the cover sheet and a revised budget for Grant #G00000375 as requested by your contracting officer. We are pleased to receive this grant to develop and implement a program in Latin American Studies at Anyville College. This revised budget for a total of $37,000 has my approval.

Very truly yours,

Bartholomew Presley
President

BP/pr
Enclosure

Exhibit 18. Revised Cover Sheet. (Application for Federal Education Assistance—ED 124).

Application for Federal Education Assistance (ED 424)

U.S. Department of Education
Form Approved
OMB No. 1890-0017
Exp. 4/30/2008

Applicant Information

1. Name and Address

Legal Name: Anyville College

Address: 0000 South Street

Organizational Unit
Modern Languages

Anyville
City

VA
State

Central
County

00000 - 000
ZIP Code + 4

2. Applicant's D-U-N-S Number 1 2 3 4 5 6 7 8 9

3. Applicant's T-I-N 0 0 - 0 0 0 0 0 0 0

4. Catalog of Federal Domestic Assistance #: 8 4

Title: Undergraduate International Studies and Foreign Language Program

5. Project Director: Dr. Jane Doe

Address: 0000 South Street

Anyville
City

VA
State

00000 - 000
ZIP Code + 4

Tel. #: 1-800-234-5678

Fax #: 1-800-432-8765

E-Mail Address: jdoe@anyville.edu

6. Novice Applicant ☑ Yes ☐ No

7. Is the applicant delinquent on any Federal debt? ☐ Yes ☑ No
(If "Yes," attach an explanation.)

8. Type of Applicant *(Enter appropriate letter in the box.)* [H]

A State
B Local
C Special District
D Indian Tribe
E Individual
F Independent School District

G Public College or University
H Private, Non-Profit College or University
I Non-Profit Organization
J Private, Profit-Making Organization
K Other (Specify): _____

9. State Application Identifier: Dept of Ed/ Training

Application Information

10. Type of Submission:

—PreApplication
☐ Construction
☐ Non-Construction

—Application
☐ Construction
☑ Non-Construction

11. Is application subject to review by Executive Order 12372 process?
☐ Yes *(Date made available to the Executive Order 12372 process for review):* _____
☑ No *(If "No," check appropriate box below.)*
☐ Program is not covered by E.O. 12372.
☑ Program has not been selected by State for review.

12. Proposed Project Dates:
Start Date: 6/1/2007
End Date: 6/1/2008

13. Are any research activities involving human subjects planned at any time during the proposed project period?

☐ Yes (Go to 13a.) ☑ No (Go to item 14.)

13a. Are all the research activities proposed designated to be exempt from the regulations?

☐ Yes (Provide Exemption(s) #): _____
☐ No (Provide Assurance #): _____

14. Descriptive Title of Applicant's Project:
Latin American Studies (LAS): Second year of program designed to bring a LAS into our international studies curriculum; 4 wk faculty training, incorp. of material on LAS into over 20 exsisting courses for ca. 300 students/yr.

Estimated Funding

15a. Federal	$	37,000 .00
b. Applicant	$	15,276 .00
c. State	$	.00
d. Local	$	.00
e. Other	$	.00
f. Program Income	$	.00
g. TOTAL	$	52,276 .00

Authorized Representative Information

16. To the best of my knowledge and belief, all data in this preapplication/application are true and correct. The document has been duly authorized by the governing body of the applicant and the applicant will comply with the attached assurances if the assistance is awarded.

a. Authorized Representative *(Please type or print name clearly.)*
Dr. Bartholomew Presley

b. Title
President

c. Tel. #: 1-800-567-8910   Fax #: 1-800-765-0198

d. E-Mail Address: bpresley@anyville.edu

e. Signature of Authorized Representative

Date: 1/1/2007

Exhibit 19. Revised Budget Detail.

Anyville College Revised Budget			AVC	ED	TOTAL
A.	Personnel.				
	1.	Project Director in-kind overload (1 course)		2886	2886
	2.	2 Faculty Group Leaders 1 term I. course released time each	2806	4838	7644
	3.	5 Faculty Participants in intro course 7105 (equivalent *1/4* course each)		7106	
	4.	1 Faculty Released 1 course to teach Contemporary Latin American Literature in translation	2886		2886
	5.	1 or 2 Faculty — 1 man month Sumner work on computer-based language instruction	0	3800	3800
	6.	7 Faculty including pa. 5 for 1 week; 2 for 1—1/2 week *at* rate of 1/9 salary/month	7500		7500
	7.	Visiting Lecturer	3000		3000
	Subtotal		23297	11524	34821
B.	Fringe Benefits (18.42 S & W)		4287	2120	6407
C.	Travel				
	1.	Consultant	975		915
	2.	Project Director	600		600
D.	Equipment		-	-	-
E.	Supplies				
	1.	Paper, binders, blank tapes, etc.	500		500
	2.	Library holdings	3200	500	3700
	3.	Duplicating	400		400
F.	Contractual		-	-	-
G.	Construction	0	-	-	-
H.	Other	0	-	-	-
	1.	Consultants	1000	400	
I.	Total Direct Costs		4259	14144	48403
S.	Indirect Costs (82 TDC)		2741	1132	3873
K.	**Project Total**	$	**37,000**	**$15,276**	**$52,276**

Exhibit 20. Federal Budget Form, Revised.

OMB APPROVAL NO. 29 R0218

PART III — BUDGET INFORMATION

SECTION A — BUDGET SUMMARY

GRANT PROGRAM, FUNCTION OR ACTIVITY (a)	FEDERAL CATALOG NO. (b)	ESTIMATED UNOBLIGATED FUNDS		NEW OR REVISED BUDGET		
		FEDERAL (c)	NON-FEDERAL (d)	FEDERAL (e)	NON-FEDERAL (f)	TOTAL (g)
1. Undergrad International Studies and Foreign Language Program	84.016	$	$	$ 37,000	$ 15,276	$ 51,195

SECTION B — BUDGET CATEGORIES

GRANT PROGRAM, FUNCTION OR ACTIVITY

6. OBJECT CLASS CATEGORIES	(1) Federal	(2) Non-Federal	TOTAL (5)
a. PERSONNEL	$ 23,297	$ 11,524	$ 34,821
b. FRINGE BENEFITS	4,287	2,120	6,407
c. TRAVEL	1,575	--	1,575
d. EQUIPMENT	--	--	--
e. SUPPLIES	4,100	500	4,600
f. CONTRACTUAL	--	--	--
g. CONSTRUCTION			
h. OTHER	1,000	--	1,000
i. TOTAL DIRECT CHARGES	34,259	14,144	48,403
j. INDIRECT CHARGES	2,741	1,132	3,873
k. TOTALS	$ 37,000	$ 15,276	$ 52,276
7. PROGRAM INCOME			

Exhibit 21. Grant Notification Award.

U.S. DEPARTMENT OF EDUCATION
WASHINGTON, D.C. 20202
GRANT AWARD NOTIFICATION

GRANTS AND CONTRACTS
SERVICE

1 RECIPIENT NAME

Anyville College
0000 South Street
Anyville, E. Va. 00000

4 AWARD INFORMATION

PR/AWARD NUMBER	GOO---375
ACTION NUMBER	01
ACTION TYPE	NEW
AWARD TYPE	DISCRETIONARY

2 PROJECT TITLE

COST CONTAINMENT IN HIGHER EDUCATION: UNBUNDLING
CHARGES TO STUDENTS DTD 03/07/88 AS AMENDED

5 AWARD PERIODS

BUDGET PERIOD	09/01/X1 – 08/31/X2
PROJECT PERIOD	09/01/X1 – 08/31/X2

3 PROJECT STAFF

RECIPIENT PROJECT DIRECTOR

JANE DOE   20?- -

EDUCATION PROGRAM STAFF

EDNA GREEN   202- -

EDUCATION GRANTS STAFF

ANNE PERKING   202- -

6 AUTHORIZED FUNDING

THIS ACTION	$37,000
CARRY OVER	-0-
BUDGET PERIOD	$37,000
PROJECT PERIOD	$37,000
RECIPIENT COST SHARE	$15,276

7 ADMINISTRATIVE INFORMATION

PAYMENT METHOD	ED PMS
ENTITY NUMBER	1-521244583-A1
REGULATIONS	34 CFR 74, 75, 77, 78
	34 CFR 630
ATTACHMENTS	AB

8 LEGISLATIVE & FISCAL DATA

AUTHORITY: Higher EDUCATION AMENDMENTS OF 1980, P.L. 96-374, TITLE VI
PROGRAM TITLE: FIPSE –UNDERGRADUATE INTERNATIONAL STUDIES   CFDA: 84.016A

APPROPRIATION	FY	CAN	OBJECT CLASS	AMOUNT
9130201		E003088	4127	37,000

9 TERMS AND CONDITIONS OF AWARD

THE FOLLOWING ITEMS ARE INCORPORATED IN THE GRANT AGREEMENT:
  1) THE RECIPIENT'S APPLICATION (BLOCK 2),
  2) THE APPLICABLE EDUCATION DEPARTMENT REGULATIONS (BLOCK 7).

OTHER INFORMATION AFFECTING THIS ACTION IS PROVIDED IN THE ATTACHMENTS SHOWN IN BLOCK 7.

GRANTS OFFICER B.R.BROWN   DATE

Ver. 1

ED - GCS 007 (9/87)   **PLEASE SEE OTHER SIDE FOR MORE INFORMATION**

Exhibit 22. Anyville Internal Grant Notification and Status Sheet.

TITLE OF PROJECT: Latin American Studies Program (Continuation)

AGENCY/ORGANIZATION:

N AME: Department of Education

A DDRESS: 400 Maryland Avenue, SW, Washington, DC 20202

C ONTACT/PROGRAM: Edna Green

CONTACT/FISCAL: Anne Perking - (202) 000-0000

PERIOD OF PROJECT:

PERIOD OF AWARD:

N EGOTIATED TERMS: Reduction

A MENDMENTS: Budget was revised on _____for a request of $37,000.

AGENCY NO. G00000375: ANYVILLE ACCOUNT NO. #330. 000

PROJECT REPORT DUE: 7/1/08   PROJECT REPORT IN: 6/25/08

FISCAL REPORT DUE: 7/1/08   FISCAL REPORT IN: 6/25/08

AUTHORIZATIONS FOR PAYMENT

    1. P1/PD: Jane Doe

    2. Other:

    3. Sponsored Program Office: George Smith

    4. Fiscal Office: Susan S. Jones

N OTE: NO PAYMENTS CAN BE MADE WITHOUT ABOVE SIGNATURES.

Exhibit 23. Sample Vouchers.

REQUEST FOR PAYMENT EXTERNAL FUNDS	ANYVILLE COLLEGE SPONSORED PROGRAM	1. VOUCHER NO. 50		
2. CONSORTIUM: FISCAL AGENT	3. AGENCY/ORGANIZATION ED:Latin American Studies	4. AGENCY GRANT NO. GOO 375		
5. SUBCONTRACTOR	6. PROJECT DIRECTOR (P.D.)/PRINCIPAL INVESTIGATOR (P.I.) Professor Doe	7. SBC ACCOUNT NO. 330.726		
8. PAYEE AND DESCRIPTION OR EXPLANATION *(ATTACH INVOICES OR PAYEE LIST)*		9. LINE ITEM	10. $ AMOUNT	
Pay to Mary I. Navarro for airfare for trip to ECC for consulting		C1	329	50

REQUEST FOR PAYMENT EXTERNAL FUNDS	ANYVILLE COLLEGE SPONSORED PROGRAM	1. VOUCHER NO. 57		
2. CONSORTIUM: FISCAL AGENT	3. AGENCY/ORGANIZATION ED:Latin American Studies	4. AGENCY GRANT NO. GOO 375		
5. SUBCONTRACTOR	6. PROJECT DIRECTOR (P.D.)/PRINCIPAL INVESTIGATOR (P.I.) Professor Doe	7. SBC ACCOUNT NO. 330.726		
8. PAYEE AND DESCRIPTION OR EXPLANATION *(ATTACH INVOICES OR PAYEE LIST)*		9. LINE ITEM	10. $ AMOUNT	
Pay to John Hap for 2 weeks @ $650/week for teaching preparation		A1	1300	00

11. P.I./P.

14. SPO

REQUEST FOR PAYMENT EXTERNAL FUNDS	ANYVILLE COLLEGE SPONSORED PROGRAM	1. VOUCHER NO. 45		
2. CONSORTIUM: FISCAL AGENT	3. AGENCY/ORGANIZATION ED:Latin American Studies	4. AGENCY GRANT NO. GOO 375		
5. SUBCONTRACTOR	6. PROJECT DIRECTOR (P.D.)/PRINCIPAL INVESTIGATOR (P.I.) Professor Doe	7. SBC ACCOUNT NO. 330.726		
8. PAYEE AND DESCRIPTION OR EXPLANATION *(ATTACH INVOICES OR PAYEE LIST)*		9. LINE ITEM	10. $ AMOUNT	
11. P.I./P.I Pay to John Hap for teaching 4 classes for introductory Latin American Studies course 14. SPON (4 of 20 courses @ 1/7 salary per course) (4/20 * 1/7 * $45,981)		A1	1313	74
11. P.I./P.D. SIGNATURE *Jane Doe*	12. DATE 12/4	13. TOTAL CHARGED TO PROJECT	$ 1313	74
14. SPONSORED PROGRAM OFFICER'S SIGNATURE *George Smith*	15. DATE 12/6	16. BUSINESS OFFICER'S SIGNATURE *Susan S Jones*		12/9

Exhibit 24. Sample Spread Sheet.

ED: LATIN AMERICAN STUDIES Grant #: G00 375
PD: Account #: 33Q726

Continuation: September 1, 19 - August 31, 19

Date	Payee	Voucher #	A1 Faculty Salaries 23297.00	B Fringe Benefits 4287.00	C1 Travel Consult. 975.00	C2 Travel PD 600.00	E1 Supplies 500.00	E2 Supplies Library 3200.00	E3 Supplies Dup. 400.00	H Consul- tants 1000.00	J Indirect Costs 2741.00	TOTAL 37000.00
11/04/	Films/Humanities	38						69.75				69.75
11/06/	The Book Shop	39						314.38				314.38
11/06/	Library	40						1403.14				1403.14
12/04/	Seaman	41	702.17									702.17
12/04/	Edwards	42	782.89									782.89
12/04/	Moran	43	370.40									370.40
12/04/	Miller	44	1196.08									1196.08
12/04/	Hap	45	1313.74									1313.74
12/04/	Grimm	46	693.25									693.25
12/04/	Husz	47	187.55									187.55
01/10/	Duff	48	3000.00									3000.00
04/01/	Payroll	49	4000.00									4000.00
04/25/	Ing	50A				306.00						306.00
05/01/	Navarro	50			329.50							329.50
05/01/	Navarro	51								500.00		500.00
05/28/	Edwards	52	650.00									650.00
05/28/	Seaman	53	650.00									650.00
05/28/	Wit	54	650.00									650.00
05/28/	Lance	55	1300.00									1300.00
05/28/	Taylor	56	1300.00									1300.00
05/28/	Hap	57	1300.00									1300.00
05/28/	Rich	58	1300.00									1300.00
05/28/	Grimm	59	1300.00									1300.00
05/28/	Miller	60	1300.00									1300.00
05/28/	Ing	61	1300.00									1300.00
06/24/	Duplicating	62							77.11			77.11
06/24/		63		4286.48								4286.48
08/01/	Library Account	64						2348.60				2348.60
08/01/	Library Account	65						791.15				791.15
08/01/	Account 210375	66							536.81			536.81
08/21/		67									2741.00	2741.00
08/30/	BALANCE		.92	.52	645.50	294.00	500.00	-1727.02	-213.92	500.00	.00	.00

Exhibit 25. Financial Status Report to the Grantor.

FINANCIAL STATUS REPORT
(Short Form)
(Follow instructions on the back)

1. Federal Agency and Organizational Element to Which Report is Submitted	2. Federal Grant or Other Identifying Number Assigned By Federal Agency	OMB Approval No. **0348–0039**	Page 1	of 1 pages
U.S. Department of Education International Education Branch	Grant # G00---375			

3. Recipient Organization (Name and complete address, including ZIP code)
Anyville College
0000 South Street
Anyville, E.Va. 00000

4. Employer Identification Number	5. Recipient Account Number or Identifying Number	6. Final Report	7. Basis
000-000-0000-A1	Govt.Acct #330.726	☒ Yes ☐ No	☐ Cash ☒ Accrual

8. Funding/Grant Period (See Instructions) From: (Month, Day, Year)	To: (Month, Day, Year)	9. Period Covered by this Report From: (Month, Day, Year)	To: (Month, Day, Year)
09/01/ 19X1	08/31/19X2	09/01/19X1	08/31/19X2

10. Transactions:	I Previously Reported	II This Period	III Cumulative
a. Total outlays	–0–	–0–	$ 52,276
b. Recipient share of outlays	–0–	–0–	15,276
c. Federal share of outlays	–0–	–0–	37,000
d. Total unliquidated obligations			–0–
e. Recipient share of unliquidated obligations			–0–
f. Federal share of unliquidated obligations			–0–
g. Total Federal share (Sum of lines c and f)			37,000
h. Total Federal funds authorized for this funding period			37,000
i. Unobligated balance of Federal funds (Line h minus line g)			–0–

11. Indirect Expense

a. Type of Rate (Place "X" in appropriate box)
☐ Provisional ☒ Predetermined ☐ Final ☐ Fixed

b. Rate	c. Base	d. Total Amount	e. Federal Share
65%	S&W used 8%TDC	$3,873	$ 2,741

12. Remarks: Attach any explanations deemed necessary or information required by Federal sponsoring agency in compliance with governing legislation.

NOTE: Item 11. This program limits indirect costs to 8% of total Direct Costs. Therefore, the predetermined rate of 65% S&W was not used.

13. Certification: I certify to the best of my knowledge and belief that this report is correct and complete and that all outlays and unliquidated obligations are for the purposes set forth in the award documents.

Typed or Printed Name and Title	Telephone (Area code, number and extension)
Ms Susan S. Jones, Vice President for Business Affairs (Chief Fiscal Officer)	20x-000-0000 ext 2

Signature of Authorized Certifying Official	Date Report Submitted
Susan S. Jones	09/31/19X2

Previous Editions not Usable

Standard Form 269A (REV 4-88)
Prescribed by OMB Circulars A-102 and A-110

Evaluation

IMPORTANCE OF EVALUATION TO THE SPONSOR

Evaluation has become a very important requirement by most funding sources, private and government, for their own purposes. We have emphasized the importance of "in-process" evaluation as an essential tool for achieving the project objectives and preparing the basis for an after-the-fact or "summative" evaluation of the work.

Now we will discuss the needs of the grantors. It is important for the grantors to know to what extent projects met expected goals. They will want information to help them determine what went right and what went wrong and why, perhaps, projects had unrealistic goals or perhaps external forces or unforeseen new information changed the expectations for the projects.

Finally, the funding sources may want to learn if there was meaningful impact beyond the projects. If the projects resulted in publications or transferable plans, were these products cost-effective and actually used by others with similar problems? The sponsors may be assessing the programs that provided the support. Should the programs be continued, revised, or abandoned in light of the evaluations of all of their awards in a given field?

Societal needs change and so do the priorities of government and private agencies charged with addressing urgent needs. One foundation officer told us "we have supported college level writing projects over the last three years. Now we need to evaluate our program based on the data provided form these grants and consider changing our priorities." In another case, a collection of data from well-managed successful projects may provide a persuasive argument for continuing to fund the current initiatives.

We mention this to stress the importance of a carefully planned evaluation to a sponsor.

AN AGENCY REQUIREMENT FOR EVALUATION

The Internet has extensive resources available on evaluation plans. Many agencies are not explicit and simply list "evaluation" as one element of a proposal. The following is an example of a fairly typical requirement for evaluation.

Institutions are required to employ external, or outside, evaluators for all funded projects as part of the evaluation process. The outside evaluator must not be employed by or affiliated with the institution submitting the proposal. The consultants are to assist the institution in evaluating the project with respect to achievement of the project's objectives and to assist in the preparation of final reports. While these evaluation plans may vary in scope and design, they must contain provisions for the employment of outside evaluators and will be considered integral parts of the proposals. Consultants, who assist with planning or implementing a funded project, should not be hired as evaluators.

Evaluation plans should meet the following guidelines:

A. Procedures for data collection must be built into the project design so that data can be collected from the outset of the program.
B. Evaluation plans must consider both formative and summative assessments of the program. Data must be collected and analyzed to monitor progress in achieving project goals and to document the level of success in attaining these goals by conclusion of the funding cycle.
C. Evaluation plans must include a balance of subjective indicators of participant satisfaction and objective indicators of project performance such as achievement test scores.
D. Evaluation plans should specify

1. the data needed to assess the effectiveness of the action taken to meet the project objectives,
2. the instruments and/or means to collect the data, and
3. the timetable for collection, analysis, and report of the data.

PREPARING AN EFFECTIVE EVALUATION PLAN

One of the most difficult problems in planning and designing a project is that of providing for competent evaluation. Everyone wants the assurance that an evaluation is going to be carried out in some objective fashion and that the evaluation will justify continuation of the funding program, or justify continued support of similar kinds of activities or projects, or perhaps even call for ending an effort.

We look at evaluation as a learning process both during periods of planning and implementation and also on completion of a project. It is an important part of the theme of this book. A sincere and well-convinced, in-progress evaluation provides the information needed to alter plans, methods, and sometimes goals and thus helps to ensure a successful end result.

We are indebted to the late Dr. Sherry Lancaster who was a Research Associate with the State Council of Higher Education for Virginia when she planned the evaluation and served as the outside evaluator for the model evaluation we will use as an example later in this chapter.

Start planning your evaluation by asking questions about the project objectives and plan of action.

1. What is the objective?
2. What information will have to be secured at the beginning before starting work, during the project, and after it is completed?
3. What are the sources of the needed information—participants, instructors, staff, other reports, databases, student records, etc.?
4. How will the information be collected—questionnaires, interviews, test, other?
5. Who will be involved in the evaluation, planning, and implementation—an outside objective evaluator, the Project Director, participants, the sponsors—and what will be expected of each individual involved in the process?
6. When will each evaluation activity take place—choosing an outside evaluator, meetings with PI/PD

and/or participant development of questionnaires, development of interview questions, distribution of questionnaires, scheduling of interviews?
7. What will be done with the data collected? Who will compile and analyze the information and how will it be done?
8. What will be done with the information—the raw data and analyses? Will they be required as separate reports, as part of the brief summaries?

We found some universally good advice in the guidelines for the Fund for Improvement of Post Secondary Education (FIPSE), http://www.ed.gov/about/offices/list/ope/fipse/index.html, worth quoting here:

> What, in your view, would count as evidence that your project has succeeded? What would count as evidence that it had failed? It may be difficult, within the terms of the grant, to assess accomplishment of long-range objectives, but you should be able to identify or develop some approximate indicators. Bear in mind that the goals of local institutionalization and wide impact may well elude you unless you can provide others with solid evidence that your project achieved its aims. Developing such evidence should not be put off until the last stages of a project. It must be a consideration from the design stage onward. . . . Evaluation can be an important tool for increasing a project's wider use. In designing a good evaluation plan, it might help if you imagine that some other institution was submitting your proposal: what would you need to learn about their project in order for your institution to benefit concretely from its results? What form should the information take in order to be sufficiently noticeable, credible, and useful? Such evaluations typically use a combination of statistical measurement and non-quantitative evidence.

In the FIPSE Web site, you will also find a bibliography on evaluation.

In summary, a competent evaluation during the progress of a project or after the fact should provide a measure of its success related to the original objectives, or expected outcomes, and even the unexpected outcomes. The failures and successes should be analyzed in terms of the methods, viewpoints of participants, and resulting products.

TWO EXAMPLE EVALUATIONS

First, we have chosen a community service project initiated and carried out by three colleges because it involves professors and administrators in those colleges and a wide range of community agencies in three countries and a small city.

Second, we have selected the evaluation of a regional teacher-training project directed by Professor Jill

Granger, Sweet Briar College. The project has been running for several years, is sponsored by The Virginia State Council of Higher Education (SCHEV), and is open to teachers in the Central Virginia counties and the city of Lynchburg.

These two evaluations provide good examples of a large cooperative project and one directed by a single institution. The Central Virginia Tomorrow project was one of the most ambitious projects for which Title I of the Higher Education Act, Community Service and Continuing Education, provided funding. It was noted just a few years ago as one of the few community service project awards which met its goals and continued to play a part in the long-range development of the region. Another project noted for its long-range impact is the Elderhostel Program. The Sweet Briar College project was funded with several smaller grants to provide needed equipment and supplies to the schools of the partici-

pating schools. This evaluation was done for the most recent year of the project. Each year it has been revised to suit the needs of the teachers as noted in the evaluation reports.

Evaluation of Central Virginia Tomorrow

The evaluation of the Central Virginia Tomorrow (CVT) project demonstrated the importance of involving all of the constituents in the process of planning and reviewing progress toward the original goals. The in-process or formative evaluation technique helped reveal shortcomings and new ideas while there was still time to change course. The community process was successfully started and the information compiled would provide a solid basis for future community development. The evaluation process itself was an important contributor to the project's success.

Exhibit 26. Sample Evaluation.

Attachment A
The Questionnaire

A team of evaluators is currently analyzing the Central Virginia Tomorrow Process in which you have participated. Your anonymous response to the following questions will help us to evaluate the project and see trends which emerge from the results. When we mention CVT below, we are referring to the process rather than the region. We would appreciate your response by April 14, 1975. Thank you.

1. In which of the following CVT programs have you participated: Please rank those you have attended in order of their significance to you. (1 - highest significance)
   ___ College A Seminar   ___ Blacksburg Conference
   ___ College B Seminar   ___ Jurisdictional Workshops
   ___ College C Seminar

2. If you have not attended all five of the above, what was your reason?
   ___ Dissatisfaction with a program   ___ Other (specify if you wish)
   ___ Conflict with a date

4. Which of the following groups do you feel are benefitting most from the CVT project?
   ___ The entire region   ___ Lower income people
   ___ Industrial leaders   ___ Middle income people
   ___ Community leaders   ___ Upper income people
   ___ College-based leaders   ___ County residents
   ___ Blacks   ___ City residents
   ___ Whites

5. What do you feel has been the role of the Consortium Colleges in CVT?
   ___ Consistent significant leadership   ___ Consistent significant participation
   ___ Marginal involvement   ___ No real contribution

6. How much of the planning and accomplishment of CVT do you feel COULD have been attained without the project?
   ___ Nearly all of it   ___ A great deal of it
   ___ Very little of it   ___ Virtually none of it

7. How much of the planning and accomplishment of CVT do you feel WOULD have been attained without the project?

8. What do you feel was the basic purpose of CVT?
   ___ a. Getting representatives together from all segments of the region's population.
   ___ b. Identifying major issues and establishing specific roles.
   ___ c. Developing multi-media devices for region-wide education and revitalization.
   ___ d. Other—Specify.

9. How much of this purpose do you feel has been accomplished to date?
   ___ 0-25%   ___ 26-50%   ___ 51-75%   ___ 76-100%

10. What would you like to have seen CVT do differently?
   ___ Smaller meetings   ___ Larger meetings
   ___ More people involved   ___ Fewer meetings
   ___ More meetings   ___ Other (specify)

11. What would you like to see CVT become in the future?
   ___ A regional governmental organization ___ A corporation ___ Other (specify)
   ___ A volunteer steering committee

12. What unexpected occurrences have surfaced as a spin-off of CVT?

13. What specific impact has resulted from your participation in CVT?

14. Please classify yourself to help us identify patterns:
   ___ County resident   ___ Black   ___ Government employee
   ___ City resident   ___ White   ___ Private businessperson
   ___ Not gainfully employed

Exhibit 26. (*Continued*)

Attachment B
Responses to the Questionnaire

	1	2	3	4	5			
1. A	21	13	16	7	3	6.	All	11
B	4	10	10	9	11		Little	57
RMWC	10	15	15	12	3		Great deal	26
BLK	48	6	2	0	1		None	17
JW	14	20	8	9	3	7.	All	5
2. Dissatisfied					5		Little	52
Conflict					70		Great deal	13
Other					23		None	38
3. Very much					52	8.	a	49
Somewhat					46		b	70
Very little					12		c	7
4. Region					62		d	9
Industrial leaders					12	9.	0-25	21
College based					15		26-50	48
Blacks					30		51-75	33
Whites					12		76-100	10
Lower income					23	10.	Smaller	21
Middle income					13		More people	47
Upper income					12		More meetings	14
County					12		Larger meetings	2
City					29		Fewer meetings	3
Other			3–6 or more				Other	25
5. Consistent leadership					49	11.	Regional Govt.	15
Marginal					16		Volunteer	56
Consistent participation					54		Corporation	26
None					3		Other	13

Attachment C
Summary of Responses to Questionnaires

1. The majority of participants preferred the two-day Blacksburg conferences in the fall and spring to the one-day seminars or evening jurisdictional workshops.

2. Five participants indicated that they did not attend a CVT meeting because of dissatisfaction with the program. All others indicated that their lack of participation was due to conflict with the date or time.

3. Five participants felt only partially involved in the CVT process. Of these, two felt very little involved and three felt only somewhat involved. Four of these five were city-white participants.

4. The majority of participants felt that the region as a whole benefitted from the CVT process.

5. The role of the three colleges was perceived consistently as being positive.

6. 74 participants felt that very little or none of the CVT accomplishments could have been attained without the project.

7. 90 participants felt that very little or none of the CVT accomplishments would have been attained without the project.

8. Participants accurately perceived 8a. and 8b. as the basic purposes of CVT.

9. Participants felt that a range of 25-75% of CVT's objectives have been accomplished to date.

10. A majority of participants requested that more meetings be held.

11. 50% of the participants want to see a volunteer committee remain to steer CVT activities.

12. Specific answers by different groups of participants follow.

Exhibit 26. (*Continued*)

Responses to Question #12

What unexpected occurrences have you seen as a spin-off of CVT?

1. Business-City-White
   a. None (4 have this as their reply).
   b. Some people becoming involved who didn't expect to be part of such a planning group—also a spread of interest around the community.
   c. People do not want to deal with real problems.
   d. Regional information made known to City and County Representatives.
   e. Tremendous amount of information has been made available regarding areas of concern for both City and County.
   f. Some catalytic effect for minority business development.
   g. Black-White face-off.
   h. Strictly for the Blacks.
   i. Data for grant proposals.
   j. Possible development of new Black-operated business. New vision and hope on citizens' part.
   k. Industrial input and participation lost by having too much "talk" and not enough action.
   l. A better understanding between people.
   m. The ability to include all elements (people) from the region and have them work together.
2. Business-County-White
   a. None (3 gave this as their reply).
   b. Criticism of local government.
   c. Improved human relations and understanding of various problems.
   d. The Blacks won't move and are not ready to put much effort out.
   e. Realized need of inter-dependence in all areas and of all jurisdictions.
   f. Blue Sky thinking in too many areas. I did not realize how many people really don't understand some areas discussed—the people for the rural areas that must accept any plan for the most part were not present.
3. Business-County-Black
   a. A discovery of a common denominator whereby all segments of a given region can work together constructively to achieve a common goal.
4. Government-City-White
   a. I have seen more positive confrontation than I expected; County and City people at a roundtable, exchanging ideas; Minorities feeling that they have a part in determining priorities—better understanding of employer-employee problems—Human Relations.
   b. Group held together so far better than I expected.
   c. Curiosity to participation.
5. Government-City-Black
   a. Minority business enterprises organization.
   b. A common ground between participants who would never have talked about important issues without being involved in the process.
6. Government-County-White
   a. None (3 gave this as their reply)
   b. Greater citizens' participation in governmental operations than before CVT.
   c. A unity in purpose and goal-setting.
   d. The absence of the decision-makers.
   e. Good relationships between Black and White leadership.
   f. Many people involved for the first time in problem identification.
   g. "You-owe-us" attitude of Blacks; trend toward regional government; the selfish attitude of central city.
7. Other-City-White
   a. Not sure.
   b. A forum for the minorities.
   c. Several programs have been influenced by the CVT process.
   d. Greater awareness of what goes into solving problems that our governmental leaders are faced with.
   e. More cooperation—city/county.
   f. None.
   g. I could only see a strong force for regional government and the complete breakdown of elected form of government.
8. Other-County-White
   a. None.
   b. Agencies using concerns identified to develop current programs.
   c. Nothing particular.
9. Educator-City-White
   a. None.
   b. Participation and goal-sharing at local meetings among individuals who formerly would not or could not remain in the same room together. Individual recognition and acknowledgement of the views and rights of the other—by Black and White—industry and community.
   c. Bringing people together.
   d. Increased drug enforcement.

Exhibit 26. (*Continued*)

10. Educator-City-Black
   a. A surprising willingness for feuding political jurisdictions to talk to each other and AGREE on some basic things.
11. Educator-County-White
   a. People have gained a sense of the region and their interdependence on one another. Also, an awareness of some problems that have still to be dealt with (race relations and poverty, for example).
12. Educator-County-Black
   a. Not enough low-income persons participating (working class).
13. Student-City-White
   a. Nothing yet.

Responses to Question #13

What specific impact has resulted from your participation in CVT?
1. Business-City-White
   a. Nothing—none (4 persons gave these answers as their reply).
   b. Better informed, interested in areas which were pointed out as needing work.
   c. Chance to meet and work with other interested citizens.
   d. Acute awareness of problems and goals of City and County.
   e. Much more aware of City-County problems and goals and the cooperative effort that must be present to alleviate the problems.
   f. A new ray of hope that the region will work collectively to develop life-support systems which will work for all people and build a dynamic community with a high quality of life for all.
   g. Disheartened by changes—the public wants the government to pay—they are so uninformed.
   h. 80% of the population forgotten.
   i. Meet new people.
   j. Understanding of the issues before the people of the region, coming to know the region and some of its citizens, more awareness of the importance and need for formal planning for the future.
   k. Process is good but very frustrating because of the time it takes.
   l. Problem knowledge—lack of understanding by majority of citizens' realization.
   m. A heightened interest in regional cooperation; an expectation of success of regional improvement.

n. Increased and renewed interest in regional development.
o. Involvement in trust-awareness.
p. Specific.
2. Business-County-White
   a. Awareness of high percent of public employees.
   b. Improved human relations and understanding of various problems.
   c. Health and business voice.
   d. Working together with diversified Central Virginia population segments.
   e. Know each problem better.
   f. More awareness of major issues. I am now more concerned about the region's future.
   g. The importance of an informed and concerned group of citizens, setting goals and working together in their attainment, has impressed me deeply.
   h. People have seen problems as having a regional basis.
   i. Realization that the different areas need to get together more in small groups and come to some realistic understanding on many issues, especially governments and government planning groups.
   j. I am more aware of the overlapping nature of the services and their interdependence and therefore of the complexity of the problem.
3. Business-County-Black
   a. An awareness of the ties between regional-city-county government and the importance of each working individually, yet collectively, to gain the best final result from any major change in a given area.
4. Government-City-White
   a. Upon me! Initial enthusiasm weakened by "group process" and evidence of provincialism leading to guarded pessimism. Upon others! Unknown.
   b. I have developed a greater understanding of the dilemma of the lower-income population of the area.
   c. Frustration because April is here and fear that once Blacksburg is over so will CVT be.
   d. More contacts with key people throughout region. It is to be hoped that more people will be made aware of the project including women in leadership and planning roles in the future.

Exhibit 26. (*Continued*)

e. Importance of involving people in determining problem, priorities, goals and such.

f. Our overall goals and objectives are much closer than I realized!

g. Met people I wouldn't otherwise have met from the area and beyond.

5. Government-City-Black

a. Realization of the region's potentials helped my individual outlook to be more realistic and not so negative.

6. Government-County-White

a. A better insight to the needs of the people.

b. More aware of problems in other jurisdictions.

c. A better understanding of the problems perceived by others in the community.

d. More respect for regional problems.

e. Became acquainted with more people from the region.

f. Only meeting a few new people and providing a forum for discussion.

g. A definite lack of interest on the part of those who really make things happen.

h. Confidence that we can work together for area problems.

i. Better understanding of the people, problems and possible solutions.

j. Once issues and goals are established, where does the funding come from?

k. Better understanding of the needs of the area.

7. Other-City-White

a. The conviction that such a project is possible.

b. A sense of involvement in what happens in the community (outside of my specific interest area), seeing the total CVT area not the city by itself.

c. Opportunity to learn about various aspects of the community and their relationships.

d. Involvement by my civic group.

e. Public looking with overview rather than none at all!

f. Immeasurable, due to the fact of my little involvement and chance for participation.

g. It has proved to me what I have always believed; that upper-class wants regional government.

8. Other-County-White

a. Greater awareness of community priority concerns.

b. Greater awareness of multiplying of problems—all interrelated—and the impact of small people in the community.

c. Made me aware that the entire area has similar problems, what benefits one county or city benefits the whole community.

d. Liberals want additional social problems.

9. Other-County-Black

a. I am sort of disappointed in the little evidence of change of opinion of members of the group from first meeting. The meetings seemed to have changed very few people in broadening their overview. The opinions expressed at the first group meetings were very much like the ones expressed at the final meeting. There seems to have been no broadening of the overview.

10. Educator-City-White

a. Growing conviction that a cross system approach can work.

b. I have a better insight into the problems facing all of us.

c. Closer working relationships and/or familiarity of nearly all participants.

d. Thinking there may be help for a region-wide approach to development of Central Virginia Tomorrow.

11. Educator-City-Black

a. Increased optimism that social problems can be solved.

12. Educator-County-Black

a. I have gained greater insight on long-range planning, as well as a better understanding of how some problem areas are left out of plans.

b. Problem areas are left out of plans.

13. Student-City-White

a. An acute awareness of the problems of the Central Virginia region.

b. Learning about the region; getting to know people; getting involved.

14. Student-City-Black

a. Virginia has some of the same problems that other states have. That is, although we are in the south, we still have some of the problems found in the west. Problems are not confined to geographical location.

Exhibit 26. (*Continued*)

	EDUCATORS			
	City		County	
	Black	White	Black	White
1. The entire region	2	5	0	1
2. Industrial leaders	1	1	0	0
3. Community leaders	1	1	0	1
4. College-based leaders	1	0	0	0
5. Blacks	1	1	0	0
6. Whites	1	0	0	1
7. Lower income people	1	1	0	0
8. Middle income people	1	1	0	0
9. Upper income people	1	1	1	1
10. County residents	1	1	0	0
11. City residents	1	1	0	1
12. Other	0	0	0	0

	OTHERS			
	City		County	
	Black	White	Black	White
1. The entire region	1	7	0	1
2. Industrial leaders	1	1	0	1
3. Community leaders	1	7	1	1
4. College-based leaders	1	2	0	1
5. Blacks	1	4	0	1
6. Whites	2	1	0	0
7. Lower income people	1	1	0	1
8. Middle income people	1	3	0	0
9. Upper income people	0	1	0	0
10. County residents	2	4	0	1
11. City residents	2	4	0	1
12. Other				

Exhibit 26. (*Continued*)

7. The Blacksburg Conferences were of great value in getting people's total time commitment to CVT for a longer period of time.

8. One of the greatest accomplishments of CVT has been to get people together to communicate their community and regional concerns to each other.

9. There is great hope that CVT will "keep moving," because it is beneficial to so many specific interests to continue to communicate and work for the future.

10. CVT is at a crucial point now, and great care must be taken to ensure its continuation.

11. CVT must attempt in any way possible to keep the top people involved in CVT, because their participation signifies top-level interest which others will follow.

12. Lynchburg College has been the most active in working with the community; RMWC has been the least.

13. CVT has provided a vehicle for relieving many suspicions held by the community towards academics.

Specific Suggestions

1. A detailed study phase should precede the implementation of any CVT recommendations, because participants do not always know the consequences of their suggestions.

2. Committee chairs and committees of each interest area (i.e., housing, education, etc.) should have an update meeting to inform participants of where they are now and where they're going. This could be in the form of a Dutch treat lunch.

3. A report should be sent to all CVT participants to inform them of the plans made by the organizational committee at the Peaks of Otter.

4. More people under 30 and not yet established should be included—as observers if not as full participants.

5. The interest and participation of each organizational committee member should be checked; if anyone hasn't the time to devote to meeting and planning, he should be replaced by someone who can be a full participant.

6. Make clear whether the CVT meetings are open to the public or by invitation only.

7. Hold more meetings in the evenings to involve more "grass roots" people. These people are not able to leave their jobs for full days to attend CVT meetings.

8. Alleviation of the drug problem should be a goal in itself rather than being considered a part of law enforcement.

9. More of the "right" people must be involved; specifically, more agency directors, more civic group leaders, and judges.

10. After sub-groups meet to discuss different issues in workshops, enough time should be left for all participants to get back together as a whole and be able to reach to the sub-groups' reports.

11. CVT could have a form letter that would go out to employers of the "little" people, requesting the employers to support CVT by giving these "little" people time off with pay and without losing annual leave to attend CVT meetings.

12. CVT should send out notices of meetings sooner than they have in the past.

13. One way to increase awareness and publicity of CVT is to set up a speakers' bureau to visit all regional civic groups periodically.

14. Give the counties more representation in CVT, and accomplish this by election rather than selection to the board of directors.

Specific Complaints

1. CVT is really a Lynchburg project—not a regional one.

2. Bedford has not given CVT a chance; it cannot see ahead.

3. The colleges are taking on too much leadership and community people are suspicious that they are being "manipulated."

4. The economist who spoke at college B's seminar was irrelevant, unprepared, and turned people off CVT.

5. Too many meetings were held on workdays. Only executives and owners of businesses had the kinds of jobs they could leave for this long. This is the reason attendance was down at the second Blacksburg Conference.

6. Enough top-level influential leaders are still not being convinced to lend their full support to the CVT process.

7. Reports of group meetings have not always been accurate summaries of what has actually occurred.

8. Outside speakers have not always been as effective or as relevant as local experts could be.

9. Title I, and the three colleges, have not received enough credit for their roles in CVT.

10. The counties are very fearful of the use of federal money for any reason, because federal dollars are bound to be accompanied by federal intervention.

Exhibit 27. Sample Evaluation: Sweet Briar College/State Council of Higher Education (SCHEV) 2006 Teacher-Training Program.

Sweet Briar/SCHEV Questionnaire, 2006

We are interested in your thinking about hands-on science and mathematics teaching.

We will compile these answers in order to assist the workshop leaders in their planning for future workshops.

Evaluators: Julia Jacobsen and Jan F. Kress

1. How many years have you attended Sweet Briar summer SCHEV workshops? _____
2. How many semesters of science have you taken since high school? Please state the year(s) of your last course (s).

    _____Biology _____year

    _____Chemistry _____year

    _____Physics _____year

    _____Environmental science _____year

    _____ Mathematics _____year
3. How many years have you been teaching science?

    _____Biology

    _____Chemistry

    _____Physics

    _____Environmental science

    _____Mathematics
4. I will be able to use these experiments in class using an inquiry-based mode?

    _____Yes

    _____No

    _____Some

    Please explain your answer:

5. This workshop has increased my understanding of inquiry-based science?

    _____Yes

    _____No

    _____Some

    Please explain your answer:

6. This workshop will change my method of teaching science.

    _____Yes, totally

    _____Partially

    _____Not at all

    Please explain your answer:

7. Further comments:

8. Suggestions for future workshops:

Exhibit 27(a). Sweet Briar College/State Council of Higher Education of Virginia (SCHEV) 2006 Teacher-Training Program.

Evaluation Report by Julia Jacobsen & Jan F. Kress, August 6, 2006

This is the evaluation report for the 2006 Inquiry-Based Approach to Mathematics and Science, grades 3–8, held at Sweet Briar College. Teachers from public and independent schools located in Central Virginia were invited to participate in a five-day workshop. The stated goal of the workshop was "to present teachers with inquiry-based teaching strategies that will engage diverse learners and will generate enthusiasm for learning among teachers and students."

The workshop evaluation was conducted in two ways. The first was to observe the program and interview the participants. The second was the analysis and summary of questionnaires returned directly to the evaluators.

Each year, the project director and faculty have revised the workshop to reflect the comments and needs of the teachers. The 2006 plan calls for five-day workshops in the summers of 2006 and 2007 and for an academic year program on nine Saturdays in the academic year 2006–2007. A one-day administrative workshop will be held in the summer of 2006 with yearlong project updates. On-site instructional support is provided during the academic year.

I (Julia Jacobsen) spent one afternoon and the following morning in workshops during the 2006 summer session. This gave me an opportunity to observe how the teachers were reacting to the curriculum and a first hand view of the teachers' attitudes toward the content and instruction provided.

The teachers who attended the workshop during the previous years clearly were beginning to understand the inquiry-based instruction method. This was reflected during group sessions and one-on-one conversations. New attendees were excited about the inquiry-based process and anxious to incorporate the information into their curriculum.

Having served as an outside evaluator since the workshop inception, I have seen a change in teachers' attitudes from " I can't do this," and opposing the concept of Standards of Learning (SOLs) to " I must learn to teach this way" and embracing this new style of teaching and learning.

All the teachers I interviewed found the workshop stimulating and very helpful, but also felt there was a disconnect between the inquiry-based approach and the required tests.

I sat in on several sessions and observed the teachers working in teams to conduct the experiments. Those who had attended the program for one or more years (range for attendance is 2–6 years) helped encourage and assisted the newcomers. Of those participants I interviewed, all told me they plan to return again next year and particularly praised Professors Granger and Yokum as a team. The materials were presented in a clear and concise manner. Plenty of time was allowed to do the experiments and discuss variations to suit their own curriculum.

A major component of the program that was especially subject to praise and made a "big difference" to the teachers was the on-site support and loaning of laboratory equipment. Funds provided for supplies and matched by the teacher's schools was also an important component of the program. Many of them told me that they often paid for materials out of pocket because the allowance from the schools was so limited.

Analysis of the Questionnaire, by Jan F. Kress

This questionnaire was given to all participants at the end of the workshop.

Question 1: *How many years have you attended Sweet Briar/ SCHEV summer workshops?*

21% of the participants were first-time attendees.

65% of the participants have attended for 2–3 years.

15% of the participants have attended for 3 or more years.

Summary: Most participants have attended this workshop in the past.

Question 2: *How many semesters of science have you taken since high school?*

Science is defined as biology, physics, mathematics, chemistry, and environmental science (ES).

Of the participants who stated the year they had taken biology:

participant took biology in the 1960s

1 participant took biology in the 1970s

participants took biology in the 1980s

participants took biology in the 1990s

Of the participants who stated the year they had taken physics:

2 participants took physics in the 1970s

participant tool physics in the 1980s

Of the participants who stated the year they had taken mathematics:

participant took mathematics in the 1960s

participants took mathematics in the 1970s

participants took mathematics in the 1980s

participants took mathematics in the 1990s

1 participant took mathematics in 2000

Of the participants who stated the year they had taken chemistry:

2 participants took chemistry in the 1970s

2 participants took chemistry in the 1980s

Of the participants who stated the year they had taken environmental sciences (ES):

participant took ES in the 1990s

participants took ES in the 1980s

1 participant took ES in the 1970s

Of the participants who stated the year they had taken astronomy:

participant took astronomy in 2000

1 participant took astronomy in the 1990s

Summary:

17 (53%) out of 32 participants had exposure to biology since high school

53%: 17 (53%) out of 32 had exposure to mathematics since high school

21%: 7 (21%) out of 32 had exposure to ES since high school

15%: 5 (15%) out of 32 had exposure to chemistry since high school

9%: 3 (9%) out of 32 participants had exposure to physics since high school

9%: 3 (9%) out of 32 participants had exposure to astronomy since high school

Question 3: *How many years have you been teaching science?*

Teaching biology (6)

1 out of 6 participants is a new teacher

1 out of 6 participants has been teaching for less than 5 years

2 out of 6 participants has been teaching for 5 or more years

2 out of 6 participants has been teaching for 10 or more years

Teaching chemistry (2)

1 out of 2 participants has been teaching for 5 or more years

1 out of 2 participants has been teaching for more than 10 years

Teaching ES (8)

1 out of 8 participants is a new teacher

1 out of 8 participants has been teaching for less than 5 years

1 out of 8 participants has been teaching for more than 5 years, but less than 10 years

4 out of 8 participants has been teaching for 10 years or more

1 out of 8 participants has been teaching for 20 years or more

Teaching physics (3)

1 out of 3 participants has been teaching for 5 or more years

2 out of 3 participants has been teaching for 10 years or more, but less than 20 years

Teaching mathematics (21)

2 out of 21 participants is a new teacher

5 out of 21 participants has been teaching for less than 5 years

4 out of 21 participants has been teaching for more than 5 years, but less than 10 years

10 out of 21 participants has been teaching for 10 years or more, but less than 20 years

Teaching physical science (1)

1 participant has been teaching for more than 16 years

Teaching general science (6)

1 out of 6 participants is a new teacher

3 out of 6 participants has been teaching less than 5 years

2 out of 6 participants has been teaching more than 10 years, but less than 20 years

Teaching life science (1)

1 participant is a new teacher

Summary:

12 (37%) out of 32 participants teach mathematics as well as another science

21%: 9 (21%) out of 32 participants teach mathematics only

18%: 6 (18%) out of 32 participants do not teach mathematics

12%: 5 (12%) out of 32 participants did not answer the question

Question 4: *I will be able to use these experiments in class using an inquiry-based mode?*

65% responded YES (21 out of 32 participants)

32% responded SOME (10 out of 32 participants)

0% responded NO

Please refer to Table 4 for individual comments

Question 5: *This workshop has increased my understanding of inquiry-based science.*

87% responded YES (28 out of 32 participants)

12% responded SOME (4 out of 32 participants)

0% responded NO

Please refer to Table 5 for individual comments.

Question 6: *This workshop will change my method of teaching science.*

21% responded YES (7 out of 32 participants)

65%: responded PARTIALLY (21 out of 32 participants)

6%: responded NOT AT ALL (2 out of 32 participants did not teach science)

Summary: 21% of participants that responded PARTIALLY are already using some inquiry-based methods in their classrooms, others that responded PARTIALLY will be using the new activities presented, or the material presented was too new, or they will modify their curriculum slowly, but all stated they will be using more of the inquiry-based method in one way or the other.

Question 7: *Further Comments Summary*:

More than 50% of the participants made comments to this question. All responses were positive, many loved the activities, many stated the workshop helped them rethink and restructure the way they think, many

loved the new topics, and most rated the workshop as "excellent."

Question 8: *Suggestions for future workshops*:

More than 50% of the participants suggested future workshop ideas. The following is compilation of ideas.

Water ecology (lakes)

Recycling

Study of insects

Human body

More math

Loved how Jill, Hank, and Marcia worked together

Games for math and science

More math

Stop the redundancy about plants, school yard science, let participants pick their top 2 or 3 choices, more elementary math

More math related workshops with hands on activities

I have already listed suggestions on another questionnaire

Water, matter, computer lab exploration, more inquiry

Already noted this on 2 other forms . . . math manipulations in general and hands on equations

Workshops are wonderful

Electricity

Inquiry facilitating questions, geology, oceans

More math, applied math

More math workshops

Fabulous workshop

Simple mathematics

65%: 21 out of 32 participants responded to this question.

Sweet Briar/SCHEV Evaluation Conclusions

The Sweet Briar/SCHEV teacher-training program is carefully designed to meet the demands of the Virginia Standards of Learning (SOLs) and the in-service needs of current teachers in grades 3–8. The project director and Sweet Briar Faculty have created a partnership atmosphere with the teachers. As a result, changes are made in the program each year to reflect the needs and suggestions of the teachers.

Results of the questionnaire showed that the varied teaching experience and limited exposure to science courses since high school did not have a negative impact on learning new methods of instruction. All participants said they benefited on some level from this inquiry-based workshop.

The timing of the award of the supporting grant has cut the recruiting time short resulting in fewer enrollees than the plan called for. The two-year funding should make it possible to increase the number next year. We recommend that the effort to recruit first-time attendees be emphasized. Participation of the teachers' school with financial support for supplies, is a strength, and represents a real commitment to the program. We recommend Sweet Briar College and the State Council of Higher Education of Virginia continue to support this excellent program.

Conclusion

A PROCESS FOR DEVELOPMENT OF IDEAS

We have attempted to lead you through a complete process for nurturing an idea from its inception to its conclusion, the conclusion being the result of an evaluation of the project's impact. Common sense dictated much of what we have written about developing a competitive proposal. Spending the sponsors,' and sometimes the taxpayers' dollars, and taking an honest look at the impact of your project are responsibilities to be taken very seriously.

The sections that follow include reference materials mentioned in the text and other useful, if not essential, information. No one guide to proposal development can provide all of the answers. We have attempted to provide you with a selection of actual forms and regulations that you can use to track down current versions or those that fit your mission.

We have fortified the text with actual examples and case studies that are adaptable to other real situations. These examples are only one way of doing the job. The management system described could be adopted for a small organization with little change. The evaluations we selected gives a thorough picture of two very different projects, their accomplishments and flaws. One feature that led us to choose these examples was the outside evaluator's effective use of the insiders in the evaluations.

Thorough and thoughtful planning, involving others in your plans and articulating the plan to bring your "idea" to fruition in clear, concise, jargon-free English will lead you to success.

Don't give up. Good ideas will eventually be recognized and implemented if they are clearly articulated and have genuine support from those they affect.

Let us conclude with the school motto of one of the authors.

"Inveniam viam aut faciam"

translated

"I will find a way or make one"

PART II: BASIC RESOURCES

Section I. Acronyms

AAAS	American Association for the Advancement of Science
AAC	Association for American Colleges
AAHA	American Association for the Humanities Administration
ACE	American Council on Education
ACLS	American Council for Learned Societies
ACS	American Chemical Society
ACUO	Association of College and University Offices, Washington Office
ADAMHA	Administration on Drug Abuse, Mental Health and Alcoholism
AFOSR	Air Force Office of Scientific Research
AFP/NSFRE	National Society of Fund Raising Executives (now Association of Fund Raising Professionals, AFP)
AOA	Administration on Aging
AOTA	American Occupational Therapy Association
APTA	American Physical Therapy Association
ARI	Army Research Institute
ARO	Army Research Office
BARC	Beltsville Agricultural Research Center
CASE	Council for the Advancement and Support of Education
CBD	Commerce Business Daily
CDC	Centers for Disease Control
CFDA	Catalog of Federal Domestic Assistance
CFR	Code of Federal Regulations
CIES	Council for the International Exchange of Scholars
CPB	Corporation for Public Broadcasting
DEA	Drug Enforcement Administration
DOD	Department of Defense
DOT	Department of Transportation
ED	Education Department or Department of Education
EDGAR	Education Department General Administrative Regulations
EEOC	Equal Employment Opportunity Commission
EPA	Environmental Protection Agency
ERIC	Education Resources Information Clearinghouse
ESEA	Elementary & Secondary Education Act
FIPSE	Fund for the Improvement of Post Secondary Education
FOB#	Federal Office Building number
FONZ	Friends of the National Zoo
GAO	Government Accounting Office
GPO	Government Printing Office
GSA	General Service Administration
HEA	Higher Education (Act) Amendments
HED	Higher Education Daily
HENA	Higher Education and National Affairs
HHS	Health and Human Services (Department of)
HUD	Housing and Urban Development (Department of)
ICA	International Communications Agency
IMF	International Monetary Fund
IPA	Intergovernmental Personnel Act
IREX	International Research and Exchange Board
LSCA	Library Services and Construction Act
MDTA	Manpower Development and Training Act
NACUBO	National Association of College and University Business Officers
NASA	National Aeronautics and Space Administration
NBS	National Bureau of Standards
NCES	National Center for Educational Statistics
NCURA	National Council of University Administrators
NCWGE	National Coalition for Women and Girls in Education
NDEA	National Defense Educational Act

NEA	National Endowment for the Arts and or National Education Association
NEH	National Endowment for the Humanities
NHPRC	National Historical Publications and Records Commission
NIA	National Institute on Aging
NIAAA	National Institute on Alcohol Abuse and Alcoholism
NIDA	National Institute on Drug Abuse
NIH	National Institutes of Health
NIHR	National Institute for Handicapped Research
NIJ	National Institute of Justice
NIMH	National Institute of Mental Health
NLRB	National Labor Relations Board
NOAA	National Oceanic and Atmospheric Administration
NRC	Nuclear Regulatory Commission
NSF	National Science Foundation
NTIA	National Telecommunication and Information Administration

OCD	Office of Child Development
OCR	Office of Civil Rights
ONR	Office of Management and Budget
ONR	Office of Naval Research
OSHA	Occupational Safety and Health Administration
OTA	Office of Technology Assessment
PHS	Public Health Service
SRA	Society of Research Administration International
SSRC	Social Science Research Council
WHO	World Health Organization

Other abbreviations of interest:

ASAP	As Soon As Possible
FY	Fiscal Year
FYI	For Your Information
NA	Not Applicable
NB	Note Bene
PTO	Please Turn Over
REP	Request for Proposal
RFA	Request for Application

Section II. Essential Basic Information Sources

A. PUBLICATIONS

In establishing a basic resource library for your organization, a number of points should be considered. First and foremost is that the library represents the needs of your agency in four areas:

1. Basic library or reference sources.
2. Periodicals from agencies and foundations.
3. Periodicals from private/ professional source.
4. Information services that provide a basic information packet, along with possible periodic update services or online newsletters.

Additionally, cost should be a factor in what your library will include. For instance, a low-budget office might consider having the following holdings for under $500. Contact the publishing organization for current options and prices.

	Price or range
Foundation Center Directory	$19.95–179.95 per month/available online
Catalog of Federal Domestic Assistance	FREE/online
NIH Guide for Grants and Contracts	FREE/online
NSF Bulletin	FREE/electronic only
Humanities	Bimonthly periodical/$24.00
Federal Agency Directories/ Reports	Call agency and/or check website
Foundation Newsletters and Annual Reports (Ford, Carnegie, Rockefeller)	FREE/online

In addition you might want to consider subscribing to the *Federal Register* at US$929.00 per year if federal programs are your primary interest. http://bookstore.gpo.gov/actions/GetPublication?stocknumber=769-004-00000-9

Locate the Web site of those agencies that deal with your particular interests and ask for their newsletters, reports, and related lists of programs and guidelines online. There is nothing wrong with seeking general information in more detail than that offered by the *Foundation Directory* and the *Catalog of Federal Domestic Assistance,* but do not send proposals off at this point.

We are merely pointing out how to gather information if your resources in terms of personnel and technical support are limited. Many people have volunteered or forced to go into fund-seeking without any support. Others have changed from educational institutions to other nonprofit groups and may have been the first people in the job. We cannot provide you with all the information that might be useful. However, the following references and resources mentioned serve as a starting point for your quest for information on sources of grant support.

The following Web address lists the President's Cabinet agencies (federal agencies). There are 15 executive departments, with programs of interest to grant seekers, that have extensive information and application forms online: http://www.whitehouse.gov/omb/inforeg/sbpra_cabinet.html.

A complete list of current grant and contract opportunities is available at www.grants.gov.

Department of Agricultrue (USDA)

Department of Defense (DOD)

Department of Education (ED)

Department of Energy (DOE)

Department of Health and Human Services (HHS).

Department of Home Land Security (DHS)

Department of Justice (USDOA)

Department of Labor (DOL)

Department of Transportation (DOT)

Department of Veteran Affairs

Environmental Protection Agency (EPA)

National Endowment for the Arts (NEA)

National Endowment for the Humanities (NEH)

National Institutes of Health (NIH)

National Science Foundation (NSF)

B. TELEPHONE BOOKS/ONLINE TELEPHONE BOOKS

An often overlooked source of information is the Washington, DC (or any city), telephone book. The most frequently called agency numbers appear in "The Blue Pages," which list state, District of Columbia and federal government numbers, and local addresses. Under each agency, a number of special phone numbers are listed as well as a general information number that can help direct your call to the appropriate section or office. At the beginning of the "The Blue Pages" section is a list of about 25 of the most frequently called telephone numbers.

Telephone numbers within a federal agency are listed in its own directory and are largely for internal use. The Web pages of government agencies tell you how to contact them.

C. GOVERNMENT PRINTING OFFICE (GPO) LIST OF PUBLICATIONS

Familiarity with GPO and its publications is essential. Visit the GPO Web site at http://www.gpo.gov/ and explore the many opportunities listed. A good place to start on this Web site is under GPO ACCESS to find most popular resources, an A–Z resource list, and an online bookstore.

Section III. Other Sources of Assistance and Training

Your institution or organization may belong to some national organizations that provide guidance and information on federal programs. Given below is a list, though incomplete, of such national organizations that will give you an idea of what might be available to your institution and to you.

If you are associated with a community college, a land-grant college, a large health organization, or a faith-based organization, chances are you will find a staff member who has information on government funding and other sources with interests directly related to the association's membership. There are experienced people in these national offices, and the government agency program officers know and respect them. In other cases, state systems provide assistance to faculty and individual campuses. And once again, the place to start is their Web site.

Educational Organizations listed online:

- http://www.ed.gov/about/contacts/gen/othersites/associations.html

- http://wdcrobcolp01.ed.gov/Programs/EROD/

- (Educational Resource Organizations Directory)

- http://www.ed.gov/about/contacts/gen/othersites/associations

- (Educational Associations and Organizations)

- http://www.ntlf.com/html/lib/assoc/index.htm

- (Higher Education Associations)

FINDING NATIONAL EDUCATIONAL ORGANIZATONS

The Web address of Washington Higher Education Secretariat (WHES), http://www.whes.org/members.html, provides a complete listing of 50 national higher education associations. This listing of associations most likely includes several organizations with which your institution is affiliated. It is worth checking to see what services may be available to you.

Section IV. Forms and Required Information

It would probably be most helpful—or at least less confusing—if every federal agency used the same application forms. Unfortunately, this is not the case, not because of any predetermined obstinacy on the part of federal agencies, but primarily because each application form was developed to provide the unique information an agency believes is needed to process proposals.

However, there is some information that seems to repeat itself from application form to application form, and there is certain unique information that certain agencies require each time an application is submitted. In this section, we have provided examples of current application forms for federal agencies that educational, training, and research institutions are most likely to be applying to for project support. In addition, we have listed some of the standard and special institutional information needed to complete each form.

While the information provided should be most helpful to completing the forms, this appendix should not be viewed as all-inclusive. It is only a reference tool to be used when preparing an application. The best sources of specific information are the sponsoring agencies' application kits. Still, we hope this additional information will help with the sometimes confusing task of "filling out the forms."

One thing to keep in mind is that many government forms are copied from copies and the small print is often illegible (as with some of the examples in this section). If you are concerned about the small print, call the appropriate government agency to locate the forms or look on their Web site. Downloading is easy. Most forms can be filled out on the Internet, most forms have a printable version, but most government forms cannot be saved for future use, so make extra copies after you enter the data and print it!

The following Web sites may help you locate government forms:

> http://www.ed.gov/fund/grant/apply/appforms/ed524.doc,
>
> http://www.whitehouse.gov/omb/grants/sf269.pdf.

One good thing that has happened and made life easier is access to the World Wide Web (WWW). Every federal agency has a Web site where guidelines and forms are available. Some were easier to find than others. The Department of Defense required a couple of phone calls and a written request for the latest version of a required form. The Department of Homeland Security (DHS) required a download designed to view the application forms.

A. CLASSIFICATION OF TYPES OF GRANT APPLICATIONS

Exhibit 28. Types of Grant Applications.

CLASSIFICATIONS OF TYPES OF GRANT APPLICATIONS				
TYPES	**DEFINITIONS**	**DISTINGUISHING FEATURES**	**LIMITATIONS**	**NON-GOV'T REVIEW REQUIRED**
NEW	An action which is being submitted by an Applicant for the first time	Not previously Submitted	Availability of funds, successful competition based upon published evaluation criteria	YES
CONTINUATIONS	A grant application which contains multiyear documentation and the original grant contemplated multiyear funding.	Multiyear scope and budget	Funds are available, Successful prior year performance, Continuation is in the best interest of the Government	NO
COMPETING CONTINUATION	A grant application which proposes to continue an assisting grant beyond the grant period on year-to-year basis	Year-to-Year application is required; treated the same as a new application	Availability of funds, successful competition based upon published evaluation criteria	YES

Exhibit 28. (*Continued*)

COMPETING EXTENSION GRANT	The first grant made in support of the project period extension, requested on a competing extension application	Multiyear project period following a multiyear project period	Availability of funds, successful completion of prior project period	YES
SUPPLEMENTAL GRANT	An action which pertains to an increase in the amount of the Federal contribution for the same period	Funding increase, No time extension	Availability of funds, Program judgment priorities.	NO
CHANGES IN EXISTING GRANT	Increase in duration Decrease in duration Decrease in Federal Funding	Grant period changes. Federal contribution decreases only	No funding increases	NO

* For the purpose of this directive "Non-Governmental" means Non- Federal.

B. DEPARTMENT OF DEFENSE (DOD)

General

Although DOD may give grants, it usually funds unsolicited research proposal via the mechanism of a contract. You will be amazed at the things for which DOD is seeking proposals. The environment in which a tank must operate could be the subject of a research grant or contract, for one example.

The current short term contract DD Form 2222-2 has a format that allows the applicant to make an "offer" and for the government to accept it. Unfortunately, this form DD 2222-2 was marked cancelled on the DOD Web site listing. Here an e-mail request for the hard copy of the form may be necessary. This form was not placed in electronic format at the time of writing this book. Contact the DOD Forms Management Program at WHS/ESD/IMD

http://www.dtic.mil/whs/directives/infomgt/forms/formsprogram.htm.

C. DEPARTMENT OF EDUCATION (ED)

General

The government has made an attempt toward application form standardization. The result has been standard form 424 prescribed by the General Service Administration (GSA), now available on the Internet at http://www.ed.gov/fund/grant/apply/appforms/ed424.doc.

Exhibit 29. ED Federal Assistance Form.

Application for Federal Education Assistance (ED 424)

U.S. Department of Education
Form Approved
OMB No. 1890-0017
Exp. 04/30/2008

Applicant Information

1. Name and Address
Legal Name:_____

Address: _____

_____

_____

| City | State | County | ZIP Code + 4 |

2. Applicant's D-U-N-S Number | | | | | | | | | | |

3. Applicant's T-I-N | | | - | | | | | | | |

4. Catalog of Federal Domestic Assistance #: 84. | | | |

Title: _____

_____

5. Project Director:_____

Address:_____

_____

| City | State | Zip code + 4 |
Tel. #: ( )_____-_____ Fax #: ( )_____-_____

E-Mail Address: _____

Organizational Unit

6. Novice Applicant ___Yes ___No

7. Is the applicant delinquent on any Federal debt? ___Yes ___No
(If "Yes," attach an explanation.)

8. Type of Applicant *(Enter appropriate letter in the box.)* |____|

A - State	F - Independent School District
B - Local	G - Public College or University
C - Special District	H - Private, Non-profit College or University
D - Indian Tribe	I - Non-profit Organization
E - Individual	J - Private, Profit-Making Organization

K - Other *(Specify)*: _____

9. State Application Identifier _____

Application Information

10. Type of Submission:

-PreApplication	*-Application*
___ Construction	___ Construction
___ Non-Construction	___ Non-Construction

11. Is application subject to review by Executive Order 12372 process?
___ Yes *(Date made available to the Executive Order 12372 process for review):* ____/____/_____

___ No *(If "No," check appropriate box below.)*
___ Program is not covered by E.O. 12372.
___ Program has not been selected by State for review.

12. Proposed Project Dates: ____/____/_____ ____/____/_____
                Start Date: **End Date:**

13. Are any research activities involving human subjects planned at any time during the proposed project period?
___ Yes (Go to 13a.) ___ No (Go to item 14.)

13a. Are all the research activities proposed designated to be exempt from the regulations?
___ Yes (Provide Exemption(s) #): _____

___ No (Provide Assurance #): _____

14. Descriptive Title of Applicant's Project:

_____

_____

_____

Estimated Funding

15a. Federal	$_____	. 00
b. Applicant	$_____	. 00
c. State	$_____	. 00
d. Local	$_____	. 00
e. Other	$_____	. 00
f. Program Income	$_____	. 00
g. TOTAL	$_____	. 00

Authorized Representative Information

16. To the best of my knowledge and belief, all data in this preapplication/application are true and correct. The document has been duly authorized by the governing body of the applicant and the applicant will comply with the attached assurances if the assistance is awarded.

a. Authorized Representative *(Please type or print name clearly.)*

_____

b. Title: _____

c. Tel. #: ( )_____-_____ **Fax #:** ( )_____-_____

d. E-Mail Address: _____

e. Signature of Authorized Representative

_____ Date:___/___/___

Exhibit 29. (*Continued*)

Definitions for Form ED 424

Novice Applicant (See 34 CFR 75.225). For discretionary grant programs under which the Secretary gives special consideration to novice applications, a novice applicant means any applicant for a grant from ED that—

- Has never received a grant or subgrant under the program from which it seeks funding;

- Has never been a member of a group application, submitted in accordance with 34 CFR 75.127-75.129, that received a grant under the program from which it seeks funding; and

- Has not had an active discretionary grant from the Federal government in the five years before the deadline date for applications under the program. For the purposes of this requirement, a grant is active until the end of the grant's project or funding period, including any extensions of those periods that extend the grantee's authority to obligate funds.

In the case of a group application submitted in accordance with 34 CFR 75.127-75.129, a group includes only parties that meet the requirements listed above.

Type of Submission. "Construction" includes construction of new buildings and acquisition, expansion, remodeling, and alteration of existing buildings, and initial equipment of any such buildings, or any combination of such activities (including architects' fees and the cost of acquisition of land). "Construction" also includes remodeling to meet standards, remodeling designed to conserve energy, renovation or remodeling to accommodate new technologies, and the purchase of existing historic buildings for conversion to public libraries. For the purposes of this paragraph, the term "equipment" includes machinery, utilities, and built-in equipment and any necessary enclosures or structures to house them; and such term includes all other items necessary for the functioning of a particular facility as a facility for the provision of library services.

Executive Order 12372. The purpose of Executive Order 12372 is to foster an intergovernmental partnership and strengthen federalism by relying on State and local processes for the coordination and review of proposed Federal financial assistance and direct Federal development. The application notice, as published in the Federal Register, informs the applicant as to whether the program is subject to the requirements of E.O. 12372. In addition, the application package contains information on the State Single Point of Contact. An applicant is still eligible to apply for a grant or grants even if its respective State, Territory, Commonwealth, etc. does not have a State Single Point of Contact. For additional information on E.O. 12372 go to http://12.46.245.173/pls/portal30/catalog.REQ_FOR_12372.show

PROTECTION OF HUMAN SUBJECTS IN RESEARCH

I. Definitions and Exemptions

A. Definitions.

A research activity involves human subjects if the activity is research, as defined in the Department's regulations, and the re-

search activity will involve use of human subjects, as defined in the regulations.

—Research

The ED Regulations for the Protection of Human Subjects, Title 34, Code of Federal Regulations, Part 97, define research as "a systematic investigation, including research development, testing and evaluation, designed to develop or contribute to generalizable knowledge." *If an activity follows a deliberate plan whose purpose is to develop or contribute to generalizable knowledge it is research.* Activities which meet this definition constitute research whether or not they are conducted or supported under a program which is considered research for other purposes. For example, some demonstration and service programs may include research activities.

—Human Subject

The regulations define human subject as "a living individual about whom an investigator (whether professional or student) conducting research obtains (1) data through intervention or interaction with the individual, or (2) identifiable private information." *(1) If an activity involves obtaining information about a living person by manipulating that person or that person's environment, as might occur when a new instructional technique is tested, or by communicating or interacting with the individual, as occurs with surveys and interviews, the definition of human subject is met. (2) If an activity involves obtaining private information about a living person in such a way that the information can be linked to that individual (the identity of the subject is or may be readily determined by the investigator or associated with the information), the definition of human subject is met.* [Private information includes information about behavior that occurs in a context in which an individual can reasonably expect that no observation or recording is taking place, and information which has been provided for specific purposes by an individual and which the individual can reasonably expect will not be made public (for example, a school health record).]

B. Exemptions.

Research activities in which the **only** involvement of human subjects will be in one or more of the following six categories of *exemptions* are not covered by the regulations:

(1) Research conducted in established or commonly accepted educational settings, involving normal educational practices, such as (a) research on regular and special education instructional strategies, or (b) research on the effectiveness of or the comparison among instructional techniques, curricula, or classroom management methods.

(2) Research involving the use of educational tests (cognitive, diagnostic, aptitude, achievement), survey procedures, interview procedures or observation of public behavior, unless: (a) information obtained is recorded in such a manner that human subjects can be identified, directly or through identifiers linked to the subjects; and (b) any disclosure of the human subjects' responses outside the research could reasonably place the subjects at risk of criminal or civil liability or be damaging to the subjects' financial standing, employability, or reputation. *If the subjects are chil-*

Exhibit 29. (*Continued*)

Instructions for Form ED 424

1. **Legal Name and Address.** Enter the legal name of applicant and the name of the primary organizational unit which will undertake the assistance activity.

2. **D-U-N-S Number.** Enter the applicant's D-U-N-S Number. If your organization does not have a D-U-N-S Number, you can obtain the number by calling 1-800-333-0505 or by completing a D-U-N-S Number Request Form. The form can be obtained via the Internet at the following URL: **http://www.dnb.com.**

3. **Tax Identification Number.** Enter the taxpayer's identification number as assigned by the Internal Revenue Service.

4. **Catalog of Federal Domestic Assistance (CFDA) Number.** Enter the CFDA number and title of the program under which assistance is requested. The CFDA number can be found in the federal register notice and the application package.

5. **Project Director.** Name, address, telephone and fax numbers, and e-mail address of the person to be contacted on matters involving this application.

6. **Novice Applicant.** Check "**Yes**" or "**No**" only if assistance is being requested under a program that gives special consideration to novice applicants. Otherwise, **leave blank**.

    Check "**Yes**" if you meet the requirements for novice applicants specified in the regulations in 34 CFR 75.225 and included on the attached page entitled "Definitions for Form ED 424." By checking "**Yes**" the applicant certifies that it meets these novice applicant requirements. Check "**No**" if you do not meet the requirements for novice applicants.

7. **Federal Debt Delinquency.** Check "**Yes**" if the applicant's organization is delinquent on any Federal debt. (This question refers to the applicant's organization and not to the person who signs as the authorized representative. Categories of debt include delinquent audit disallowances, loans and taxes.) Otherwise, check "**No**."

8. **Type of Applicant.** Enter the appropriate letter in the box provided.

9. **State Application Identifier.** State use only (if applicable).

10. **Type of Submission.** See "Definitions for Form ED 424" attached.

11. **Executive Order 12372.** See "Definitions for Form ED 424" attached. Check "**Yes**" if the application is subject to review by E.O. 12372. Also, please enter the month, day, and four (4) digit year (mm/dd/yyyy). Otherwise, check "**No**."

12. **Proposed Project Dates.** Please enter the month, day, and four (4) digit year (mm/dd/yyyy).

13. **Human Subjects Research.** (See I.A. "Definitions" in attached page entitled "Definitions for Form ED 424.")

If Not Human Subjects Research. Check "No" if research activities involving human subjects are not planned at any time during the proposed project period. The remaining parts of Item 12 are then not applicable.

If Human Subjects Research. Check "Yes" if research activities involving human subjects are planned at any time during the proposed project period, either at the applicant organization or at any other performance site or collaborating institution. Check "Yes" even if the research is exempt from the regulations for the protection of human subjects. (See I.B. "Exemptions" in attached page entitled "Definitions for Form ED 424.")

13a. **If Human Subjects Research is Exempt from the Human Subjects Regulations.** Check "Yes" if all the research activities proposed are designated to be exempt from the regulations. Insert the exemption number(s) corresponding to one or more of the six exemption categories listed in I.B. "Exemptions." In addition, follow the instructions in II.A. "Exempt Research Narrative" in the attached page entitled "Definitions for Form ED 424." Insert this narrative immediately following the ED 424 face page.

13a. **If Human Subjects Research is Not Exempt from Human Subjects Regulations.** Check "No" if some or all of the planned research activities are covered (not exempt). In addition, follow the instructions in II.B. "Nonexempt Research Narrative" in the page entitled "Definitions for Form ED 424." Insert this narrative immediately following the ED 424 face page.

13a. **Human Subjects Assurance Number.** If the applicant has an approved Federal Wide (FWA) or Multiple Project Assurance (MPA) with the Office for Human Research Protections (OHRP), U.S. Department of Health and Human Services, that covers the specific activity, insert the number in the space provided. If the applicant does not have an approved assurance on file with OHRP, enter "None." In this case, the applicant, by signature on the face page, is declaring that it will comply with 34 CFR 97 and proceed to obtain the human subjects assurance upon request by the designated ED official. If the application is recommended/selected for funding, the designated ED official will request that the applicant obtain the assurance within 30 days after the specific formal request.

Note about Institutional Review Board Approval. ED does not require certification of Institutional Review Board approval with the application. However, if an application that involves non-exempt human subjects research is recommended/selected for funding, the designated ED official will request that the applicant obtain and send the certification to ED within 30 days after the formal request.

14. **Project Title.** Enter a brief descriptive title of the project. If more than one program is involved, you should append an explanation on a separate sheet. If appropriate (e.g., construction or real property projects), attach a map showing project location. For preapplications, use a separate sheet to provide a summary description of this project.

Exhibit 29. (*Continued*)

15. **Estimated Funding**. Amount requested or to be contributed during the first funding/budget period by each contributor. Value of in-kind contributions should be included on appropriate lines as applicable. If the action will result in a dollar change to an existing award, indicate **only** the amount of the change. For decreases, enclose the amounts in parentheses. If both basic and supplemental amounts are included, show breakdown on an attached sheet. For multiple program funding, use totals and show breakdown using same categories as item 15.

16. **Certification**. To be signed by the authorized representative of the applicant. A copy of the governing body's authorization for you to sign this application as official representative must be on file in the applicant's office. Be sure to enter the telephone and fax number and e-mail address of the authorized representative. Also, in item 16e, please enter the month, day, and four (4) digit year (mm/dd/yyyy) in the date signed field.

Paperwork Burden Statement. According to the Paperwork Reduction Act of 1995, no persons are required to respond to a collection of information unless such collection displays a valid OMB control number. The valid OMB control number for this information collection is 1890-0017. The time required to complete this information collection is estimated to average between 15 and 45 minutes per response, including the time to review instructions, search existing data resources, gather the data needed, and complete and review the information collection. **If you have any comments concerning the accuracy of the estimate(s) or suggestions for improving this form, please write to:** U.S. Department of Education, Washington, D.C. 20202-4700. **If you have comments or concerns regarding the status of your individual submission of this form write directly to:** Joyce I. Mays, Application Control Center, U.S. Department of Education, Potomac Center Plaza, 550 12th Street SW, Room 7076, Washington, DC 20202-4260.

Institutional Information Required

Along with the standard project information, there are several items of information needed to complete the application form that may not be readily accessible. Therefore, you should have them in advance to make completion of the forms easier. These are

1. Congressional district,
2. Federal Employer Identification No. (IRS #),
3. type of organization of applicant (list is provided: select one),
4. estimated number of persons benefiting from the assistance,
5. sources of funding for project,
6. applicant's TIN (Tax Identification Number), and
7. applicant's DUNS number (http://www.dnb.com/US/duns).

Project Questions

If the project is subject to a State Clearinghouse submission pursuant to the OMB Circular A-95, the responses must be attached to the application.

Exhibit 30. Financial Status Report.

FINANCIAL STATUS REPORT
(Short Form)
(Follow instructions on the back)

1. Federal Agency and Organizational Element to Which Report is Submitted	2. Federal Grant or Other Identifying Number Assigned By Federal Agency	OMB Approval No. 0348-0038	Page of pages

3. Recipient Organization (Name and complete address, including ZIP code)

4. Employer Identification Number	5. Recipient Account Number or Identifying Number	6. Final Report ☐ Yes ☐ No	7. Basis ☐ Cash ☐ Accrual

8. Funding/Grant Period *(See instructions)* From: (Month, Day, Year)	To: (Month, Day, Year)	9. Period Covered by this Report From: (Month, Day, Year)	To: (Month, Day, Year)

10. Transactions:	I Previously Reported	II This Period	III Cumulative
a. Total outlays			0.00
b. Recipient share of outlays			0.00
c. Federal share of outlays			0.00
d. Total unliquidated obligations			
e. Recipient share of unliquidated obligations			
f. Federal share of unliquidated obligations			
g. Total Federal share *(Sum of lines c and f)*			0.00
h. Total Federal funds authorized for this funding period			
i. Unobligated balance of Federal funds *(Line h minus line g)*			0.00

11. Indirect Expense	a. Type of Rate *(Place "X" in appropriate box)* ☐ Provisional ☐ Predetermined ☐ Final ☐ Fixed			
	b. Rate	c. Base	d. Total Amount	e. Federal Share

12. *Remarks: Attach any explanations deemed necessary or information required by Federal sponsoring agency in compliance with governing legislation.*

13. Certification: **I certify to the best of my knowledge and belief that this report is correct and complete and that all outlays and unliquidated obligations are for the purposes set forth in the award documents.**

Typed or Printed Name and Title	Telephone (Area code, number and extension)
Signature of Authorized Certifying Official	Date Report Submitted January 26, 2007

NSN 7540-01-218-4387   269-202   Standard Form 269A (Rev. 7-97)
Prescribed by OMB Circulars A-102 and A-110

Exhibit 30. (*Continued*)

FINANCIAL STATUS REPORT
(Short Form)

Public reporting burden for this collection of information is estimated to average 90 minutes per response, including time for reviewing instructions, searching existing data sources, gathering and maintaining the data needed, and completing and reviewing the collection of information. Send comments regarding the burden estimate or any other aspect of this collection of information, including suggestions for reducing this burden, to the Office of Management and Budget, Paperwork Reduction Project (0348-0038), Washington, DC 20503.

PLEASE DO NOT RETURN YOUR COMPLETED FORM TO THE OFFICE OF MANAGEMENT AND BUDGET. SEND IT TO THE ADDRESS PROVIDED BY THE SPONSORING AGENCY.

Please type or print legibly. The following general instructions explain how to use the form itself. You may need additional information to complete certain items correctly, or to decide whether a specific item is applicable to this award. Usually, such information will be found in the Federal agency's grant regulations or in the terms and conditions of the award. You may also contact the Federal agency directly.

Item	Entry	Item	Entry

1, 2 and 3. Self-explanatory.

4. Enter the Employer Identification Number (EIN) assigned by the U.S. Internal Revenue Service.

5. Space reserved for an account number or other identifying number assigned by the recipient.

6. Check *yes* only if this is the last report for the period shown in item 8.

7. Self-explanatory.

8. Unless you have received other instructions from the awarding agency, enter the beginning and ending dates of the current funding period. If this is a multi-year program, the Federal agency might require cumulative reporting through consecutive funding periods. In that case, enter the beginning and ending dates of the grant period, and in the rest of these instructions, substitute the term "grant period" for "funding period."

9. Self-explanatory.

10. The purpose of columns I, II, and III is to show the effect of this reporting period's transactions on cumulative financial status. The amounts entered in column I will normally be the same as those in column III of the previous report in *the same funding period*. If this is the first or only report of the funding period, leave columns I and II blank. If you need to adjust amounts entered on previous reports, footnote the column I entry on this report and attach an explanation.

10a. Enter total program outlays less any rebates, refunds, or other credits. For reports prepared on a cash basis, outlays are the sum of actual cash disbursements for direct costs for goods and services, the amount of indirect expense charged, the value of in-kind contributions applied, and the amount of cash advances and payments made to subrecipients. For reports prepared on an accrual basis, outlays are the sum of actual cash disbursements for direct charges for goods and services, the amount of indirect expense incurred,

the value of in-kind contributions applied, and the net increase or decrease in the amounts owed by the recipient for goods and other property received, for services performed by employees, contractors, subgrantees and other payees, and other amounts becoming owed under programs for which no current services or performances are required, such as annuities, insurance claims, and other benefit payments.

10b. Self-explanatory.

10c. Self-explanatory.

10d. Enter the total amount of unliquidated obligations, including unliquidated obligations to subgrantees and contractors.

Unliquidated obligations on a cash basis are obligations incurred, but not yet paid. On an accrual basis, they are obligations incurred, but for which an outlay has not yet been recorded.

Do not include any amounts on line 10d that have been included on lines 10a, b, or c.

On the final report, line 10d must be zero.

10e. f, g, h, h and i. Self-explanatory.

11a. Self-explanatory.

11b. Enter the indirect cost rate in effect during the reporting period.

11c. Enter the amount of the base against which the rate was applied.

11d. Enter the total amount of indirect costs charged during the report period.

11e. Enter the Federal share of the amount in 11d.

Note: If more than one rate was in effect during the period shown in item 8, attach a schedule showing the bases against which the different rates were applied, the respective rates, the calendar periods they were in effect, amounts of indirect expense charged to the project, and the Federal share of indirect expense charged to the project to date.

*U. S. Government Printing Office: 1993 - 342-197/81289

SF-269A (Rev. 7-97) Back

Exhibit 30. (*Continued*)

APPLICATION FOR FEDERAL ASSISTANCE		Version 7/03
	2. DATE SUBMITTED	Applicant Identifier

APPLICATION FOR FEDERAL ASSISTANCE Version 7/03

1. TYPE OF SUBMISSION:		**2. DATE SUBMITTED**	Applicant Identifier
Application	Pre-application	**3. DATE RECEIVED BY STATE**	State Application Identifier
☐ Construction	☐ Construction	**4. DATE RECEIVED BY FEDERAL AGENCY**	Federal Identifier
☐ Non-Construction	☐ Non-Construction		

5. APPLICANT INFORMATION

Legal Name:	**Organizational Unit:**
	Department:
Organizational DUNS:	Division:
Address: Street:	**Name and telephone number of person to be contacted on matters involving this application (give area code)**
	Prefix: / First Name:
City:	Middle Name
County:	Last Name
State: / Zip Code	Suffix:
Country:	Email:

6. EMPLOYER IDENTIFICATION NUMBER (*EIN*): ☐☐–☐☐☐☐☐☐☐	Phone Number (give area code)	Fax Number (give area code)

8. TYPE OF APPLICATION:	**7. TYPE OF APPLICANT:** (See back of form for Application Types)
☐ New ☐ Continuation ☐ Revision If Revision, enter appropriate letter(s) in box(es) (See back of form for description of letters.) ☐ ☐ Other (specify)	Other (specify)
	9. NAME OF FEDERAL AGENCY:

10. CATALOG OF FEDERAL DOMESTIC ASSISTANCE NUMBER: ☐☐–☐☐☐ TITLE (Name of Program):	**11. DESCRIPTIVE TITLE OF APPLICANT'S PROJECT:**

12. AREAS AFFECTED BY PROJECT (*Cities, Counties, States, etc.*):

13. PROPOSED PROJECT		**14. CONGRESSIONAL DISTRICTS OF:**	
Start Date:	Ending Date:	a. Applicant	b. Project

15. ESTIMATED FUNDING:		**16. IS APPLICATION SUBJECT TO REVIEW BY STATE EXECUTIVE ORDER 12372 PROCESS?**	
a. Federal	$ .00	a. Yes. ☐ THIS PREAPPLICATION/APPLICATION WAS MADE AVAILABLE TO THE STATE EXECUTIVE ORDER 12372 PROCESS FOR REVIEW ON	
b. Applicant	$ .00		
c. State	$ .00	DATE:	
d. Local	$ .00	b. No. ☐ PROGRAM IS NOT COVERED BY E. O. 12372	
e. Other	$ .00	☐ OR PROGRAM HAS NOT BEEN SELECTED BY STATE FOR REVIEW	
f. Program Income	$ .00	**17. IS THE APPLICANT DELINQUENT ON ANY FEDERAL DEBT?**	
g. TOTAL	$ .00	☐ Yes If "Yes" attach an explanation. ☐ No	

18. TO THE BEST OF MY KNOWLEDGE AND BELIEF, ALL DATA IN THIS APPLICATION/PREAPPLICATION ARE TRUE AND CORRECT. THE DOCUMENT HAS BEEN DULY AUTHORIZED BY THE GOVERNING BODY OF THE APPLICANT AND THE APPLICANT WILL COMPLY WITH THE ATTACHED ASSURANCES IF THE ASSISTANCE IS AWARDED.

a. Authorized Representative		
Prefix	First Name	Middle Name
Last Name		Suffix
b. Title		c. Telephone Number (give area code)
d. Signature of Authorized Representative		e. Date Signed

Previous Edition Usable
Authorized for Local Reproduction

Standard Form 424 (Rev.9-2003)
Prescribed by OMB Circular A-102

Exhibit 30. (*Continued*)

INSTRUCTIONS FOR THE SF-424

Public reporting burden for this collection of information is estimated to average 45 minutes per response, including time for reviewing instructions, searching existing data sources, gathering and maintaining the data needed, and completing and reviewing the collection of information. Send comments regarding the burden estimate or any other aspect of this collection of information, including suggestions for reducing this burden, to the Office of Management and Budget, Paperwork Reduction Project (0348-0043), Washington, DC 20503.

PLEASE DO NOT RETURN YOUR COMPLETED FORM TO THE OFFICE OF MANAGEMENT AND BUDGET. SEND IT TO THE ADDRESS PROVIDED BY THE SPONSORING AGENCY.

This is a standard form used by applicants as a required face sheet for pre-applications and applications submitted for Federal assistance. It will be used by Federal agencies to obtain applicant certification that States which have established a review and comment procedure in response to Executive Order 12372 and have selected the program to be included in their process, have been given an opportunity to review the applicant's submission.

Item:	Entry:	Item:	Entry:
1.	Select Type of Submission.	11.	Enter a brief descriptive title of the project. If more than one program is involved, you should append an explanation on a separate sheet. If appropriate (e.g., construction or real property projects), attach a map showing project location. For preapplications, use a separate sheet to provide a summary description of this project.
2.	Date application submitted to Federal agency (or State if applicable) and applicant's control number (if applicable).	12.	List only the largest political entities affected (e.g., State, counties, cities).
3.	State use only (if applicable).	13	Enter the proposed start date and end date of the project.
4.	Enter Date Received by Federal Agency Federal identifier number: If this application is a continuation or revision to an existing award, enter the present Federal Identifier number. If for a new project, leave blank.	14.	List the applicant's Congressional District and any District(s) affected by the program or project
5.	Enter legal name of applicant, name of primary organizational unit (including division, if applicable), which will undertake the assistance activity, enter the organization's DUNS number (received from Dun and Bradstreet), enter the complete address of the applicant (including country), and name, telephone number, e-mail and fax of the person to contact on matters related to this application.	15	Amount requested or to be contributed during the first funding/budget period by each contributor. Value of in kind contributions should be included on appropriate lines as applicable. If the action will result in a dollar change to an existing award, indicate only the amount of the change. For decreases, enclose the amounts in parentheses. If both basic and supplemental amounts are included, show breakdown on an attached sheet. For multiple program funding, use totals and show breakdown using same categories as item 15.
6.	Enter Employer Identification Number (EIN) as assigned by the Internal Revenue Service.	16.	Applicants should contact the State Single Point of Contact (SPOC) for Federal Executive Order 12372 to determine whether the application is subject to the State intergovernmental review process.

7.	Select the appropriate letter in the space provided.
	  A. State
	  B. County
	  C. Municipal
	  D. Township
	  E. Interstate
	  F. Intermunicipal
	  G. Special District
	  H. Independent School District
	  I. State Controlled Institution of Higher Learning
	  J. Private University
	  K. Indian Tribe
	  L. Individual
	  M. Profit Organization
	  N. Other (Specify)
	  O. Not for Profit Organization
		17.	This question applies to the applicant organization, not the person who signs as the authorized representative. Categories of debt include delinquent audit disallowances, loans and taxes.

8.	Select the type from the following list:
	• "New" means a new assistance award.
	• "Continuation" means an extension for an additional funding/budget period for a project with a projected completion date.
	• "Revision" means any change in the Federal Government's financial obligation or contingent liability from an existing obligation. If a revision enter the appropriate letter:
	  A. Increase Award B. Decrease Award
	  C. Increase Duration D. Decrease Duration
		18	To be signed by the authorized representative of the applicant. A copy of the governing body's authorization for you to sign this application as official representative must be on file in the applicant's office. (Certain Federal agencies may require that this authorization be submitted as part of the application.)

9.	Name of Federal agency from which assistance is being requested with this application.		
10.	Use the Catalog of Federal Domestic Assistance number and title of the program under which assistance is requested.		

SF-424 (Rev. 7-97) Back

Exhibit 30. (*Continued*)

			OMB APPROVAL NO.		PAGE	OF
			0348-0004			PAGES

REQUEST FOR ADVANCE OR REIMBURSEMENT

(See instructions on back)

1. TYPE OF PAYMENT REQUESTED	a. "X" one or both boxes	2. BASIS OF REQUEST
	☐ ADVANCE ☐ REIMBURSE-MENT	☐ CASH
	b. "X" the applicable box	
	☐ FINAL ☐ PARTIAL	☐ ACCRUAL

3. FEDERAL SPONSORING AGENCY AND ORGANIZATIONAL ELEMENT TO WHICH THIS REPORT IS SUBMITTED	4. FEDERAL GRANT OR OTHER IDENTIFYING NUMBER ASSIGNED BY FEDERAL AGENCY	5. PARTIAL PAYMENT REQUEST NUMBER FOR THIS REQUEST

6. EMPLOYER IDENTIFICATION NUMBER	7. RECIPIENT'S ACCOUNT NUMBER OR IDENTIFYING NUMBER	8. PERIOD COVERED BY THIS REQUEST
		FROM *(month, day, year)* / TO *(month, day, year)*

9. RECIPIENT ORGANIZATION	10. PAYEE *(Where check is to be sent if different than item 9)*
Name:	Name:
Number and Street:	Number and Street:
City, State and ZIP Code:	City, State and ZIP Code:

11. COMPUTATION OF AMOUNT OF REIMBURSEMENTS/ADVANCES REQUESTED

PROGRAMS/FUNCTIONS/ACTIVITIES ▶	(a)	(b)	(c)	TOTAL
a. Total program outlays to date *(As of date)*	$	$	$	$ 0.00
b. *Less:* Cumulative program income				0.00
c. Net program outlays (*Line a minus line b*)	0.00	0.00	0.00	0.00
d. Estimated net cash outlays for advance period				0.00
e. Total *(Sum of lines c & d)*	0.00	0.00	0.00	0.00
f. Non-Federal share of amount on line e				0.00
g. Federal share of amount on line e				0.00
h. Federal payments previously requested				0.00
i. Federal share now requested (*Line g minus line h*)	0.00	0.00	0.00	0.00
j. Advances required by month, when requested by Federal grantor agency for use in making prescheduled advances — 1st month				0.00
2nd month				0.00
3rd month				0.00

12. ALTERNATE COMPUTATION FOR ADVANCES ONLY

a. Estimated Federal cash outlays that will be made during period covered by the advance	$
b. *Less:* Estimated balance of Federal cash on hand as of beginning of advance period	
c. Amount requested (*Line a minus line b*)	$ 0.00

AUTHORIZED FOR LOCAL REPRODUCTION   *(Continued on Reverse)*   STANDARD FORM 270 (Rev. 7-97)
Prescribed by OMB Circulars A-102 and A-110

Exhibit 30. (*Continued*)

13.	CERTIFICATION	
I certify that to the best of my knowledge and belief the data on the reverse are correct and that all outlays were made in accordance with the grant conditions or other agreement and that payment is due and has not been previously requested.	SIGNATURE OR AUTHORIZED CERTIFYING OFFICIAL	DATE REQUEST SUBMITTED January 26, 2007
	TYPED OR PRINTED NAME AND TITLE	TELEPHONE (AREA CODE, NUMBER, EXTENSION)

This space for agency use

Public reporting burden for this collection of information is estimated to average 60 minutes per response, including time for reviewing instructions, searching existing data sources, gathering and maintaining the data needed, and completing and reviewing the collection of information. Send comments regarding the burden estimate or any other aspect of this collection of information, including suggestions for reducing this burden, to the Office of Management and Budget, Paperwork Reduction Project (0348-0004), Washington, DC 20503.

PLEASE DO NOT RETURN YOUR COMPLETED FORM TO THE OFFICE OF MANAGEMENT AND BUDGET. SEND IT TO THE ADDRESS PROVIDED BY THE SPONSORING AGENCY.

INSTRUCTIONS

Please type or print legibly. Items 1, 3, 5, 9, 10, 11e, 11f, 11g, 11i, 12 and 13 are self-explanatory; specific instructions for other items are as follows:

Item	Entry

2 Indicate whether request is prepared on cash or accrued expenditure basis. All requests for advances shall be prepared on a cash basis.

4 Enter the Federal grant number, or other identifying number assigned by the Federal sponsoring agency. If the advance or reimbursement is for more than one grant or other agreement, insert N/A; then, show the aggregate amounts. On a separate sheet, list each grant or agreement number and the Federal share of outlays made against the grant or agreement.

6 Enter the employer identification number assigned by the U.S. Internal Revenue Service, or the FICE (institution) code if requested by the Federal agency.

7 This space is reserved for an account number or other identifying number that may be assigned by the recipient.

8 Enter the month, day, and year for the beginning and ending of the period covered in this request. If the request is for an advance or for both an advance and reimbursement, show the period that the advance will cover. If the request is for reimbursement, show the period for which the reimbursement is requested.

Note: The Federal sponsoring agencies have the option of requiring recipients to complete items 11 or 12, but not both. Item 12 should be used when only a minimum amount of information is needed to make an advance and outlay information contained in item 11 can be obtained in a timely manner from other reports.

11 The purpose of the vertical columns (a), (b), and (c) is to provide space for separate cost breakdowns when a project has been planned and budgeted by program, function, or

activity. If additional columns are needed, use as many additional forms as needed and indicate page number in space provided in upper right; however, the summary totals of all programs, functions, or activities should be shown in the "total" column on the first page.

11a Enter in "as of date," the month, day, and year of the ending of the accounting period to which this amount applies. Enter program outlays to date (net of refunds, rebates, and discounts), in the appropriate columns. For requests prepared on a cash basis, outlays are the sum of actual cash disbursements for goods and services, the amount of indirect expenses charged, the value of in-kind contributions applied, and the amount of cash advances and payments made to subcontractors and subrecipients. For requests prepared on an accrued expenditure basis, outlays are the sum of the actual cash disbursements, the amount of indirect expenses incurred, and the net increase (or decrease) in the amounts owed by the recipient for goods and other property received and for services performed by employees, contracts, subgrantees and other payees.

11b Enter the cumulative cash income received to date, if requests are prepared on a cash basis. For requests prepared on an accrued expenditure basis, enter the cumulative income earned to date. Under either basis, enter only the amount applicable to program income that was required to be used for the project or program by the terms of the grant or other agreement.

11d Only when making requests for advance payments, enter the total estimated amount of cash outlays that will be made during the period covered by the advance.

13 Complete the certification before submitting this request.

STANDARD FORM 270 (Rev. 7-97) Back

Exhibit 30. (*Continued*)

FINANCIAL STATUS REPORT
(Short Form)
(Follow instructions on the back)

1. Federal Agency and Organizational Element to Which Report is Submitted	2. Federal Grant or Other Identifying Number Assigned By Federal Agency	OMB Approval No. **0348-0038**	Page of pages

3. Recipient Organization (Name and complete address, including ZIP code)

4. Employer Identification Number	5. Recipient Account Number or Identifying Number	6. Final Report ☐ Yes ☐ No	7. Basis ☐ Cash ☐ Accrual

8. Funding/Grant Period *(See instructions)* From: (Month, Day, Year)	To: (Month, Day, Year)	9. Period Covered by this Report From: (Month, Day, Year)	To: (Month, Day, Year)

10. Transactions:	I Previously Reported	II This Period	III Cumulative
a. Total outlays			0.00
b. Recipient share of outlays			0.00
c. Federal share of outlays			0.00
d. Total unliquidated obligations			
e. Recipient share of unliquidated obligations			
f. Federal share of unliquidated obligations			
g. Total Federal share *(Sum of lines c and f)*			0.00
h. Total Federal funds authorized for this funding period			
i. Unobligated balance of Federal funds *(Line h minus line g)*			0.00

11. Indirect Expense

a. Type of Rate *(Place "X" in appropriate box)*
☐ Provisional ☐ Predetermined ☐ Final ☐ Fixed

b. Rate	c. Base	d. Total Amount	e. Federal Share

12. Remarks: *Attach any explanations deemed necessary or information required by Federal sponsoring agency in compliance with governing legislation.*

13. Certification: **I certify to the best of my knowledge and belief that this report is correct and complete and that all outlays and unliquidated obligations are for the purposes set forth in the award documents.**

Typed or Printed Name and Title	Telephone (Area code, number and extension)

Signature of Authorized Certifying Official	Date Report Submitted December 16, 2006

NSN 7540-01-218-4387   269-202   Standard Form 269A (Rev. 7-97)
Prescribed by OMB Circulars A-102 and A-110

Exhibit 30. (*Continued*)

Please type or print legibly. The following general instructions explain how to use the form itself. You may need additional information to complete certain items correctly, or to decide whether a specific item is applicable to this award. Usually, such information will be found in the Federal agency's grant regulations or in the terms and conditions of the award. You may also contact the Federal agency directly.

Item	Entry

1, 2 and 3. Self-explanatory.

4. Enter the Employer Identification Number (EIN) assigned by the U.S. Internal Revenue Service.

5. Space reserved for an account number or other identifying number assigned by the recipient.

6. Check *yes* only if this is the last report for the period shown in item 8.

7. Self-explanatory.

8. Unless you have received other instructions from the awarding agency, enter the beginning and ending dates of the current funding period. If this is a multi-year program, the Federal agency might require cumulative reporting through consecutive funding periods. In that case, enter the beginning and ending dates of the grant period, and in the rest of these instructions, substitute the term "grant period" for "funding period."

9. Self-explanatory.

10. The purpose of columns I, II, and III is to show the effect of this reporting period's transactions on cumulative financial status. The amounts entered in column I will normally be the same as those in column III of the previous report in *the same funding period*. If this is the first or only report of the funding period, leave columns I and II blank. If you need to adjust amounts entered on previous reports, footnote the column I entry on this report and attach an explanation.

10a. Enter total program outlays less any rebates, refunds, or other credits. For reports prepared on a cash basis, outlays are the sum of actual cash disbursements for direct costs for goods and services, the amount of indirect expense charged, the value of in-kind contributions applied, and the amount of cash advances and payments made to subrecipients. For reports prepared on an accrual basis, outlays are the sum of actual cash disbursements for direct charges for goods and services, the amount of indirect expense incurred,

the value of in-kind contributions applied, and the net increase or decrease in the amounts owed by the recipient for goods and other property received, for services performed by employees, contractors, subgrantees and other payees, and other amounts becoming owed under programs for which no current services or performances are required, such as annuities, insurance claims, and other benefit payments.

10b. Self-explanatory.

10c. Self-explanatory.

10d. Enter the total amount of unliquidated obligations, including unliquidated obligations to subgrantees and contractors.

Unliquidated obligations on a cash basis are obligations incurred, but not yet paid. On an accrual basis, they are obligations incurred, but for which an outlay has not yet been recorded.

Do not include any amounts on line 10d that have been included on lines 10a, b, or c.

On the final report, line 10d must be zero.

10e. f, g, h, h and i. Self-explanatory.

11a. Self-explanatory.

11b. Enter the indirect cost rate in effect during the reporting period.

11c. Enter the amount of the base against which the rate was applied.

11d. Enter the total amount of indirect costs charged during the report period.

11e. Enter the Federal share of the amount in 11d.

Note: If more than one rate was in effect during the period shown in item 8, attach a schedule showing the bases against which the different rates were applied, the respective rates, the calendar periods they were in effect, amounts of indirect expense charged to the project, and the Federal share of indirect expense charged to the project to date.

D. DEPARTMENT OF HEALTH AND HUMAN SERVICES (HHS)

General

HHS uses several forms—similar, but different nevertheless. Form PHS 398 (Rev. 10-88) is most familiar as it is used to apply for all new, competing continuation, and supplemental research and training grant and cooperative agreement support except as shown in the next exhibit.

Continuation grants by HHS definition are for projects previously funded but whose funding term is finishing, thereby putting it in a "competitive" situation with new proposals. However, if an applicant has the information to complete a PHS 398 application, all others will be routine. Therefore, discussion will focus on PHS 398.

Institutional Information Required

Along with the standard application and project information there are several items of information needed to complete the application forms but may not be readily accessible. Therefore, you should have them in advance to make completion of the forms easier. These are as follows:

1. Entity Identification # (EIN # assigned by IRS).
2. Name of official in business office to be notified of award.
3. Clearance by Institutional Review Boards if human subjects or animals are involved in the research?
4. Does the project involve recombinant DNA?

Exhibit 31. Types of HHS Forms.

Forms

Use Form PHS 398 to apply for all new, competing continuation, and supplemental research and research training grant and cooperative agreement support, except as shown in the table below:

Type of Application	Use Form Number
Small Business Innovation Research Program—Phase I	PHS 6246-1
Small Business Innovation Research Program—Phase II	PHS 6246-2
Individual National Research Service Award or Senior International Fellowship Award	PHS 416-1
International Research Fellowship Award	NIH 1541-1
Nonresearch Training Grant	PHS 6025
Grant to State or Local Government Agency	PHS 5161-1
Health Services Project	PHS 5161-1
Construction Grant	NIH 2575
Biomedical Research Support Grant	NIH 147-1

Most of the above application forms have corresponding forms to be used when applying for noncompeting continuation support during an approved project period. The form corresponding to PHS 398 is Form PHS 2590.

Exhibit 32. HHS Grant Application.

Form Approved Through 09/30/2007 OMB No. 0925-0001

Department of Health and Human Services Public Health Services **Grant Application** *Do not exceed character length restrictions indicated.*	LEAVE BLANK—FOR PHS USE ONLY.		
	Type	Activity	Number
	Review Group		Formerly
	Council/Board (Month, Year)		Date Received

1. TITLE OF PROJECT *(Do not exceed 81 characters, including spaces and punctuation.)*

2. RESPONSE TO SPECIFIC REQUEST FOR APPLICATIONS OR PROGRAM ANNOUNCEMENT OR SOLICITATION ☐ NO ☐ YES
(If "Yes," state number and title)
Number: Title:

3. PRINCIPAL INVESTIGATOR/PROGRAM DIRECTOR	New Investigator ☐ No ☐ Yes	
3a. NAME (Last, first, middle)	3b. DEGREE(S)	3h. eRA Commons User Name
3c. POSITION TITLE	3d. MAILING ADDRESS *(Street, city, state, zip code)*	
3e. DEPARTMENT, SERVICE, LABORATORY, OR EQUIVALENT		
3f. MAJOR SUBDIVISION		
3g. TELEPHONE AND FAX *(Area code, number and extension)* TEL: FAX:	E-MAIL ADDRESS:	

4. HUMAN SUBJECTS RESEARCH	4b. Human Subjects Assurance No.	5. VERTEBRATE ANIMALS ☐ No ☐ Yes	
☐ No ☐ Yes	4c. Clinical Trial ☐ No ☐ Yes	4d. NIH-defined Phase III Clinical Trial ☐ No ☐ Yes	5a. If "Yes," IACUC approval Date
4a. Research Exempt ☐ No ☐ Yes	If "Yes," Exemption No.		5b. Animal welfare assurance no.

6. DATES OF PROPOSED PERIOD OF SUPPORT *(month, day, year—MM/DD/YY)*		7. COSTS REQUESTED FOR INITIAL BUDGET PERIOD		8. COSTS REQUESTED FOR PROPOSED PERIOD OF SUPPORT	
From	Through	7a. Direct Costs ($)	7b. Total Costs ($)	8a. Direct Costs ($)	8b. Total Costs ($)

9. APPLICANT ORGANIZATION Name Address	10. TYPE OF ORGANIZATION
	Public: → ☐ Federal ☐ State ☐ Local
	Private: → ☐ Private Nonprofit
	For-profit: → ☐ General ☐ Small Business
	☐ Woman-owned ☐ Socially and Economically Disadvantaged
	11. ENTITY IDENTIFICATION NUMBER DUNS NO. Cong. District

12. ADMINISTRATIVE OFFICIAL TO BE NOTIFIED IF AWARD IS MADE Name Title Address Tel: FAX: E-Mail:	13. OFFICIAL SIGNING FOR APPLICANT ORGANIZATION Name Title Address Tel: FAX: E-Mail:

14. APPLICANT ORGANIZATION CERTIFICATION AND ACCEPTANCE: I certify that the statements herein are true, complete and accurate to the best of my knowledge, and accept the obligation to comply with Public Health Services terms and conditions if a grant is awarded as a result of this application. I am aware that any false, fictitious, or fraudulent statements or claims may subject me to criminal, civil, or administrative penalties.	SIGNATURE OF OFFICIAL NAMED IN 13. *(In ink. "Per" signature not acceptable.)*	DATE

PHS 398 (Rev. 04/06)   Face Page   Form Page 1

Exhibit 32. (*Continued*)

Use only if responding to a **Multiple PI pilot initiative.** See http://grants.nih.gov/grants/multi_pi/index.htm for details.

Contact Principal Investigator/Program Director (Last, First, Middle):

3. PRINCIPAL INVESTIGATOR

3a. NAME (Last, first, middle)	3b. DEGREE(S)	3h. NIH Commons User Name
3c. POSITION TITLE	3d. MAILING ADDRESS (Street, city, state, zip code)	
3e. DEPARTMENT, SERVICE, LABORATORY, OR EQUIVALENT		
3f. MAJOR SUBDIVISION		
3g. TELEPHONE AND FAX (Area code, number and extension) TEL: FAX:	E-MAIL ADDRESS:	

3. PRINCIPAL INVESTIGATOR

3a. NAME (Last, first, middle)	3b. DEGREE(S)	3h. NIH Commons User Name
3c. POSITION TITLE	3d. MAILING ADDRESS (Street, city, state, zip code)	
3e. DEPARTMENT, SERVICE, LABORATORY, OR EQUIVALENT		
3f. MAJOR SUBDIVISION		
3g. TELEPHONE AND FAX (Area code, number and extension) TEL: FAX:	E-MAIL ADDRESS:	

3. PRINCIPAL INVESTIGATOR

3a. NAME (Last, first, middle)	3b. DEGREE(S)	3h. NIH Commons User Name
3c. POSITION TITLE	3d. MAILING ADDRESS (Street, city, state, zip code)	
3e. DEPARTMENT, SERVICE, LABORATORY, OR EQUIVALENT		
3f. MAJOR SUBDIVISION		
3g. TELEPHONE AND FAX (Area code, number and extension) TEL: FAX:	E-MAIL ADDRESS:	

3. PRINCIPAL INVESTIGATOR

3a. NAME (Last, first, middle)	3b. DEGREE(S)	3h. NIH Commons User Name
3c. POSITION TITLE	3d. MAILING ADDRESS (Street, city, state, zip code)	
3e. DEPARTMENT, SERVICE, LABORATORY, OR EQUIVALENT		
3f. MAJOR SUBDIVISION		
3g. TELEPHONE AND FAX (Area code, number and extension) TEL: FAX:	E-MAIL ADDRESS:	

PHS 398 (Rev. 04/06) Face Page-continued Form Page 1-continued

Exhibit 32. (*Continued*)

Principal Investigator/Program Director (Last, First, Middle):

DESCRIPTION: See instructions. State the application's broad, long-term objectives and specific aims, making reference to the health relatedness of the project (i.e., relevance to the **mission of the agency**). Describe concisely the research design and methods for achieving these goals. Describe the rationale and techniques you will use to pursue these goals.

In addition, in two or three sentences, describe in plain, lay language the relevance of this research to **public** health. If the application is funded, this description, as is, will become public information. Therefore, do not include proprietary/confidential information. **DO NOT EXCEED THE SPACE PROVIDED.**

PERFORMANCE SITE(S) (organization, city, state)

Exhibit 32. (*Continued*)

Principal Investigator/Program Director (Last, First, Middle):

KEY PERSONNEL. See instructions. *Use continuation pages as needed* to provide the required information in the format shown below. Start with Principal Investigator(s). List all other key personnel in alphabetical order, last name first.

Name	eRA Commons User Name	Organization	Role on Project

OTHER SIGNIFICANT CONTRIBUTORS

Name	Organization	Role on Project

Human Embryonic Stem Cells ☐ No   ☐ Yes

If the proposed project involves human embryonic stem cells, list below the registration number of the specific cell line(s) from the following list: http://stemcells.nih.gov/registry/index.asp. *Use continuation pages as needed.*

If a specific line cannot be referenced at this time, include a statement that one from the Registry will be used.

Cell Line

PHS 398 (Rev. 04/06)   Page <u>3</u>   **Form Page 2-continued**

Number the *following* pages consecutively throughout
the application. Do not use suffixes such as 4a, 4b.

Exhibit 32. (*Continued*)

Principal Investigator/Program Director (Last, First, Middle):

The name of the principal investigator/program director must be provided at the top of each printed page and each continuation page.

RESEARCH GRANT
TABLE OF CONTENTS

Appendix (*Five collated sets. No page numbering necessary for Appendix.*)

□ Check if Appendix is Included

Number of publications and manuscripts accepted for publication (*not to exceed 10*)   ___

    Other items (list):

Exhibit 32. (*Continued*)

Principal Investigator/Program Director (last, First, Middle):

CHECKLIST

TYPE OF APPLICATION *(Check all that apply.)*

☐ NEW application. *(This application is being submitted to the PHS for the first time.)*

☐ REVISION/RESUBMISSION of application number: _____

(This application replaces a prior unfunded version of a new, competing continuation/renewal, or supplemental/revision application.)

☐ COMPETING CONTINUATION/RENEWAL of grant number: _____

(This application is to extend a funded grant beyond its current project period.)

INVENTIONS AND PATENTS
(Competing continuation/renewal appl. only)

☐ No   ☐ Previously reported

☐ SUPPLEMENT/REVISION to grant number: _____

☐ Yes. If "Yes,"   ☐ Not previously reported

(This application is for additional funds to supplement a currently funded grant.)

☐ CHANGE of principal investigator/program director.

Name of former principal investigator/program director: _____

☐ CHANGE of Grantee Institution.   Name of former institution: _____

☐ FOREIGN application   ☐ Domestic Grant with foreign involvement   List Country(ies) Involved: _____

1. PROGRAM INCOME *(See instructions.)*

All applications must indicate whether program income is anticipated during the period(s) for which grant support is request. If program income is anticipated, use the format below to reflect the amount and source(s).

Budget Period	Anticipated Amount	Source(s)

2. ASSURANCES/CERTIFICATIONS *(See instructions.)*

In signing the application Face Page, the authorized organizational representative agrees to comply with the following policies, assurances and/or certifications when applicable. Descriptions of individual assurances/certifications are provided in Part III. If unable to certify compliance, where applicable, provide an explanation and place it after this page.
•Human Subjects Research •Research Using Human Embryonic Stem Cells •Research on Transplantation of Human Fetal Tissue •Women and Minority Inclusion Policy •Inclusion of Children Policy •Vertebrate Animals•

•Debarment and Suspension •Drug- Free Workplace *(applicable to new [Type 1] or revised/resubmission [Type 1] applications only)* •Lobbying •Non-Delinquency on Federal Debt •Research Misconduct •Civil Rights (Form HHS 441 or HHS 690) •Handicapped Individuals (Form HHS 641 or HHS 690) •Sex Discrimination (Form HHS 639-A or HHS 690) •Age Discrimination (Form HHS 680 or HHS 690) •Recombinant DNA Research, Including Human Gene Transfer Research •Financial Conflict of Interest •Smoke Free Workplace •Prohibited Research •Select Agent Research •PI Assurance

3. FACILITIES AND ADMINSTRATIVE COSTS (F&A)/ INDIRECT COSTS. See specific instructions.

☐ DHHS Agreement dated: _____   ☐ No Facilities And Administrative Costs Requested.

☐ DHHS Agreement being negotiated with _____ Regional Office.

☐ No DHHS Agreement, but rate established with _____ Date _____

CALCULATION* *(The entire grant application, including the Checklist, will be reproduced and provided to peer reviewers as confidential information.)*

a. Initial budget period: Amount of base $ _____ x Rate applied _____ % = F&A costs $ _____

b. 02 year   Amount of base $ _____ x Rate applied _____ % = F&A costs $ _____

c. 03 year   Amount of base $ _____ x Rate applied _____ % = F&A costs $ _____

d. 04 year   Amount of base $ _____ x Rate applied _____ % = F&A costs $ _____

e. 05 year   Amount of base $ _____ x Rate applied _____ % = F&A costs $ _____

TOTAL F&A Costs $ _____

*Check appropriate box(es):

☐ Salary and wages base   ☐ Modified total direct cost base   ☐ Other base *(Explain)*

☐ Off-site, other special rate, or more than one rate involved *(Explain)*

Explanation *(Attach separate sheet, if necessary.)*:

PHS 398 (Rev. 04/06)   Page ____   **Checklist Form Page**

E. NATIONAL ENDOWMENT FOR THE ARTS (NEA)

General

NEA uses several versions of its form (OMB #128R0001). There is one new version for submissions from individuals and one for organizations, also modified slightly by programs, i.e., literature or museum. Still, they are all similar. Included here are three sets of forms.

Institutional Information Required

Along with the normal project information, NEA has added the requirement that project budget information be included in the application form. Therefore, the institution representative must be prepared to understand the budget completely to ensure the line items are completely correct. The budgets include requests not only for information on expenditures, but also contributions, revenues, and grants that might be relevant to the project. Then they ask the institutional authorizing official to sign a statement that the information is true and correct to the best of his or her knowledge.

Project Questions

As the last bit of information, the applicant requires completion of an assurance that the applicant institution will comply with the Title VI of the Civil Rights Act of 1964, Section 504 of the Rehabilitation Act of 1973, and Title IX of the Educational Amendments of 1972. These are standard compliances but the institutional application preparer should be familiar with what will be required if the grant is received. This is particularly important in view of legislation and regulations placing restrictions on NEA-funded projects.

Exhibit 33. NEA Individual Grant Application Form—Literature.

OMB No. 3135-0049 Expires 9/30/91   **47**

Literature Program Fiscal Year 1992	**Individual Grant Application Form NEA-2 (Rev.)** This application form must be submitted in triplicate together with other required materials and mailed to: Information Management Division/LIT FEL, 8th floor, National Endowment for the Arts, Nancy Hanks Center, 1100 Pennsylvania Avenue, N.W., Washington, D.C. 20506

1. Name (last, first, middle initial)

4. Literature Program Fellowships
Check one:
☐ Fiction
☐ Poetry
☐ Creative Non-Fiction
☐ Translation   Specify Language: _____
☐ Collaboration

2. Permanent mailing address/phone

5. U.S. Citizenship
☐ Yes   ☐ No   (Visa Number: _____)

6. Professional field or discipline:

3. Present mailing address/phone

7.
_____
Birthdate
_____
Place of birth
— —
_____
Social Security Number

8. Period of support requested
Starting
_____
month   day   year
Ending
_____
month   day   year

9. Fellowship for Creative Writer: Amount requested: $20,000. No project description necessary.

10. Translators: Amount requested (circle one): $10,000 $20,000
Description of proposed activity

11. Summary of Publications (Use this space to document your eligibility.) You may attach one additional sheet if necessary.

Titles   Name of Magazine or Press   Publication Dates
                          (include address and phone number)

(Continued on reverse)

Exhibit 33. (*Continued*)

11. Summary of publications (continued)

2

12. Education

Name of institution	Major area of study	Inclusive dates	Degree

13. Fellowships or grants previously awarded

Name of award	Area of study	Inclusive dates	Amount

14. Present employment

Employer	Position/Occupation

15. Prizes/Honors received   **Membership/professional societies**

16. Final Reports

Have you submitted required Final Report packages on all completed Arts Endowment grants since (and including) Fiscal Year 1984?

_____ Yes _____ No   If no, please mail immediately, under separate cover, to Grants Office/Final Reports Section to maintain eligibility. <u>Do not include with your application package.</u>

17. Delinquent Debt

Are you delinquent on repayment of any Federal debt (e.g. student loans, delinquent taxes)? _____ Yes _____ No. If yes, provide explanatory information on a separate sheet.

18. Certification: I certify that the foregoing statements are true and complete to the best of my knowledge. I also certify that, in compliance with the Drug-Free Workplace Act of 1988, I will not engage in the unlawful manufacture, distribution, dispensation, possession, or use of a controlled substance in conducting any activity with the grant.

x_____   _____

Signature of applicant   Date

BE SURE TO DOUBLE CHECK THE "HOW TO APPLY" SECTION ON PAGE 43. AND, IF APPLICABLE, THE SPECIAL APPLICATION REQUIREMENTS FOR YOUR CATEGORY FOR ALL MATERIALS TO BE INCLUDED IN YOUR APPLICATION PACKAGE. LATE APPLICATIONS WILL BE REJECTED. INCOMPLETE APPLICATIONS ARE UNLIKELY TO BE FUNDED.

Privacy Act

The Privacy Act of 1974 requires us to furnish you with the following information:

The Endowment is authorized to solicit the requested information by Section 5 of the National Foundation on the Arts and the Humanities Act of 1965, as amended. The information is used for grant processing, statistical research, analysis of trends, and for congressional oversight hearings. Failure to provide the requested information could result in rejection of your application.

Exhibit 34. NEA Organizational Grant Application Form—Literature.

OMB No. 3135-0049 Expires 9/30/91　49

Literature Program Fiscal Year 1992	**Organization Grant Application Form NEA-3 (Rev.)** Applications must be submitted in triplicate together with other required materials and mailed to: Information Management Division/LIT, 8th floor, National Endowment for the Arts, Nancy Hanks Center, 1100 Pennsylvania Avenue, N.W., Washington, D.C. 20506

I. Applicant organization (name, address, zip)

II. Category under which support is requested:

☐ **Literary Publishing**
_____ **Literary Magazines**
_____ **Small Presses**
_____ **Distribution Projects**

☐ **Audience Development**
_____ **Residencies for Writers and Reading Series**
_____ **Literary Centers**
_____ **Audience Development Projects**

☐ **Professional Development**

III. Period of support requested:

Starting _____
　　　　　month　　day　　year

Ending _____
　　　　　month　　day　　year

IV. Employer Identification Number: _____

V. Summary of project description. Specify clearly how the requested funds will be spent. (Complete in space provided unless "Application Requirements" for your category specify otherwise).

VI. Estimated number of persons expected to benefit from this project

VII. Summary of estimated costs (recapitulation of budget items in Section X)　　　　　　**Total costs of activity**

A. **Direct costs**
　Salaries and wages _____ $ _____
　Fringe benefits _____
　Supplies and materials _____
　Travel _____
　Permanent equipment _____
　Fees and other _____
B. **Indirect costs** _____
　　　　　　　　　　　　　　　Total direct costs $ _____
　　　　　　　　　　　　　　　　　　　　　　　　　 $ _____
　　　　　　　　　　　　　Total project costs $ _____
　　　　　　　　　　　　　(rounded to nearest $10)

VIII. Total amount requested from the National Endowment for the Arts　　$ _____

　　NOTE: This amount (amount requested): $ _____
　　PLUS Total contributions, grants, and revenues (XI., page 3): + _____
　　MUST EQUAL Total project costs (VII. above): = _____

IX. Organization total fiscal activity　　Most recently completed fiscal year　　Estimated for fiscal year related to grant

　A. Expenses　　1. $ _____　　2. $ _____

　B. Contributions, grants, & revenues　　1. $ _____　　2. $ _____

Do not write in this space
PYS: $

Exhibit 34. (*Continued*)

X. Budget breakdown of summary of estimated costs

A. Direct costs

1. Salaries and wages

Title and/or type of personnel	Number of personnel	Annual or average salary range	% of time devoted to this project	Amount $

Total salaries and wages	$
Add fringe benefits	$
Total salaries and wages including fringe benefits	$

2. Supplies and materials (list each major type separately)

	Amount $

Total supplies and material	$

3. Travel

Transportation of personnel

No. of travelers	from	to	Amount $

Total transportation of personnel	$

Subsistence

No. of travelers	No. of days	Daily rate	$

Total subsistence	$
Total travel	$

Exhibit 34. (*Continued*)

X. Budget breakdown of summary of estimated costs (continued)

3

4. Permanent equipment

Amount
$

Total permanent equipment $ _____

5. Fees for services and other expenses (list each item separately)

Amount
$

Total fees and other $ _____

B. Indirect costs

Amount

Rate established by attached negotiation agreement with
National Endowment for the Arts or another Federal agency
Rate _____ % Base _____

$ _____

XI. Contributions, grants, and revenues (for this project)

A. Contributions

Amount

1. Cash

$ _____

2. In-kind contributions (list each major item)

Total contributions $ _____

B. Grants (do not list anticipated grant from the Arts Endowment)

Total grants $ _____

C. Revenues

Total revenues $ _____
Total contributions, grants, and revenues for this project $ _____

Exhibit 34. (*Continued*)

XII. Final Reports

4

Have you submitted required Final Report packages on all completed grants
from any Arts Endowment Program since (and including) Fiscal Year 1984? (i.e., any grant letter dated on or after October 1, 1983)

_____ Yes _____ No   If no, please mail immediately, under separate cover, to Grants Office/Final Reports Section
to maintain eligibility. <u>Do not include with your application package.</u>

XIII. Delinquent Debt

Are you delinquent on repayment of any Federal debt? _____ Yes _____ No
If yes, provide explanatory information on a separate sheet.

XIV. Certification

The Authorizing Official(s) certify that the information contained in this application, including all attachments and supporting
materials, is true and correct to the best of our knowledge. The Authorizing Official(s) also certify that the applicant will comply
with the Federal requirements specified under "Assurance of Compliance" on pages 39-42.

<u>Authorizing Official(s)</u>

Signature   X _____ Date signed _____
Name (print or type)   _____
Title (print or type)   _____
Telephone (area code)   _____

Signature   X _____ Date signed _____
Name (print or type)   _____
Title (print or type)   _____
Telephone (area code)   _____

<u>Project director</u>

Signature   X _____ Date signed _____
Name (print or type)   _____
Title (print or type)   _____
Telephone (area code)   _____

<u>*Payee</u> (to whom grant payments will be sent if other than authorizing official)

Signature   X _____ Date signed _____
Name (print or type)   _____
Title (print or type)   _____
Telephone (area code)   _____

*If payment is to be made to anyone other than the grantee, it is understood that the grantee is financially, administratively, and
programmatically responsible for all aspects of the grant and that all reports must be submitted through the grantee.

BE SURE TO DOUBLE CHECK THE "HOW TO APPLY" SECTION ON PAGE 43 AND THE APPLICATION PACKAGE.

LATE APPLICATIONS WILL BE REJECTED.

INCOMPLETE APPLICATIONS ARE UNLIKELY TO BE FUNDED.

Privacy Act

The Privacy Act of 1974 requires us to furnish you with the following information:

The Endowment is authorized to solicit the requested information by Section 5 of the National
Foundation on the Arts and the Humanities Act of 1965, as amended. The information is used for
grant processing, statistical research, analysis of trends, and for congressional oversight hearings.
Failure to provide the requested information could result in rejection of your application.

Exhibit 35. NEA Organizational Grant Application Form—Museum.

X. Budget breakdown of summary of estimated costs (continued)

    4. Permanent equipment ($5,000 or more per unit)   **Amount**
                                                                                  $

                                      Total permanent equipment $ _____

    5. Fees for services and other expenses (list each item separately) $

                                      Total fees and other $ _____

B. Indirect costs   **Amount**

Rate established by attached rate negotiation agreement with
National Endowment for the Arts or another Federal agency
Rate _____ % Base _____ Negotiated with _____ $ _____

XI. Contributions, grants, and revenues (for this project)

    A. Contributions   **Amount**

        1. Cash $

                                      Total cash $ _____

        2. In-kind contributions (list each major item)

                                      Total contributions $ _____

    B. Grants (do not list anticipated grant from the Arts Endowment)

                                        Total grants $ _____

    C. Revenues

                                          Total revenues $ _____
        Total contributions, grants, and revenues for this project $ _____

(Continued on reverse)

Exhibit 35. (*Continued*)

OMB No. 3135-0053 Expires 8/31/92   **45**

Museum
Fiscal Year 1992

Organization Grant Application Form NEA-3 (Rev.)

Applications must be submitted in triplicate and mailed together with other required materials to: Information Management Division/MM, 8th floor, National Endowment for the Arts, Nancy Hanks Center, 1100 Pennsylvania Avenue, N.W., Washington, D.C. 20506 (overnight mail zip code: 20004)

I. Applicant Organization: IRS name (popular name, if different), address, zip	II. Category under which support is requested:	III. Period of support requested:
		Starting _____ month day year Ending _____ month day year
		IV. Employer I.D. number:

V. Summary of project activity: (Complete in space provided. DO NOT reduce copy or continue on additional pages.)

VI. Estimated number of persons expected to benefit from this activity:

VII. Summary of estimated costs: (recapitulation of budget items in Section X)

	Total costs of project
A. Direct costs	
Salaries and wages _____	$ _____
Fringe benefits _____	$ _____
Supplies and materials _____	$ _____
Travel _____	$ _____
Permanent equipment _____	$ _____
Fees and other _____	$ _____
Total direct costs	$ _____
B. Indirect costs _____	$ _____
Total project costs	$ _____
(rounded to nearest hundred dollars)	

VIII. Total amount requested from the National Endowment for the Arts : . . . . $ _____

NOTE: Amount requested from Arts Endowment (VIII.): $ _____
PLUS Total contributions, grants, and revenues (XI., page 3):   + _____
MUST EQUAL Total project costs (VII. above):   = _____

IX. Organization total fiscal activity:	Most recently completed fiscal year	Estimated for fiscal year relating to grant period
A. Expenses	1. $ _____	2. $ _____
B. Contributions, grants, and revenues	1. $ _____	2. $ _____

(Continued on reverse)

FORMS AND REQUIRED INFORMATION   **111**

Exhibit 35. (*Continued*)

X. Budget breakdown of summary of estimated costs

2

   A. Direct costs

      1. Salaries and wages

Title and/or type of personnel	Number of personnel	Annual or average salary range exclusive of incidentals	% of time devoted to this project	Amount $

                                                 Total salaries and wages $ _____

                                                     Add fringe benefits $ _____

                  Total salaries and wages including fringe benefits $ _____

      2. Supplies and materials (list each major type separately)

Amount $

	Amount $

                                        Total supplies and materials $ _____

      3. Travel

Transportation of personnel

No. of travelers	from	to	Amount $

                          Total transportation of personnel $ _____

Subsistence

No. of travelers	No. of days	Daily rate	$

                                     Total subsistence $ _____

                                              Total travel $ _____

Exhibit 35. (*Continued*)

48

XII. To what other Federal funding sources (including other Arts Endowment programs) have you applied since October 1, 1990, **4**
or do you intend to apply this year or next, for support of this project or program? _____

XIII. Final Reports

Have you submitted required Final Report packages on all completed Arts Endowment
grants since (and including) Fiscal Year 1984?

_____ Yes _____ No   If no, please mail immediately, under separate cover, to Grants Office / Final Reports Section to
maintain eligibility. Do **not** include with your application package.

XIV. Delinquent Debt

Are you delinquent on repayment of any Federal debt? _____ Yes _____ No.
If yes, provide explanatory information on a separate sheet.

XV. Certification

The Authorizing Official(s) certify that the information contained in this
application, including all attachments and supporting materials, is true
and correct to the best of our knowledge. The Authorizing Official(s) also
certify that the applicant will comply with the Federal requirements
specified under "Assurance of Compliance" on pages 37-39.

<u>Authorizing Official(s)</u>

Signature   X _____   Date signed _____
Name (print or type)   _____
Title (print or type)   _____
Telephone (area code)   _____

Signature   X _____   Date signed _____
Name (print or type)   _____
Title (print or type)   _____
Telephone (area code)   _____

<u>Project director</u>

Signature   X _____   Date signed _____
Name (print or type)   _____
Title (print or type)   _____
Telephone (area code)   _____

*<u>Payee</u> (to whom grant payments will be sent if other than authorizing official)

Signature   X _____   Date signed _____
Name (print or type)   _____
Title (print or type)   _____
Telephone (area code)   _____

*If payment is to be made to anyone other than the grantee, it is understood that
the grantee is financially, administratively, and programmatically responsible for
all aspects of the grant and that all reports must be submitted through the grantee.

BE SURE TO DOUBLE CHECK THE "SUBMITTING YOUR APPLICATION" SECTION ON PAGE 41 AND "SPECIAL
APPLICATION REQUIREMENTS" SECTION UNDER THE APPROPRIATE CATEGORY FOR ALL MATERIALS TO BE INCLUDED
IN YOUR APPLICATION PACKAGE. LATE APPLICATIONS WILL BE REJECTED. INCOMPLETE APPLICATIONS ARE UNLIKELY
TO BE FUNDED.

Privacy Act

The Privacy Act of 1974 requires us to furnish you with the following information:

The Endowment is authorized to solicit the requested information by Section 5 of
the National Foundation on the Arts and the Humanities Act of 1965, as amended.
The information is used for grant processing, statistical research, analysis of
trends, and for congressional oversight hearings. Failure to provide the requested
information could result in rejection of your application.

F. NATIONAL ENDOWMENT FOR THE HUMANITIES (NEH)

General

NEH uses the same application form for all programs (form OMB # 3136.0059 exp. 6/30/90).

Institutional Information Required

NEH requires minimal budget information on its application form, certainly to a lesser degree of detail than NEA, but nevertheless requiring a knowledge of where the *total* resources for the project will come from. In addition, the application form requests information on the direct beneficiaries of the program and the institution's congressional district.

Project Questions

The application asks if the project has been submitted to another NEH program, another government agency, or a private entity.

Exhibit 36. NEH Application Form.

F. NATIONAL ENDOWMENT FOR THE HUMANITIES (NEH)

General

NEH uses the same application form for all programs (form OMB# 3136.0059 exp. 6/30/90)

Institutional Information Required

NEH requires some minimal budget information on its applications form, certainly to a lesser degree of detail than NEA, but nevertheless requiring a knowledge of where the *total* resources for the project will come from. In addition, the application form requests information on the direct beneficiaries of the program and the institution's congressional district.

Project Questions

The application asks if the project has been submitted to another NEH program, another government agency, or a private entity.

Exhibit 36. (*Continued*)

NEH APPLICATION COVER SHEET

OMB No. 3136–0059
Expires 6/30/92

1. Individual applicant or project director
a. Name and mailing address

Name _____
(last)   (first)   (initial)

Address _____

_____

_____
(city)   (state)   (zip code)

b. Form of address: ☐

c. Social
Security # ____n/a____   Date of
birth ____n/a____
(mo./day/yr.)

d. Telephone number
Office: _____/_____   Home: _____/_____
(area code)   (area code)

e. Major field of applicant
or project director _____ ☐
(code)

f. Citizenship ☐ U.S.
☐ Other _____
(specify)

2. Type of applicant
a. ☐ by an individual   **b.** ☐ through an org./institute
If a, indicate an institutional affiliation, if applicable, on line 11a.
If b, complete block 11 below and indicate here:
c. Type
d. Status

3. Type of application
a. ☐ new   **c.** ☐ renewal
b. ☐ revision and resubmission   **d.** ☐ supplement
If either **c** or **d**, indicate previous grant number:

_____

4. Program to which application is being made

Endowment Initiatives: _____
(code)

5. Requested grant period
From: _____   To: _____
(month/year)   (month/year)

6. Project funding
a. Outright funds $ _____
b. Federal match $ _____
c. Total from NEH $ _____
d. Cost sharing $ _____
e. Total project costs $ _____

7. Field of project ☐   **8. Descriptive title of project**

9. Description of project (do not exceed space provided)

10. Will this proposal be submitted to another government agency or private entity for funding?
(if yes, indicate where and when):

11. Institutional data
a. Institution or organization: _____
(name)   (city)   (state)
b. Name of authorizing official: _____
(last)   (first)   (initial)
Title: _____   Signature: _____   Date _____
c. Institutional grant administrator—name and mailing address:

_____
(last)   (first)   (initial)

_____

_____
(city)   (state)   (zip code)

Form of address ☐

Telephone: _____/_____
(area code)

12. Student loan status
Is the individual applicant or project director currently delinquent on repayments of any federally backed student loans?
Note: Knowingly providing false information may subject the applicant to criminal penalties of up to $10,000 or imprisonment of up to five years, or both. 18 U.S.C. §1001.

Not applicable

For NEH use only
Date received
Application #
Initials

Exhibit 36. (*Continued*)

National Endowment for the Humanities
BUDGET INSTRUCTIONS

Before developing a project budget, applicants should review those sections of the program guidelines and application instructions that discuss cost-sharing requirements, the different kinds of Endowment funding, limitations on the length of the grant period, and any restrictions on the types of costs that may appear in the project budget.

Requested Grant Period

Grant periods begin on the first day of the month and end on the last day of the month. All project activities must take place during the requested grant period.

Project Costs

The budget should include the project costs that will be charged to grant funds as well as those that will be supported by applicant or third-party cash and in-kind contributions.

All of the items listed, whether supported by grant funds or cost-sharing contributions, must be reasonable, necessary to accomplish project objectives, allowable in terms of the applicable federal cost principles, auditable, and incurred during the grant period. Charges to the project for items such as salaries, fringe benefits, travel, and contractual services must conform to the written policies and established practices of the applicant organization.

When indirect costs are charged to the project, care should be taken that expenses that are included in the organization's indirect cost pool (see Indirect Costs) are not charged to the project as direct costs.

Fringe Benefits

Fringe benefits may include contributions for social security, employee insurance, pension plans, etc. Only those benefits that are not included in an organization's indirect cost pool may be shown as direct costs.

Travel Costs

Less-than-first-class accommodations must be used and foreign travel must be undertaken on U.S. flag carriers when such services are available.

Equipment

Only when an applicant can demonstrate that the purchase of permanent equipment will be less expensive than rental may charges be made to the project for such purchases. Permanent equipment is defined as an item costing more than $500 with an estimated useful life of more than two years.

Indirect Costs (Overhead)

These are costs that are incurred for common or joint objectives and therefore cannot be readily identified with a specific project or activity of an organization. Typical examples of indirect cost type items are the salaries of executive officers, the costs of operating and maintaining facilities, local telephone service, office supplies, and accounting and legal services.

Indirect costs are computed by applying a negotiated indirect cost rate to a distribution base (usually the direct costs of the project). Organizations that wish to include overhead charges in the budget but do not have a current federally negotiated indirect cost rate or have not submitted a pending indirect cost proposal to a federal agency may choose one of the following options:

1. The Endowment will not require the formal negotiation of an indirect cost rate, provided the charge for indirect costs does not exceed 10 percent of direct costs, less distorting items (e.g., capital expenditures, major subcontracts), up to a maximum charge of $5,000. (Applicants who choose this option should understand that they must maintain documentation to support overhead charges claimed as part of project costs.)

2. If your organization wishes to use a rate higher than 10 percent or claim more than $5,000 in indirect costs, an estimate of the indirect cost rate and the charges should be provided on the budget form. If the application is approved for funding, you will be instructed to contact the NEH Audit Office to develop an indirect cost proposal.

SAMPLE BUDGET COMPUTATIONS

				NEH Funds (a)	Cost Sharing (b)	Total (c)
Salaries and Wages						
Jane Doe/Project Director	[ ]	9 months x 100% @ $27,000/academic yr.		$13,500	$13,500	$27,000
Jane Doe	[ ]	1 summer month x 100% @ $3,000		3,000		3,000
John Smith/Research Assistant	[ ]	6 months x 50% @ $25,000/yr.		6,250		6,250
Secretarial Support	[1]	3 months x 100% @ $14,000/yr.		3,500		3,500
Fringe Benefits						
11 % of $36,250				2,503	1,485	3,988
8 % of $ 3,500				280		280

Travel	no. of persons	total travel days	subsistence costs	transport. + costs =			
New York City/Chicago	[2]	[4]	$300	$430	730		730
Various/Washington D.C. conf.	[5]	[10]	$750	500	1,250		1,250

Consultant Fees						
Serbo-Croatian Specialist		5	$100	500		500
Services						
Long Distance Telephone	est. 40 toll calls @ $3.00			120		120
Conference Brochure	50 copies @ $3.50/copy			175		175
T O T A L D I R E C T C O S T S				$31,808	$14,985	$46,793
Indirect Costs						
20% of $46,793				$ 6,362	$ 2,997	$ 9,359
T O T A L P R O J E C T C O S T S (Direct and Indirect)				$38,170	$17,982	$56,152

Exhibit 36. (*Continued*)

National Endowment for the Humanities

BUDGET FORM

OMB No. 3136-0071

Project Director	If this is a revised budget, indicate the NEH application/grant number:
Applicant Organization	Requested Grant Period From _____ to _____ mo/yr mo/yr

The three-column budget has been developed for the convenience of those applicants who wish to identify the project costs that will be charged to NEH funds and those that will be cost shared. FOR NEH PURPOSES, THE ONLY COLUMN THAT NEEDS TO BE COMPLETED IS COLUMN C. The method of cost computation should clearly indicate how the total charge for each budget item was determined. If more space is needed for any budget category, please follow the budget format on a separate sheet of paper.

When the requested grant period is eighteen months or longer, separate budgets for each twelve-month period of the project must be developed on duplicated copies of the budget form.

SECTION A — budget detail for the period from _____ to _____
                                                                        mo/yr   mo/yr

1. Salaries and Wages

Provide the names and titles of principal project personnel. For support staff, include the title of each position and indicate in brackets the number of persons who will be employed in that capacity. For persons employed on an academic year basis, list separately any salary charge for work done outside the academic year.

name/title of position	no.	method of cost computation (see sample)	NEH Funds (a)	Cost Sharing (b)	Total (c)
_____	[ ]	_____	$_____	$_____	$_____
_____	[ ]	_____	_____	_____	_____
_____	[ ]	_____	_____	_____	_____
_____	[ ]	_____	_____	_____	_____
_____	[ ]	_____	_____	_____	_____
_____	[ ]	_____	_____	_____	_____
_____	[ ]	_____	_____	_____	_____
_____	[ ]	_____	_____	_____	_____
		SUBTOTAL	$_____	$_____	$_____

2. Fringe Benefits

If more than one rate is used, list each rate and salary base.

rate		salary base	(a)	(b)	(c)
_____ %	of	$_____	$_____	$_____	$_____
_____ %	of	$_____	_____	_____	_____
		SUBTOTAL	$_____	$_____	$_____

3. Consultant Fees

Include payments for professional and technical consultants and honoraria.

name or type of consultant	no. of days on project	daily rate of compensation	(a)	(b)	(c)
_____	_____	$_____	$_____	$_____	$_____
_____	_____	$_____	_____	_____	_____
_____	_____	$_____	_____	_____	_____
_____	_____	$_____	_____	_____	_____
_____	_____	$_____	_____	_____	_____
		SUBTOTAL	$_____	$_____	$_____

Exhibit 36. (*Continued*)

4. Travel

For each trip, indicate the number of persons traveling, the total days they will be in travel status, and the total subsistence and transportation costs for that trip. When a project will involve the travel of a number of people to a conference, institute, etc., these costs may be summarized on one line by indicating the point of origin as "various." All foreign travel must be listed separately.

from/to	no. of persons	total travel days	subsistence costs +	transportation costs =	NEH Funds (a)	Cost Sharing (b)	Total (c)
_____	[ ]	[ ]	$ _____	$ _____	$ _____	$ _____	$ _____
_____	[ ]	[ ]	_____	_____	_____	_____	_____
_____	[ ]	[ ]	_____	_____	_____	_____	_____
_____	[ ]	[ ]	_____	_____	_____	_____	_____
_____	[ ]	[ ]	_____	_____	_____	_____	_____
_____	[ ]	[ ]	_____	_____	_____	_____	_____
_____	[ ]	[ ]	_____	_____	_____	_____	_____
				SUBTOTAL	$ _____	$ _____	$ _____

5. Supplies and Materials

Include consumable supplies, materials to be used in the project, and items of expendable equipment; i.e., equipment items costing less than $500 or with an estimated useful life of less than two years.

item	basis/method of cost computation	(a)	(b)	(c)
_____	_____	$ _____	$ _____	$ _____
_____	_____	_____	_____	_____
_____	_____	_____	_____	_____
_____	_____	_____	_____	_____
_____	_____	_____	_____	_____
_____	_____	_____	_____	_____
_____	_____	_____	_____	_____
_____	_____	_____	_____	_____
	SUBTOTAL	$ _____	$ _____	$ _____

6. Services

Include the cost of duplication and printing, long distance telephone, equipment rental, postage, and other services related to project objectives that are not included under other budget categories or in the indirect cost pool. For subcontracts over $10,000, provide an itemization of subcontract costs on this form or on an attachment.

item	basis/method of cost computation	(a)	(b)	(c)
_____	_____	$ _____	$ _____	$ _____
_____	_____	_____	_____	_____
_____	_____	_____	_____	_____
_____	_____	_____	_____	_____
_____	_____	_____	_____	_____
_____	_____	_____	_____	_____
_____	_____	_____	_____	_____
_____	_____	_____	_____	_____
	SUBTOTAL	$ _____	$ _____	$ _____

Exhibit 36. (*Continued*)

7. Other Costs

Include participant stipends and room and board, equipment purchases, and other items not previously listed. Please note that "miscellaneous" and "contingency" are not acceptable budget categories. Refer to the budget instructions for the restriction on the purchase of permanent equipment.

item	basis/method of cost computation	NEH Funds (a)	Cost Sharing (b)	Total (c)
		$_____	$_____	$_____
		_____	_____	_____
		_____	_____	_____
		_____	_____	_____
		_____	_____	_____
		_____	_____	_____
		_____	_____	_____
		_____	_____	_____
	SUBTOTAL	$_____	$_____	$_____

8. Total Direct Costs (add subtotals of items 1 through 7)

$_____ $_____ $_____

9. Indirect Costs [This budget item applies only to institutional applicants.]

If indirect costs are to be charged to this project, check the appropriate box below and provide the information requested. Refer to the budget instructions for explanations of these options.

☐ Current indirect cost rate(s) has/have been negotiated with a federal agency. (Complete items A and B.)

☐ Indirect cost proposal has been submitted to a federal agency but not yet negotiated. (Indicate the name of the agency in item A and show proposed rate(s) and base(s), and the amount(s) of indirect costs in item B.)

☐ Indirect cost proposal will be sent to NEH if application is funded. (Provide an estimate in item B of the rate that will be used and indicate the base against which it will be charged and the amount of indirect costs.)

☐ Applicant chooses to use a rate not to exceed 10% of direct costs, less distorting items, up to a maximum charge of $5,000. (Under item B, enter the proposed rate, the base against which the rate will be charged, and the computation of indirect costs or $5,000, whichever sum is less.)

A. _____   _____
   name of federal agency   date of agreement

B.		NEH Funds (a)	Cost Sharing (b)	Total (c)
rate(s)	base(s)			
_____ %	of $_____	$_____	$_____	$_____
_____ %	of $_____	_____	_____	_____
	TOTAL INDIRECT COSTS	$_____	$_____	$_____

10. Total Project Costs (direct and indirect) for Budget Period

$_____ $_____ $_____

Exhibit 36. (*Continued*)

NEH Budget Form

SECTION B — Summary Budget and Project Funding

SUMMARY BUDGET

Transfer from section A the total costs (column c) for each category of project expense. When the proposed grant period is eighteen months or longer, project expenses for each twelve-month period are to be listed separately and totaled in the last column of the summary budget. For projects that will run less than eighteen months, only the last column of the summary budget should be completed.

Budget Categories	First Year/ from: to:	Second Year/ from: to:	Third Year/ from: to:		TOTAL COSTS FOR ENTIRE GRANT PERIOD
1. Salaries and Wages	$_____	$_____	$_____	=	$_____
2. Fringe Benefits	_____	_____	_____	=	_____
3. Consultant Fees	_____	_____	_____	=	_____
4. Travel	_____	_____	_____	=	_____
5. Supplies and Materials	_____	_____	_____	=	_____
6. Services	_____	_____	_____	=	_____
7. Other Costs	_____	_____	_____	=	_____
8. **Total Direct Costs (items 1-7)**	$_____	$_____	$_____	=	$_____
9. Indirect Costs	$_____	$_____	$_____	=	$_____
10. **Total Project Costs (Direct & Indirect)**	$_____	$_____	$_____	=	$_____

PROJECT FUNDING FOR ENTIRE GRANT PERIOD

Requested from NEH:[1]

Outright $_____

Federal Matching $_____

TOTAL NEH FUNDING $_____

Cost Sharing:[2]

Cash Contributions $_____

In-Kind Contributions $_____

Project Income $_____

TOTAL COST SHARING $_____

Total Project Funding (NEH Funds + Cost Sharing)[3] = $_____

[1] Indicate the amount of outright and/or federal matching funds that is requested from the Endowment.

[2] Indicate the amount of cash contributions that will be made by the applicant or third parties to support project expenses that appear in the budget. Include in this amount third-party cash gifts that will be raised to release federal matching funds. (Consult the program guidelines for information on cost-sharing requirements.)

Occasionally, in-kind (noncash) contributions are included in a project budget as a part of the applicant's cost sharing; e.g., the value of services or equipment that is donated to the project free of charge. If this is the case, the total value of in-kind contributions should be indicated.

When a project will generate income that will be used during the grant period to support expenses listed in the budget, indicate the amount of income that will be expended on budgeted project activities.

[3] Total Project Funding should equal Total Project Costs.

Institutional Grant Administrator

Complete the information requested below when a revised budget is submitted. Block 11 of the application cover sheet instructions contains a description of the functions of the institutional grant administrator. The signature of this person indicates approval of the budget submission and the agreement of the organization to cost share project expenses at the level indicated under "Project Funding."

_____

Name and Title (please type or print)

Telephone (___) _____
         area code

_____

Signature

Date _____

NEH Application/Grant Number: _____

G. NATIONAL SCIENCE FOUNDATION (NSF)

General

NSF uses the same proposal cover sheet for all programs. It is probably the simplest of all federal agency application forms (no OMB#) and should be no problem to complete.

Institutional Information Required

There is none beyond normal address and mailing information.

Project Questions

There are none, except you are to check a box if the proposal involves any of the following: Animal Welfare, Endangered Species, Human Subjects, Historical Sites, Marine Mammal Protection, Pollution Control, National Environmental Policy Act, Recombinant DNA, and Proprietary and Privileged Information.

Exhibit 37. NSF Grant Application.

THE CLEVELAND FOUNDATION
Grant Inquiry Form

ORGANIZATION INFORMATION

Applicant Organization:		
Mailing Address:		
City:	**State:**	**Zip:**
Telephone:	**Fax:**	**County:**
Website:		
Executive Director:	**Email:**	
Project Director (*if different*):	**Email:**	
Title:	**Phone:**	

ORGANIZATION'S MISSION

Brief statement of organization's objectives and/or activities:

Annual operating budget: $ **Audited?**   ☐ **Yes**   ☐ **No**

TAX STATUS

Tax Status (choose one):   ☐ **501(c)(3)**   ☐ **Church (by definition)**   ☐ **Agency of Government**

☐ **Not a nonprofit organization, per IRS; we have a fiscal sponsor.**
    Sponsoring Organization:

Legal Name, per IRS determination:

Tax ID #:   **Date of incorporation:**

SUMMARY OF REQUEST

Project/Program Title:
Total Project/Program Budget:
Amount requested from The Cleveland Foundation: $
Timeframe for amount requested: **From:**   **To:**

Describe use of funds requested: (i.e. staff costs, consultant fees, materials)

PROJECT/PROGRAM SUMMARY

Summary of Project or Program (*suitable description to be shared with Foundation staff, Board, donors*) (short paragraph)

Exhibit 37. (*Continued*)

| **Who will this project/program serve?** |
| (special populations, geographic area, community focus, organizational focus, etc.) |

| **Specific Process Objectives** |
| (what will be provided, to whom, by when) |
| • |
| • |
| • |

| **Specific, Measurable Short-Term Outcomes** |
| (changes clients will make as a result of what you do, during the life of the grant) |
| • |
| • |
| • |

| **Measurable Long-Term Objectives** |
| (changes clients or a larger target population will make as a result of what you do, beyond the term of the grant) |
| • |
| • |
| • |

COLLABORATIONS AND OTHER SUPPORT

Please tell us if you are collaborating with any other organizations.

Please list other support you are seeking from foundations/government agencies.

COMMENTS

Is there any other information we might need to better understand your request and/or the unique needs of the community that this request will serve?

SEND THIS FORM

Please email (*preferred*), fax or mail your completed form to:

> **Grants Management**
> **The Cleveland Foundation**
> **1422 Euclid Avenue, Suite 1300**
> **Cleveland, OH 44115**
> **Phone: (216) 615-7254**
> **Fax: (216) 861-1729**
> **Email:** *grantsmgmt@clevefdn.org*

This form may be downloaded from our website at **www.clevelandfoundation.org** under Grants/Grantseekers, Forms and Resources.

If the Foundation can be of assistance to you as you prepare your grant inquiry, please feel free to contact **Grants Management at (216) 615-7254.**

Thank you! The Foundation will review your inquiry and make a determination within a few weeks of receipt, at which time you will either be requested to submit additional information or a full proposal, or be informed that the Foundation is not able to fund your request.

The Cleveland Foundation – Grant Inquiry Form   6.14.06   Page 2

Exhibit 37. (*Continued*)

PROPOSAL COVER SHEET

NAME OF APPLICANT
_____

MAILING ADDRESS (STREET)	CITY	STATE	ZIP

STREET ADDRESS (IF DIFFERENT)	CITY	STATE	ZIP

PHONE	FAX	ORGANIZATIONAL E-MAIL

NAME OF EXECUTIVE DIRECTOR (OR PRIMARY CONTACT)

IN THE SPACE BELOW, PLEASE STATE YOUR MISSION:

_____

_____

_____

_____

IN THE SPACE BELOW, LIST THE PRIMARY PURPOSE(S) OF THIS GRANT REQUEST:

_____

_____

_____

_____

TOTAL AMOUNT OF REQUEST: $_____ OVER (CIRCLE ONE) 1 YEAR, 2 YEARS, OR 3 YEARS.

ORGANIZATIONAL/FINANCIAL INFORMATION

IN WHAT YEAR WAS THE ORGANIZATION FOUNDED? _____

WHAT WERE YOUR TOTAL EXPENDITURES FOR THE LAST THREE COMPLETED FISCAL YEARS?

YEAR ENDED _____: $_____

YEAR ENDED _____: $_____

YEAR ENDED _____: $_____

WHAT WAS THE DATE OF YOUR LAST OUTSIDE AUDIT? _____ ATTACH A COPY.

☐ IF YOU HAVE A FISCAL AGENT; PLEASE PROVIDE ORGANIZATIONAL INFORMATION AS REQUIRED ABOVE ON A SEPARATE SHEET. ALSO INCLUDE REQUIRED ENCLOSURES AS SPECIFIED IN APPLICATION GUIDELINES.

Exhibit 37. (*Continued*)

Application Guidelines

Final proposals and all required enclosures must be postmarked or received electronically by the following deadlines:
- February 1 for June review by the Foundation board; or
- July 1 for October review by the Foundation board.

If you are mailing your application, please send one copy only.

The narrative should:
- Answer the following questions.
- Be no more than eight pages.
- Use type size no smaller than 12-point.
- Present realistic long-term outcomes your organization can accomplish, indicators that let you know you are making progress toward accomplishing long-term outcomes, and specific plans for assessing your progress.

Current Mission, Analysis and Impact

1. What is your mission? Include constituency and geography served.

2a. What is your organization's understanding of the underlying causes of persistent poverty where you work?

2b. What are the challenges and opportunities for moving people and places out of poverty where you work?

3. What are your organization's major strategies (not programs or activities)?

4. Over the past five years, what have been your specific outcomes related to helping low-wealth people build assets and transform economic conditions in low-wealth communities? Specifically, what have you achieved?

Constituency and Partners

5. Describe your connections to low-wealth people and communities. What roles do low-wealth people play in governance and decision making?

6. Who are the most important strategic partners in your current work, and what is the role of each?

7. If you are a network, partnership, collaborative or alliance, describe your structure and how decisions get made.

Proposed Outcomes and Activities

8a. Briefly describe the primary purpose of your grant request.

Exhibit 37. (*Continued*)

8b. Explain the rationale for this request at this time. Include organizational factors (e.g., analysis, mission, strategies, capacity) and external factors (e.g., policy environment, community situation, partnership opportunities).

9a. List your short-term (one to two years) indicators of progress toward long-term outcomes. What will change in this grant period to let you know you are making progress toward the long-term outcomes? See Outcomes and Indicators attachment.

9b. List your long-term (five years) outcomes: Specifically, how will people and/or places be better off economically OR what new changed policies or systems will be in place? See Outcomes and Indicators attachment.

10. How will you achieve each outcome? Be specific about activities. Include activities for data collection and assessing progress toward outcomes. (This may be a work plan attached to the nine-page proposal. Activities should clearly connect to the proposed budget.)

11. For the work described in this proposal, who will do what? (Include names and qualifications of key staff.) Describe key partners for the proposed activities, including roles they play and capacity they bring?

Required Enclosures

1. Proposal cover sheet (attached).
2. Outcomes and indicators (if separate from proposal).
3. Letter signed by executive director and board chair of applying organization or fiscal agent, stating organizational support for this proposal.
4. Budgets:
   a. If application is for general operating support, include organizational or network budget (including income and expenses) for the current year and for the proposed grant period. Income statement should specify sources of income and which resources are in-hand and which are pending.
   b. If application is for project support, include a line-item budget for the project (including income and expenses for the grant period). Also include organizational budget (including income and expenses) for the current year and the next year. Both income statements should specify sources of income and which resources are in-hand and which are pending.
5. Copy of your last audit.
6. Board list for applying organization or network, noting race, gender and affiliation of each member.
   a. If applicant is a network or collaborative, include a list of organizational members and board lists for key organizational partners.
   b. If applicant is a fiscal agent, include board lists for both fiscal agent and project or sponsored organization.
7. IRS letter noting tax-exempt status for applicant or fiscal agent.

Exhibit 37. (*Continued*)

Outcomes and Indicators

Please state your long-term outcomes (five years) and short-term indicators (one to two years) of progress toward these long-term outcomes. You may use the format on the next page as an attachment to your proposal or you may include the outcomes and indicators in the text of your proposal (Question 9 a&b). Before completing this section of your proposal, please review the following notes on the Babcock Foundation's expectations for statements of outcomes.

1. Some significant outcomes and indicators related to helping people build assets and transform communities are quantifiable. For these, we expect to see numerical targets in this proposal and then hard data later in grant reports. For those outcomes and indicators that are not quantifiable, we expect to see clear goals in proposals and descriptive data later in reports.

2. If you are requesting general operating support, state the organizational outcomes you seek to achieve in the grant period. If you are requesting support for a specific project, state its specific outcomes for the grant period.

3. If your organization or network needs to build new capacity or partnerships in order to complete the proposed work successfully, we encourage you to include capacity-building or organizational development outcomes. Include activities matched to these outcomes in your answers to Questions 8-10 and in your proposed budget.

Outcomes and Indicators	
9b. Long-term (five years) outcomes: Specifically, how will people and/or places be better off economically OR what new or changed policies or systems will be in place?	*9a. Short-term (one to two years) indicators of progress toward long-term outcomes: What will change in this grant period that lets you know you are making progress toward the long-term outcomes?*

H. U.S. DEPARTMENT OF AGRICULTURE (USDA)

General

The USDA requires the submission of OMB form # 0524-00022 for competitive, special, or other research grants from the Cooperative State Research Service. The application kit can also be used for other funds awarded by CSRS.

Institutional Information Required

Along with standard application and project information, there are several items of information needed to complete the application forms that may not be readily accessible. Therefore, you should have them in advance to make completion of the form easier.

These are

1. Congressional district,
2. program to which you are applying (as listed in the *Federal Register* announcement),
3. Federal (IRS)#, i.e., Employment Identification Number, and
4. type of performing organization the applicant is (list provided—select one).

Project Questions

There are two questions relating to submission that must be answered by the submitting institution:

1. Does the project involve recombinant DNA or human subjects?
2. Was the proposal sent to another federal agency and which one?

Other required and useful information with suggested form: example of a budget, letter of transmittal, and protection of human subjects certification.

Exhibit 38. USDA Grant Application Form (secure from Web site when available).

UNITED STATES DEPARTMENT OF AGRICULTURE
COOPERATIVE STATE RESEARCH SERVICE

GRANT APPLICATION

OMB Approved 0524-0022
Expires 8/92

FOR CSRS USE ONLY	
Program Area Code	Proposal Code

1. Legal Name of Organization to Which Award Should be Made

3. Name of Authorized Organizational Representative

4. Telephone Number (Include Area Code)

2. Address (Give complete mailing address and Zip Code-including County)

5. Address of Authorized Organizational Representative (If different from Item 2.)

6. Title of Proposal (80-character Maximum, including spaces)

7. Program to Which You are Applying (Refer to Federal Register Announcement where applicable)

8. Program Area and Number (Refer to Federal Register Announcement where applicable)

9. IRS No.

10. Congressional District No.

11. Period of Proposed Project Dates
From: Through:

12. Duration Requested

13. Type of Request

☐ New   ☐ Resubmission   ☐ Renewal   ☐ Supplement   ☐ Continuing Grant Increment

☐ PI Transfer   ☐ (of/to USDA Grant No. _____   ☐ Other

14. Funds Requested (From Form CSRS-55)

15. Principal Investigator(s)/Project Director(s)
a. PI/PD #1 Name (First, Middle, Last) and Social Security Number* (Correspondent PI)

16. PI/PD #1 Phone Number (Include Area Code)

b. PI/PD #2 Name (First, Middle, Last) and Social Security Number*

17. PI/PD #1 Business Address (Include Department/Zip Code)

c. PI/PD #3 Name (First, Middle, Last) and Social Security Number*

Submission of the Social Security Number is voluntary and will not affect the organization's eligibility for an award. However, it is an integral part of the CSRS information system and will assist in the processing of the proposal.

18. Type of Performing Organization
(Check one only)

01 ☐ USDA/S&E Laboratory
02 ☐ Other Federal Research Laboratory
03 ☐ State Agricultural Experiment Station (SAES)
04 ☐ Land-Grant University 1862
05 ☐ Land-Grant University 1890 or Tuskegee University
06 ☐ Private University or College
07 ☐ Public University or College (Non Land-Grant)
08 ☐ Private Profit-making
09 ☐ Private Non-profit
10 ☐ State or Local Government
11 ☐ Veterinary School or College
12 ☐ Other (Specify)

19. Will the Work in This Proposal Involve Recombinant DNA?
☐ No   ☐ Yes (If yes, complete Form CSRS-662)

20. Will the Work in This Proposal Involve Living Vertebrate Animals?
☐ No   ☐ Yes (If yes, complete Form CSRS-662)

21. Will the Work in This Proposal Involve Human Subjects?
☐ No   ☐ Yes (If yes, complete Form CSRS-662)

22. Will This Proposal be Sent or has it Been Sent to Other Funding Agencies, Including Other USDA Agencies?
☐ No   ☐ Yes (If yes, list Agency acronym(s) & program(s))

By signing and submitting this proposal, the prospective grantee is providing the required certifications set forth in 7 CFR Part 3017, as amended, regarding Debarment and Suspension and Drug-Free Workplace; and 7 CFR Part 3018 regarding Lobbying. **Submission of the individual forms is not required.** (Please read the Certifications and Instructions included in this kit before signing this form.)

In addition, the prospective grantee certifies that the information contained herein is true and complete to the best of its knowledge and accepts as to any grant award, the obligation to comply with the terms and conditions of Cooperative State Research Service in effect at the time of the award.

Signature of Principal Investigator(s)/Project Director(s) (All PI's/PD's listed in block 15 must sign if they are to be included in award document.)

Date

Signature of Authorized Organizational Representative
(Same as Item 3)

Title

Date

Form CSRS-661 (9/89)

Exhibit 38. (*Continued*)

UNITED STATES DEPARTMENT OF AGRICULTURE
COOPERATIVE STATE RESEARCH SERVICE
BUDGET

OMB Approved 0524-0022
Expires 8/92

Organization and Address	USDA Grant No.	
	Duration Proposed Months: _____ **FUNDS REQUESTED BY PROPOSER**	Duration Awarded Months: _____ **FUNDS APPROVED BY CSRS** (If different)

Principal Investigator(s)/Project Director(s)

		CSRS FUNDED WORK MONTHS			FUNDS REQUESTED BY PROPOSER	FUNDS APPROVED BY CSRS
		Calendar	Academic	Summer		
A.	Salaries and Wages					
	1. No. of Senior Personnel					
	a. _____ (Co)-PI(s)/PD(s)...................				$	$
	b. _____ Senior Associates...................					
	2. No. of Other Personnel (Non-Faculty)					
	a. _____ Research Associates-Postdoctorate......					
	b. _____ Other Professionals					
	c. _____ Graduate Students					
	d. _____ Prebaccalaureate Students............					
	e. _____ Secretarial-Clerical					
	f. _____ Technical, Shop and Other					
	Total Salaries and Wages ....➤					
B.	Fringe Benefits (If charged as Direct Costs)					
C.	**Total Salaries, Wages, and Fringe Benefits** (A plus B) ....➤					
D.	Nonexpendable Equipment (Attach supporting data. List items and dollar amounts for **each** item.)					
E.	Materials and Supplies					
F.	Travel 1. Domestic (Including Canada).........................					
	2. Foreign (List destination and amount for each trip.)					
G.	Publication Costs/Page Charges					
H.	Computer (ADPE) Costs					
I.	All Other Direct Costs (Attach supporting data. List items and dollar amounts. Details of subcontracts, including work statements and budget, should be explained in full in proposal.)					
J.	**Total Direct Costs** (C through I) ....➤					
K.	**Indirect Costs** (Specify rate(s) and base(s) for on/off campus activity. Where both are involved, identify itemized costs included in on/off campus bases.)					
L.	**Total Direct and Indirect Costs** (J plus K) ....➤					
M.	**Other** ....➤					
N.	**Total Amount of This Request** ....➤				$	$
O.	**Cost Sharing**	$			███████	███████

NOTE: Signatures required only for Revised Budget   *This is Revision No.* ➤

Name and Title (Type or print)	Signature	Date
Principal Investigator/Project Director		
Authorized Organizational Representative		

Form CSRS-55 (9/89)

I. OTHER REQUIRED FORMS AND NECESSARY INFORMATION

1. Examples of Application Forms and Guidelines from Two Private Foundations

Exhibit 39. Information from Private Foundations.

COVER SHEET FOR PROPOSAL TO THE NATIONAL SCIENCE FOUNDATION

PROGRAM ANNOUNCEMENT/SOLICITATION NO./CLOSING DATE/If not in response to a program announcement/solicitation enter NSF 99-2	**FOR NSF USE ONLY** NSF PROPOSAL NUMBER
FOR CONSIDERATION BY NSF ORGANIZATIONAL UNIT(S) (Indicate the most specific unit known, i.e., program, division, etc.)	

DATE RECEIVED	NUMBER OF COPIES	DIVISION ASSIGNED	FUND CODE	DUNS # (Data Universal Numbering System)	FILE LOCATION

EMPLOYER IDENTIFICATION NUMBER (EIN) OR TAXPAYER IDENTIFICATION NUMBER (TIN)	SHOW PREVIOUS AWARD NO. IF THIS IS ☐ A RENEWAL ☐ AN ACCOMPLISHMENT-BASED RENEWAL	IS THIS PROPOSAL BEING SUBMITTED TO ANOTHER FEDERAL AGENCY? YES ☐ NO ☐ IF YES, LIST ACRONYM(S)

NAME OF ORGANIZATION TO WHICH AWARD SHOULD BE MADE	ADDRESS OF AWARDEE ORGANIZATION, INCLUDING 9 DIGIT ZIP CODE
AWARDEE ORGANIZATION CODE (IF KNOWN)	
NAME OF PERFORMING ORGANIZATION, IF DIFFERENT FROM ABOVE	ADDRESS OF PERFORMING ORGANIZATION, IF DIFFERENT, INCLUDING 9 DIGIT ZIP CODE
PERFORMING ORGANIZATION CODE (IF KNOWN)	

IS AWARDEE ORGANIZATION (Check All That Apply)
(See GPG II.D.1 For Definitions)   ☐ FOR-PROFIT ORGANIZATION   ☐ SMALL BUSINESS   ☐ MINORITY BUSINESS   ☐ WOMAN-OWNED BUSINESS

TITLE OF PROPOSED PROJECT

REQUESTED AMOUNT $	PROPOSED DURATION (1-60 MONTHS) months	REQUESTED STARTING DATE	SHOW RELATED PREPROPOSAL NO., IF APPLICABLE

CHECK APPROPRIATE BOX(ES) IF THIS PROPOSAL INCLUDES ANY OF THE ITEMS LISTED BELOW

☐ BEGINNING INVESTIGATOR (GPG I.A.3)
☐ DISCLOSURE OF LOBBYING ACTIVITIES (GPG II.D.1)
☐ PROPRIETARY & PRIVILEGED INFORMATION (GPG I.B, II.D.7)
☐ NATIONAL ENVIRONMENTAL POLICY ACT (GPG II.D.10)
☐ HISTORIC PLACES (GPG II.D.10)
☐ SMALL GRANT FOR EXPLOR. RESEARCH (SGER) (GPG II.D.12)
☐ GROUP PROPOSAL (GPG II.D.12)

☐ VERTEBRATE ANIMALS (GPG II.D.12) IACUC App. Date _____
☐ HUMAN SUBJECTS (GPG II.D.12)
  Exemption Subsection____or IRB App. Date _____
☐ INTERNATIONAL COOPERATIVE ACTIVITIES: COUNTRY/COUNTRIES
  _____
☐ FACILITATION FOR SCIENTISTS/ENGINEERS WITH DISABILITIES (GPG V.G.)
☐ RESEARCH OPPORTUNITY AWARD (GPG V.H)

PI/PD DEPARTMENT	PI/PD POSTAL ADDRESS
PI/PD FAX NUMBER	

NAMES (TYPED)	High Degree	Yr of Degree	Telephone Number	Electronic Mail Address
PI/PD NAME				
CO-PI/PD				
CO-PI/PD				
CO-PI/PD				
CO-PI/PD				

NSF Form 1207 (10/98)   Page 1 of 2

Exhibit 39. (*Continued*)

CERTIFICATION PAGE

Certification for Principal Investigators and Co-Principal Investigators

I certify to the best of my knowledge that:

(1) the statements herein (excluding scientific hypotheses and scientific opinions) are true and complete, and

(2) the text and graphics herein as well as any accompanying publications or other documents, unless otherwise indicated, are the original work of the signatories or individuals working under their supervision. I agree to accept responsibility for the scientific conduct of the project and to provide the required project reports if an award is made as a result of this proposal.

I understand that the willful provision of false information or concealing a material fact in this proposal or any other communication submitted to NSF is a criminal offense (U.S.Code, Title 18, Section 1001).

Name (Typed)	Signature	Social Security No.*	Date
PI/PD			
Co-PI/PD			
Co-PI/PD			
Co-PI/PD			
Co-PI/PD			

Certification for Authorized Organizational Representative or Individual Applicant

By signing and submitting this proposal, the individual applicant or the authorized official of the applicant institution is: (1) certifying that statements made herein are true and complete to the best of his/her knowledge; and (2) agreeing to accept the obligation to comply with NSF award terms and conditions if an award is made as a result of this application. Further, the applicant is hereby providing certifications regarding Federal debt status, debarment and suspension, drug-free workplace, and lobbying activities (see below), as set forth in the *Grant Proposal Guide (GPG)*, NSF 99-2. Willful provision of false information in this and its supporting documents or in reports required under an ensuing award is a criminal offense (U.S. Code, Title 18, Section 1001).

In addition, if the applicant institution employs more than fifty persons, the authorized official of the applicant institution is certifying that the institution has implemented a written and enforced conflict of interest policy that is consistent with the provisions of *Grant Policy Manual* Section 510; that to the best of his/her knowledge, all financial disclosures required by that conflict of interest policy have been made; and that all identified conflicts of interest will have been satisfactorily managed, reduced or eliminated prior to the institution's expenditure of any funds under the award, in accordance with the institution's conflict of interest policy. Conflicts that cannot be satisfactorily managed, reduced or eliminated must be disclosed to NSF.

Debt and Debarment Certifications   (If answer "yes" to either, please provide explanation.)

Is the organization delinquent on any Federal debt?   Yes ☐   No ☐

Is the organization or its principals presently debarred, suspended, proposed for debarment, declared ineligible, or voluntarily excluded from covered transactions by any Federal Department or agency?   Yes ☐   No ☐

Certification Regarding Lobbying

This certification is required for an award of a Federal contract, grant or cooperative agreement exceeding $100,000 and for an award of a Federal loan or a commitment providing for the United States to insure or guarantee a loan exceeding $150,000.

Certification for Contracts, Grants, Loans and Cooperative Agreements

The undersigned certifies, to the best of his or her knowledge and belief, that:

(1) No Federal appropriated funds have been paid or will be paid, by or on behalf of the undersigned, to any person for influencing or attempting to influence an officer or employee of any agency, a Member of Congress, an officer or employee of Congress, or an employee of a Member of Congress in connection with the awarding of any federal contract, the making of any Federal grant, the making of any Federal loan, the entering into of any cooperative agreement, and the extension, continuation, renewal, amendment, or modification of any Federal contract, grant, loan, or cooperative agreement.

(2) If any funds other than Federal appropriated funds have been paid or will be paid to any person for influencing or attempting to influence an officer or employee of any agency, a Member of Congress, and officer or employee of Congress, or an employee of a Member of Congress in connection with this Federal contract, grant, loan, or cooperative agreement, the undersigned shall complete and submit Standard Form LLL, "Disclosure of Lobbying Activities," in accordance with its instructions.

(3) The undersigned shall require that the language of this certification be included in the award documents for all subawards at all tiers including subcontracts, subgrants, and contracts under grants, loans, and cooperative agreements and that all subrecipients shall certify and disclose accordingly.

This certification is a material representation of fact upon which reliance was placed when this transaction was made or entered into. Submission of this certification is a prerequisite for making or entering into this transaction imposed by Section 1352, Title 31, U.S. Code. Any person who fails to file the required certification shall be subject to a civil penalty of not less than $10,000 and not more than $100,000 for each such failure.

AUTHORIZED ORGANIZATIONAL REPRESENTATIVE	SIGNATURE	DATE
NAME/TITLE (TYPED)		

TELEPHONE NUMBER	ELECTRONIC MAIL ADDRESS	FAX NUMBER

*SUBMISSION OF SOCIAL SECURITY NUMBERS IS VOLUNTARY AND WILL NOT AFFECT THE ORGANIZATION'S ELIGIBILITY FOR AN AWARD. HOWEVER, THEY ARE AN INTEGRAL PART OF THE NSF INFORMATION SYSTEM AND ASSIST IN PROCESSING THE PROPOSAL. SSN SOLICITED UNDER NSF ACT OF 1950, AS AMENDED.

Page 2 of 2

Exhibit 39. (*Continued*)

DO NOT DUPLICATE THIS PAGE AS PART OF THE PROPOSAL

Every prospective grantee must complete the section on certification on the Cover Sheet (NSF Form 1207 (Rev. 10/98) submitted with each proposal. Instructions for the two certifications are below:

INSTRUCTIONS ON CERTIFICATION OF NON-DELINQUENCY BY APPLICANTS FOR FEDERAL ASSISTANCE

The certification of non-delinquency applies only to the organization requesting financial assistance and not to the individual Principal Investigator.

For the purposes of this certification, the following definitions of delinquency apply:

Direct loans — a debt more than 31 days past due on a scheduled payment

Grants — recipients of a "Notice of Grants

Cost Disallowance" who have not repaid the disallowed amount or who have not resolved the disallowance

Guaranteed and insured loans — recipients of a loan guaranteed by the Federal Government that the Federal Government has repurchased from a lender because the borrower breached the loan agreement and is in default.

Examples of debts include delinquent taxes, audit disallowances, guaranteed and direct student loans, housing loans, farm loans, business loans, Department of Education institutional loans, benefit overpayments and other miscellaneous administrative debts.

INSTRUCTIONS ON CERTIFICATION REGARDING DEBARMENT AND SUSPENSION

1. By signing and submitting this proposal, the prospective primary participant is providing the certification set out below.

2. The inability of a person to provide the certification required below will not necessarily result in denial of participation in this covered transaction. The prospective participant shall submit an explanation of why it cannot provide the certification set out below. The certification or explanation will be considered in connection with the department or agency's determination whether to enter into this transaction. However, failure of the prospective primary participant to furnish a certification or an explanation shall disqualify such person from participation in this transaction.

3. The certification in this clause is any material representation of fact upon which reliance was placed when the department or agency determined to enter into this transaction. If it is later determined that the prospective primary participant knowingly rendered an erroneous certification, in addition to other remedies available to the Federal Government, the department or agency may terminate this transaction for cause of default.

4. The prospective primary participant shall provide immediate written notice to the department or agency to whom this proposal is submitted if at any time the prospective primary participant learns that its certification was erroneous when submitted or has

become erroneous by reason of changed circumstances.

5. The terms covered transaction, debarred, suspended ineligible, lower tier-covered transaction, participant, person, primary covered transaction, principal, proposal, and voluntarily excluded, as used in this clause, have the meanings set out in the Definitions and Coverage sections of the rules implementing Executive Order 12549. You may contact the department or agency to which this proposal is being submitted for assistance in obtaining a copy of those regulations.

6. The prospective primary participant agrees by submitting this proposal that, should the proposed covered transaction be entered into, it shall not knowingly enter into any lower tier covered transaction with a person who is debarred, suspended, declared ineligible, or voluntarily excluded from participation in this covered transaction, unless authorized by the department or agency entering into this transaction.

7. The prospective primary participant further agrees by submitting this proposal that it will include the clause titled "Certification Regarding Debarment, Suspension, Ineligibility and Voluntary Exclusion - Lower Tier Covered Transaction," provided by the department or agency entering into this covered transaction, without modification, in all lower tier covered transactions.

8. A participant in a covered transaction may rely upon a certification of a prospective participant in a lower tier covered transaction that it is not debarred, suspended, ineligible, or voluntarily excluded from the covered transaction, unless it knows that the certification is erroneous. A participant may decide the method and frequency by which it determines the eligibility of its principals. Each participant may, but is not required to, check the Nonprocurement List.

9. Nothing contained in the foregoing shall be construed to require establishment of a system of records in order to render in good faith the certification required by this clause. The knowledge and information of a participant is not required to exceed that which is normally possessed by a prudent person in the ordinary course of business dealings.

10. Except for transactions authorized under paragraph 6 of these instructions, if a participant in a covered transaction knowingly enters into a lower tier covered transaction with a person who is suspended, debarred, ineligible, or voluntarily excluded from participation in this transaction, in addition to other remedies available to the Federal Government, the department or agency may terminate this transaction for cause or default.

CERTIFICATION

(1) The prospective primary participant certifies to the best of its knowledge and belief, that it and its principals:

(a) Are not presently debarred, suspended, proposed for debarment, declared ineligible, or voluntarily excluded from covered transactions by any Federal department or agency;

(b) Have not within a three-year period preceding this proposal been convicted of or had a civil judgment rendered against them for commission of fraud or a criminal offense in connection with obtaining, attempting to obtain, or performing a public (Federal, State or local) transaction or contract under a public transaction; violation of Federal or State antitrust statutes or commission of embezzlement, theft, forgery, bribery, falsification or

destruction of records, making false statements, or receiving stolen property;

(c) Are not presently indicted for or otherwise criminally or civilly charged by a governmental entity (Federal, State or local) with commission of any of the offenses enumerated in paragraph (1)(b) of this certification; and

(d) Have not within a three-year period preceding this application/proposal had one or more public transactions (Federal, State or local) terminated for cause or default.

(2) Where the prospective primary participant is unable to certify to any of the statements in this certification, such prospective participant shall attach an explanation to this proposal.

Exhibit 39. (*Continued*)

Instructions for Certification

1. By signing the NSF Proposal Cover Sheet, NSF Form 1207, and submitting this proposal, the grantee is providing the certifications set out below.
2. The certification set out below is a material representation of fact upon which reliance was placed when the agency determined to award the grant. If it is later determined that the grantee knowingly rendered a false certification, or otherwise violates the requirements of the Drug-Free Workplace Act, the agency, in addition to any other remedies available to the Federal Government, may take action authorized under the Drug-Free Workplace Act.
3. For grantees other than individuals, Alternate I applies.
4. For grantees who are individuals, Alternate II applies.

Certification Regarding Drug-Free Workplace Requirements

Alternate I (Grantees Other Than Individuals)

The grantee certifies that it will or will continue to provide a drug-free workplace by:

(a) Publishing a statement notifying employees that the unlawful manufacture, distribution, dispensing, possession or use of a controlled substance is prohibited in the grantee's workplace and specifying the actions that will be taken against employees for violation of such prohibition;

(b) Establishing an ongoing drug-free awareness program to inform employees about —

(1) The dangers of drug abuse in the workplace;

(2) The grantee's policy of maintaining a drug-free workplace;

(3) Any available drug counseling, rehabilitation and employee assistance programs; and

(4) The penalties that may be imposed upon employees for drug abuse violations occurring in the workplace;

(c) Making it a requirement that each employee to be engaged in the performance of the grant be given a copy of the statement required by paragraph (a);

(d) Notifying the employee in the statement required by paragraph (a) that, as a condition of employment under the grant, the employee will —

(1) Abide by the terms of the statement; and

(2) Notify the employer in writing of his or her conviction for a violation of a criminal drug statute occurring in the workplace, no later than five calendar days after such conviction;

(e) Notifying the agency in writing, within 10 calendar days after receiving notice under subparagraph (d)(2) from an employee or otherwise receiving actual notice of such conviction.

Employers of convicted employees must provide notice, including position title, to every grant officer or other designee on whose grant activity the convicted employee was working, unless the Federal agency has designated a central point for the receipt of such notices. Notice shall include the identification number(s) of each affected grant;

(f) Taking one of the following actions, within 30 calendar days of receiving notice under subparagraph (d)(2), with respect to any employee who is so convicted —

(1) Taking appropriate personnel action against such an employee, up to and including termination, consistent with the requirements of the Rehabilitation Act of 1973, as amended; or

(2) Requiring such employee to participate satisfactorily in a drug abuse assistance or rehabilitation program approved for such purposes by a Federal, State, or local health, law enforcement, or other appropriate agency;

(g) Making a good faith effort to continue to maintain a drug-free workplace through implementation of paragraphs (a), (b), (c), (d), (e) and (f).

Alternate II (Grantees Who Are Individuals)

(a) The grantee certifies that, as a condition of the grant, he or she will not engage in the unlawful manufacture, distribution, dispensing, possession or use of a controlled substance in conducting any activity with the grant.

(b) If convicted of a criminal drug offense resulting from a violation occurring during the conduct of any grant activity, he or she will report the conviction, in writing, within 10 calendar days of the conviction, to every grant officer or other designee, unless the Federal agency designates a central point for the receipt of such notices. When notice is made to such a central point, it shall include the identification number(s) of each affected grant.

(For NSF, grantee notification should be made to the Cost Analysis/Audit Resolution Branch, Division of Contracts, Policy & Oversight, NSF, Arlington, VA 22230)

2. A Format for *Curriculum Vitae*

Use of a standardized and easy-to-follow form helps the reviewer. Your *curriculum vitae* should provide a good profile of your background and current activities. If you are applying for support for some project not directly related to your professional experience, or if you are presenting a research project, add a statement giving information demonstrating your competency in the activities described in the proposal.

Exhibit 40. *Curriculum Vitae.*

This is a recommended format for curriculum vitae. Provide the information in the order suggested following headlines and instructions. Space headings as required by the answers.

CURRICULUM VITAE

NAME: *(first, middle, last) (repeat name on each sheet)*

ADDRESS: PHONE: (off.) (---)---/----
                                    (home) (---)---/----

PRESENT POSITION: *(title, rank, department as appropriate)*

EDUCATION: **Degree**   **Institution**   **Location**   **Date**   **Major**
             (undergraduate first)   *(state/branch)*   *(of degree)*
             (A.B.) _____   _____   ____   ____
             (M.A.) _____   _____   ____   ____
             (Ph.D.) _____   _____   ____   ____

PROFESSIONAL EXPERIENCE:

    19__ to present   *(repeat present position)*

    19__ to 19__   *(start with latest position and work backwards)*

                              (include all paid positions, full-time and part-time in your present field of work and all other work experience including military service)

AWARDS, GRANTS & SPECIAL PROJECTS: *(fellowships, traineeships, research not included under publication section. Add a heading for research if you prefer)*

MEMBERSHIPS & VOLUNTEER ACTIVITIES   *(list most important to you for any date and those which are current)*

PUBLICATIONS: *(start with current publications and work backwards. Some agencies ask that you limit publications to those completed in the last three to ten years. Continue on additional pages if needed.)*

       Name of institution: *(repeat on each sheet*
       Date: *(date when this information was prepared)*

---

3. Acknowledgment Card

Most agencies use such cards that you address to yourself, your Chief Administrative Officer, and your Grants Officer. The returned receipt will have a document number to identify your proposal. *Don't lose it!* It is the only way your proposal can be found if you have questions. It is also proof that your proposal was received on time.

Exhibit 41. Acknowledgment Card.

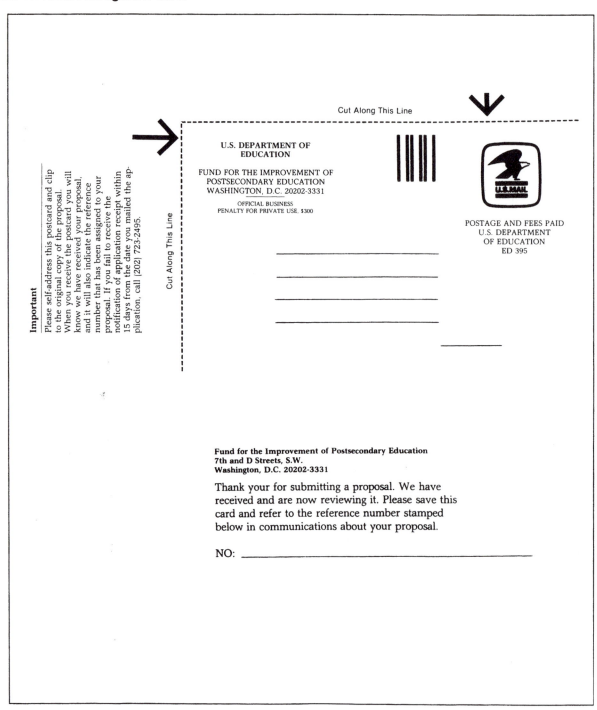

4. Certification and Assurance Forms and Regulations

The information and forms included here cover most of the federal compliance requirements:

Exhibit 42. List of Required Assurances.

Assurances

The Applicant hereby assures and certifies that it will comply with the regulations, policies, guidelines and requirements, as they relate to the application, acceptance and use of Federal funds for this Federally assisted project. Also the Applicant assures and certifies that:

1. It possesses legal authority to apply for the grant; that a resolution, motion or similar action has been dully adopted or passed as an official act of the applicant's governing body, authorizing the filing of the application, including all understandings and assurances contained therein, and directing and authorizing the person identified as the official representative of the applicant to act in connection with the application and to provide such additional information as may be required.

2. It will comply with Title VI of the Civil Rights Act of 1964 (P.L. 88-352) and in accordance with Title VI of the Act, no person in the United States shall, on the grounds of race, color or national origin, be excluded from participation in, be denied the benefits of, or be otherwise subjected to discrimination under any program or activity for which the applicant receives Federal financial assistance and will immediately take any measures necessary to effect this agreement.

3. It will comply with Title VI of the Civil Rights Act of 1964 (42 U.S.C. 2000d) prohibiting employment discrimination where (1) the primary purpose of a grant is to provide employment or (2) discriminatory employment practices will result in unequal treatment of persons who are or should be benefiting from the grant-aided activity.

4. It will comply with Section 504 of the Rehabilitation Act of 1973, as amended, 29 U.S.C. 794, which prohibits discrimination on the basis of handicap in programs and activities receiving Federal financial assistance.

5. It will comply with Title IX of the Education Amendments of 1972, as amended, 20 U.S.C. 1681 et seq., which prohibits discrimination on the basis of sex in education programs and activities receiving Federal financial assistance.

6. It will comply with the Age Discrimination Act of 1975, as amended, 42 U.S.C. 6101 et seq., which prohibits discrimination on the basis of age in programs or activities receiving Federal financial assistance.

7. It will comply with requirements of the provisions of the Uniform Relocation Assistance and Real Property Acquisitions Act of 1970 (P.L. 91-646) which provides for fair and equitable treatment of persons displaced as a result of Federal and Federally-assisted programs.

8. It will comply with provisions of the Hatch Act which limit the political activity of employees.

9. It will comply with the minimum wage and maximum hours provisions of the Federal Fair Labor Standards Act, as they apply to hospital and educational institution employees of State and local governments.

10. It will establish safeguards to prohibit employees from using their positions for a purpose that is or gives the appearance of being motivated by a desire for private gain for themselves or others, particularly those with whom they have family, business, or other ties.

11. It will give the sponsoring agency or the Comptroller General through any authorized representative the access to and the right to examine all records, books, papers, or documents related to the grant.

12. It will comply with all requirements imposed by the Federal sponsoring agency concerning special requirements of law, program requirements, and other administrative requirements.

13. It will insure that the facilities under its ownership, lease or supervision which shall be utilized in the accomplishment of the project are not listed on the Environmental Protection Agency's (EPA) list of Violating Facilities and that it will notify the Federal grantor agency of the receipt of any communication from the Director of the EPA Office of Federal Activities indicating that a facility to be used in the project is under consideration for listing by the EPA.

14. It will comply with the flood insurance purchase requirements of Section 102(a) of the Flood Disaster Protection Act of 1973, P.L. 93-234, 87 Stat. 975, approved December 31, 1976. Section 102(a) requires, on or after March 2, 1975, the purchase of flood insurance in communities where such insurance is available as a condition for the receipt of any Federal financial assistance for construction or acquisition purposes for use in any area that has been identified by the Secretary of the Department of Housing and Urban Development as an area having special flood hazards. The phrase "Federal financial assistance" includes any form of loan, grant, guaranty, insurance payment, rebate subsidy, disaster assistance loan or grant, or any other form of direct or indirect Federal assistance.

15. It will assist the Federal grantor agency in its compliance with Section 106 of the National Historic Preservation Act of 1966 as amended (16 U.S.C. 470), Executive Order 11593, and the Archeological and Historic Preservation Act of 1966 (16 U.S.C. 469a-1 et seq.) by (a) consulting with the State Historic Preservation Officer on the conduct of investigations, as necessary, to identify properties listed in or eligible for inclusion in the National Register of Historic Places that are subject to adverse effects (see 36 CFR Part 800.8) by the activity, and notifying the Federal grantor agency of the existence of any such properties, and by (b) complying with all requirements established by the Federal grantor agency to avoid or mitigate adverse effects upon such property.

Exhibit 43. Civil Rights Certificate.

OMB Approval No. 0348-0040

ASSURANCES - NON-CONSTRUCTION PROGRAMS

NOTE: Certain of these assurances may not be applicable to your project or program. If you have questions, please contact the awarding agency. Further, certain Federal awarding agencies may require applicants to certify to additional assurances. If such is the case, you will be notified.

As the duly authorized representative of the applicant, I certify that the applicant:

1. Has the legal authority to apply for Federal assistance and the institutional, managerial and financial capability (including funds sufficient to pay the non-Federal share of project cost) to ensure proper planning, management and completion of the project described in this application.

2. Will give the awarding agency, the Comptroller General of the United States and, if appropriate, the State, through any authorized representative, access to and the right to examine all records, books, papers, or documents related to the award; and will establish a proper accounting system in accordance with generally accepted accounting standards or agency directives.

3. Will establish safeguards to prohibit employees from using their positions for a purpose that constitutes or presents the appearance of personal or organizational conflict of interest, or personal gain.

4. Will initiate and complete the work within the applicable time frame after receipt of approval of the awarding agency.

5. Will comply with the Intergovernmental Personnel Act of 1970 (42 U.S.C. §§4728-4763) relating to prescribed standards for merit systems for programs funded under one of the 19 statutes or regulations specified in Appendix A of OPM's Standards for a Merit System of Personnel Administration (5 C.F.R. 900, Subpart F).

6. Will comply with all Federal statutes relating to nondiscrimination. These include but are not limited to: (a) Title VI of the Civil Rights Act of 1964 (P.L. 88-352) which prohibits discrimination on the basis of race, color or national origin; (b) Title IX of the Education Amendments of 1972, as amended (20 U.S.C. §§1681-1683, and 1685-1686), which prohibits discrimination on the basis of sex; (c) Section 504 of the Rehabilitation Act of 1973, as amended (29 U.S.C. §794), which prohibits discrimination on the basis of handicaps; (d) the Age Discrimination Act of 1975, as amended (42 U.S.C. §§6101-6107), which prohibits discrimination on the basis of age; (e) the Drug Abuse Office and Treatment Act of 1972 (P.L. 92-255), as amended, relating to nondiscrimination on the basis of drug abuse; (f) the Comprehensive Alcohol Abuse and Alcoholism Prevention, Treatment and Rehabilitation Act of 1970 (P.L. 91-616), as amended, relating to nondiscrimination on the basis of alcohol abuse or alcoholism; (g) §§523 and 527 of the Public Health Service Act of 1912 (42 U.S.C. §§290 dd-3 and 290 ee 3), as amended, relating to confidentiality of alcohol and drug abuse patient records; (h) Title VIII of the Civil Rights Act of 1968 (42 U.S.C. §§3601 et seq.), as amended, relating to nondiscrimination in the sale, rental or financing of housing; (i) any other nondiscrimination provisions in the specific statute(s) under which application for Federal assistance is being made; and, (j) the requirements of any other nondiscrimination statute(s) which may apply to the application.

7. Will comply, or has already complied, with the requirements of Titles II and III of the Uniform Relocation Assistance and Real Property Acquisition Policies Act of 1970 (P.L. 91-646) which provide for fair and equitable treatment of persons displaced or whose property is acquired as a result of Federal or federally-assisted programs. These requirements apply to all interests in real property acquired for project purposes regardless of Federal participation in purchases.

8. Will comply, as applicable, with provisions of the Hatch Act (5 U.S.C. §§1501-1508 and 7324-7328) which limit the political activities of employees whose principal employment activities are funded in whole or in part with Federal funds.

Previous Edition Usable

Authorized for Local Reproduction

Standard Form 424B (Rev. 7-97)
Prescribed by OMB Circular A-102

Exhibit 43. (*Continued*)

9. Will comply, as applicable, with the provisions of the Davis-Bacon Act (40 U.S.C. §§276a to 276a-7), the Copeland Act (40 U.S.C. §276c and 18 U.S.C. §874), and the Contract Work Hours and Safety Standards Act (40 U.S.C. §§327-333), regarding labor standards for federally-assisted construction subagreements.

10. Will comply, if applicable, with flood insurance purchase requirements of Section 102(a) of the Flood Disaster Protection Act of 1973 (P.L. 93-234) which requires recipients in a special flood hazard area to participate in the program and to purchase flood insurance if the total cost of insurable construction and acquisition is $10,000 or more.

11. Will comply with environmental standards which may be prescribed pursuant to the following: (a) institution of environmental quality control measures under the National Environmental Policy Act of 1969 (P.L. 91-190) and Executive Order (EO) 11514; (b) notification of violating facilities pursuant to EO 11738; (c) protection of wetlands pursuant to EO 11990; (d) evaluation of flood hazards in floodplains in accordance with EO 11988; (e) assurance of project consistency with the approved State management program developed under the Coastal Zone Management Act of 1972 (16 U.S.C. §§1451 et seq.); (f) conformity of Federal actions to State (Clean Air) Implementation Plans under Section 176(c) of the Clean Air Act of 1955, as amended (42 U.S.C. §§7401 et seq.); (g) protection of underground sources of drinking water under the Safe Drinking Water Act of 1974, as amended (P.L. 93-523); and, (h) protection of endangered species under the Endangered Species Act of 1973, as amended (P.L. 93-205).

12. Will comply with the Wild and Scenic Rivers Act of 1968 (16 U.S.C. §§1271 et seq.) related to protecting components or potential components of the national wild and scenic rivers system.

13. Will assist the awarding agency in assuring compliance with Section 106 of the National Historic Preservation Act of 1966, as amended (16 U.S.C. §470), EO 11593 (identification and protection of historic properties), and the Archaeological and Historic Preservation Act of 1974 (16 U.S.C. §§469a-1 et seq.).

14. Will comply with P.L. 93-348 regarding the protection of human subjects involved in research, development, and related activities supported by this award of assistance.

15. Will comply with the Laboratory Animal Welfare Act of 1966 (P.L. 89-544, as amended, 7 U.S.C. §§2131 et seq.) pertaining to the care, handling, and treatment of warm blooded animals held for research, teaching, or other activities supported by this award of assistance.

16. Will comply with the Lead-Based Paint Poisoning Prevention Act (42 U.S.C. §§4801 et seq.) which prohibits the use of lead-based paint in construction or rehabilitation of residence structures.

17. Will cause to be performed the required financial and compliance audits in accordance with the Single Audit Act Amendments of 1996 and OMB Circular No. A-133, "Audits of States, Local Governments, and Non-Profit Organizations."

18. Will comply with all applicable requirements of all other Federal laws, executive orders, regulations, and policies governing this program.

SIGNATURE OF AUTHORIZED CERTIFYING OFFICIAL	TITLE
APPLICANT ORGANIZATION	DATE SUBMITTED

Standard Form 424B (Rev. 7-97) Back

Exhibit 44. Protection of Human Subjects Assurance.

ASSURANCE OF COMPLIANCE

ASSURANCE OF COMPLIANCE WITH TITLE VI OF THE CIVIL RIGHTS ACT OF 1964, SECTION 504 OF THE REHABILITATION ACT OF 1973, TITLE IX OF THE EDUCATION AMENDMENTS OF 1972, AND THE AGE DISCRIMINATION ACT OF 1975

The Applicant provides this assurance in consideration of and for the purpose of obtaining Federal grants, loans, contracts, property, discounts or other Federal financial assistance from the Department of Health and Human Services.

THE APPLICANT HEREBY AGREES THAT IT WILL COMPLY WITH:

1. Title VI of the Civil Rights Act of 1964 (Pub. L. 88-352), as amended, and all requirements imposed by or pursuant to the Regulation of the Department of Health and Human Services (45 C.F.R. Part 80), to the end that, in accordance with Title VI of that Act and the Regulation, no person in the United States shall, on the ground of race, color, or national origin, be excluded from participation in, be denied the benefits of, or be otherwise subjected to discrimination under any program or activity for which the Applicant receives Federal financial assistance from the Department.

2. Section 504 of the Rehabilitation Act of 1973 (Pub. L. 93-112), as amended, and all requirements imposed by or pursuant to the Regulation of the Department of Health and Human Services (45 C.F.R. Part 84), to the end that, in accordance with Section 504 of that Act and the Regulation, no otherwise qualified handicapped individual in the United States shall, solely by reason of his handicap, be excluded from participation in, be denied the benefits of, or be subjected to discrimination under any program or activity for which the Applicant receives Federal financial assistance from the Department.

3. Title IX of the Educational Amendments of 1972 (Pub. L. 92-318), as amended, and all requirements imposed by or pursuant to the Regulation of the Department of Health and Human Services (45 C.F.R. Part 86), to the end that, in accordance with Title IX and the Regulation, no person in the United States shall, on the basis of sex, be excluded from participation in, be denied the benefits of, or be otherwise subjected to discrimination under any education program or activity for which the Applicant receives Federal financial assistance from the Department.

4. The Age Discrimination Act of 1975 (Pub. L. 94-135), as amended, and all requirements imposed by or pursuant to the Regulation of the Department of Health and Human Services (45 C.F.R. Part 91), to the end that, in accordance with the Act and the Regulation, no person in the United States shall, on the basis of age, be denied the benefits of, be excluded from participation in, or be subjected to discrimination under any program or activity for which the Applicant receives Federal financial assistance from the Department.

The Applicant agrees that compliance with this assurance constitutes a condition of continued receipt of Federal financial assistance, and that it is binding upon the Applicant, its successors, transferees and assignees for the period during which such assistance is provided. If any real property or structure thereon is provided or improved with the aid of Federal financial assistance extended to the Applicant by the Department, this assurance shall obligate the Applicant, or in the case of any transfer of such property, any transferee, for the period during which the real property or structure is used for a purpose for which the Federal financial assistance is extended or for another purpose involving the provision of similar services or benefits. If any personal property is so provided, this assurance shall obligate the Applicant for the period during which it retains ownership or possession of the property. The Applicant further recognizes and agrees that the United States shall have the right to seek judicial enforcement of this assurance.

The person or persons whose signature(s) appear(s) below is/are authorized to sign this assurance, and commit the Applicant to the above provisions.

_____
Date

_____
Signature and Title of Authorized Official

_____
Name of Applicant or Recipient

_____
Street

_____
City, State, Zip Code

Mail Form to:
DHHS/Office for Civil Rights
Office of Program Operations
Humphrey Building, Room 509F
200 Independence Ave., S.W.
Washington, D.C. 20201

Form HHS-690
5/97

Exhibit 44. (*Continued*)

OMB Approval 0524-0026
Expires 8/31/2006

UNITED STATES DEPARTMENT OF AGRICULTURE
COOPERATIVE STATE RESEARCH, EDUCATION, AND EXTENSION SERVICE

ASSURANCE OF COMPLIANCE
with the
DEPARTMENT OF AGRICULTURE REGULATIONS
ASSURING CIVIL RIGHTS COMPLIANCE

Legal name of the proposed applicant _____ (Hereinafter called the Applicant) hereby agrees that it will offer its programs to all eligible persons without regard to race, color, national origin, sex, disability, age, political beliefs, religion, marital status, or familial status and that people will not be excluded from participation in, be denied the benefits of, or be otherwise subjected to discrimination under any program or activity for which the Applicant receives Federal financial assistance from the Department of Agriculture; and hereby gives assurance that it will immediately take any measures necessary to effectuate this agreement.

This assurance is given in consideration of and for the purpose of obtaining any and all Federal grants, loans, contracts, property, discounts or other Federal financial assistance extended after the date hereof to the Applicant by the Department, including installment payments after such date on account of applications for Federal financial assistance which were approved before such date. The Applicant recognizes and agrees that such Federal assistance will be extended in reliance on the representations and agreements made in this assurance, and that the United States shall have the right to seek judicial enforcement of this assurance. This assurance is binding on the Applicant, its successors, transferees, and assignees.

TYPED NAME AND TITLE OF AUTHORIZED ORGANIZATIONAL REPRESENTATIVE

SIGNATURE	DATE

APPLICANT'S MAILING ADDRESS

According to the Paperwork Reduction Act of 1995, an agency may not conduct or sponsor, and a person is not required to respond to a collection of information unless it displays a valid OMB control number. The valid OMB control number for this information collection is 0524-0026. The time required to complete this information collection is estimated to average .5 hours per response, including the time for reviewing instructions, searching existing data sources, gathering and maintaining the data needed, and completing and reviewing the collection of information.

FORM CSREES-665
Revised 8/2003

Exhibit 45. Certification Regarding Lobbying, Debarment, Suspension, and Other Responsibility Matters (and a similar form from the USDA).

OMB No. 0925-0637

DEPARTMENT OF HEALTH AND HUMAN SERVICES

PROTECTION OF HUMAN SUBJECTS
ASSURANCE/CERTIFICATION/DECLARATION

☐ GRANT ☐ CONTRACT ☐ FELLOW ☐ OTHER

☐ New ☐ Competing continuation ☐ Noncompeting continuation ☐ Supplemental

☐ ORIGINAL ☐ FOLLOWUP ☐ EXEMPTION (previously undesignated)

APPLICATION IDENTIFICATION NO. *(if known)*

POLICY: *A research activity involving human subjects that is not exempt from HHS regulations may not be funded unless an Institutional Review Board (IRB) has reviewed and approved the activity in accordance with Section 474 of the Public Health Service Act as implemented by Title 45, Part 46 of the Code of Federal Regulations (45 CFR 46—as revised). The applicant institution must submit certification of IRB approval to HHS unless the applicant institution has designated a specific exemption under Section 46.101(b) which applies to the proposed research activity. Institutions with an assurance of compliance on file with HHS which covers the proposed activity should submit certification of IRB review and approval with each application. (In exceptional cases, certification may be accepted up to 60 days after the receipt date for which the application is submitted.) In the case of institutions which do not have an assurance of compliance on file with HHS covering the proposed activity, certification of IRB review and approval must be submitted within 30 days of the receipt of a written request from HHS for certification.*

1. TITLE OF APPLICATION OR ACTIVITY

2. PRINCIPAL INVESTIGATOR, PROGRAM DIRECTOR, OR FELLOW

3. FOOD AND DRUG ADMINISTRATION REQUIRED INFORMATION *(see reverse side)*

4. HHS ASSURANCE STATUS

☐ This institution has an approved assurance of compliance on file with HHS which covers this activity.

_____ Assurance identification number _____ IRB identification number

☐ No assurance of compliance which applies to this activity has been established with HHS but the applicant institution will provide written assurance of compliance and certification of IRB review and approval in accordance with 45 CFR 46 upon request.

5. CERTIFICATION OF IRB REVIEW OR DECLARATION OF EXEMPTION

☐ This activity has been reviewed and approved by an IRB in accordance with the requirements of 45 CFR 46, including its relevant Subparts. This certification fulfills, when applicable, requirements for certifying FDA status for each investigational new drug or device *(see reverse side of this form)*.

_____ Date of IRB review and approval. *(If approval is pending, write "pending". Followup certification is required.)*
(month/day/year)

☐ Full Board Review ☐ Expedited Review

☐ This activity contains multiple projects, some of which have not been reviewed. The IRB has granted approval on condition that all projects covered by 45 CFR 46 will be reviewed and approved before they are initiated and that appropriate further certification *(form HHS 596)* will be submitted.

☐ Human subjects are involved but this activity qualifies for exemption under 46.101(b) in accordance with paragraph _____ *(insert paragraph number of exemption in 46.101(b), 1 through 5)*, but the institution did not designate that exemption on the application.

6. **Each official signing below certifies that the information provided on this form is correct and that each institution assumes responsibility for assuring required future reviews, approvals, and submissions of certification.**

APPLICANT INSTITUTION	COOPERATING INSTITUTION
NAME, ADDRESS, AND TELEPHONE NO.	NAME, ADDRESS, AND TELEPHONE NO.
NAME AND TITLE OF OFFICIAL *(print or type)*	NAME AND TITLE OF OFFICIAL *(print or type)*
SIGNATURE OF OFFICIAL LISTED ABOVE *(and date)*	SIGNATURE OF OFFICIAL LISTED ABOVE *(and date)*

HHS 596 (Rev. 1/82)   *(If additional space is needed, please use reverse side under "Notes.")*

5. Sample Drug-Free Workplace Policy Statement

Exhibit 46. Drug-Free Workplace Requirements; Form for Disclosure of Lobbying Activities.

CERTIFICATION REGARDING LOBBYING

Applicants must review the requirements for certification regarding lobbying included in the regulations cited below before completing this form. Applicants must sign this form to comply with the certification requirements under 34 CFR Part 82, "New Restrictions on Lobbying." This certification is a material representation of fact upon which the Department of Education relies when it makes a grant or enters into a cooperative agreement.

As required by Section 1352, Title 31 of the U.S. Code, and implemented at 34 CFR Part 82, for persons entering into a Federal contract, grant or cooperative agreement over $100,000, as defined at 34 CFR Part 82, Sections 82.105 and 82.110, the applicant certifies that:

(a) No Federal appropriated funds have been paid or will be paid, by or on behalf of the undersigned, to any person for influencing or attempting to influence an officer or employee of any agency, a Member of Congress, an officer or employee of Congress, or an employee of a Member of Congress in connection with the making of any Federal grant, the entering into of any cooperative agreement, and the extension, continuation, renewal, amendment, or modification of any Federal grant or cooperative agreement;

(b) If any funds other than Federal appropriated funds have been paid or will be paid to any person for influencing or attempting to influence an officer or employee of any agency, a Member of Congress, an officer or employee of Congress, or an employee of a Member of Congress in connection with this Federal grant or cooperative agreement, the undersigned shall complete and submit Standard Form - LLL, "Disclosure Form to Report Lobbying," in accordance with its instructions;

(c) The undersigned shall require that the language of this certification be included in the award documents for all subawards at all tiers (including subgrants and contracts under grants and cooperative agreements) and that all subrecipients shall certify and disclose accordingly.

As the duly authorized representative of the applicant, I hereby certify that the applicant will comply with the above certification.

NAME OF APPLICANT	PR/AWARD NUMBER AND / OR PROJECT NAME
PRINTED NAME AND TITLE OF AUTHORIZED REPRESENTATIVE	
SIGNATURE	DATE

ED 80-0013   06/04

Exhibit 46. (*Continued*)

CERTIFICATIONS REGARDING LOBBYING; DEBARMENT, SUSPENSION AND OTHER RESPONSIBILITY MATTERS; AND DRUG-FREE WORKPLACE REQUIREMENTS

Applicants should refer to the regulations cited below to determine the certification to which they are required to attest. Applicants should also review the instructions for certification included in the regulations before completing this form. Signature of this form provides for compliance with certification requirements under 34 CFR Part 82, "New Restrictions on Lobbying," and 34 CFR Part 85, "Government-wide Debarment and Suspension (Nonprocurement) and Government-wide Requirements for Drug-Free Workplace (Grants)." The certifications shall be treated as a material representation of fact upon which reliance will be placed when the Department of Education determines to award the covered transaction, grant, or cooperative agreement.

1. LOBBYING

As required by Section 1352, Title 31 of the U.S. Code, and implemented at 34 CFR Part 82, for persons entering into a grant or cooperative agreement over $100,000, as defined at 34 CFR Part 82, Sections 82.105 and 82.110, the applicant certifies that:

(a) No Federal appropriated funds have been paid or will be paid, by or on behalf of the undersigned, to any person for influencing or attempting to influence an officer or employee of any agency, a Member of Congress, an officer or employee of Congress, or an employee of a Member of Congress in connection with the making of any Federal grant, the entering into of any cooperative agreement, and the extension, continuation, renewal, amendment, or modification of any Federal grant or cooperative agreement;

(b) If any funds other than Federal appropriated funds have been paid or will be paid to any person for influencing or attempting to influence an officer or employee of any agency, a Member of Congress, an officer or employee of Congress, or an employee of a Member of Congress in connection with this Federal grant or cooperative agreement, the undersigned shall complete and submit Standard Form - LLL, "Disclosure Form to Report Lobbying," in accordance with its instructions;

(c) The undersigned shall require that the language of this certification be included in the award documents for all subawards at all tiers (including subgrants, contracts under grants and cooperative agreements, and subcontracts) and that all subrecipients shall certify and disclose accordingly.

2. DEBARMENT, SUSPENSION, AND OTHER RESPONSIBILITY MATTERS

As required by Executive Order 12549, Debarment and Suspension, and implemented at 34 CFR Part 85, for prospective participants in primary covered transactions, as defined at 34 CFR Part 85, Sections 85.105 and 85.110--

A. The applicant certifies that it and its principals:

(a) Are not presently debarred, suspended, proposed for debarment, declared ineligible, or voluntarily excluded from covered transactions by any Federal department or agency;

(b) Have not within a three-year period preceding this application been convicted of or had a civil judgement rendered against them for commission of fraud or a criminal offense in connection with obtaining, attempting to obtain, or performing a public (Federal, State, or local) transaction or contract under a public transaction; violation of Federal or State antitrust statutes or commission of embezzlement, theft, forgery, bribery, falsification or destruction of records, making false statements, or receiving stolen property;

(c)Are not presently indicted for or otherwise criminally or civilly charged by a governmental entity (Federal, State, or local) with commission of any of the offenses enumerated in paragraph (1)(b) of this certification; and

(d) Have not within a three-year period preceding this application had one or more public transaction (Federal, State, or local) terminated for cause or default; and

B. Where the applicant is unable to certify to any of the statements in this certification, he or she shall attach an explanation to this application.

3. DRUG-FREE WORKPLACE (GRANTEES OTHER THAN INDIVIDUALS)

As required by the Drug-Free Workplace Act of 1988, and implemented at 34 CFR Part 85, Subpart F, for grantees, as defined at 34 CFR Part 85, Sections 85.605 and 85.610 -

A. The applicant certifies that it will or will continue to provide a drug-free workplace by:

(a) Publishing a statement notifying employees that the unlawful manufacture, distribution, dispensing, possession, or use of a controlled substance is prohibited in the grantee_s workplace and specifying the actions that will be taken against employees for violation of such prohibition;

(b) Establishing an on-going drug-free awareness program to inform employees about-

(1) The dangers of drug abuse in the workplace;

(2) The grantee's policy of maintaining a drug-free workplace;

(3) Any available drug counseling, rehabilitation, and employee assistance programs; and

(4) The penalties that may be imposed upon employees for drug abuse violations occurring in the workplace;

(c) Making it a requirement that each employee to be engaged in the performance of the grant be given a copy of the statement required by paragraph (a);

Exhibit 46. (*Continued*)

(d) Notifying the employee in the statement required by paragraph (a) that, as a condition of employment under the grant, the employee will-

(1) Abide by the terms of the statement; and

(2) Notify the employer in writing of his or her conviction for a violation of a criminal drug statute occurring in the workplace no later than five calendar days after such conviction;

(e) Notifying the agency, in writing, within 10 calendar days after receiving notice under subparagraph (d)(2) from an employee or otherwise receiving actual notice of such conviction. Employers of convicted employees must provide notice, including position title, to: Director, Grants Policy and Oversight Staff, U.S. Department of Education, 600 Independence Avenue, S.W. (Room 3652, GSA Regional Office Building No. 3), Washington, DC 20202-4248. Notice shall include the identification number(s) of each affected grant;

(f) Taking one of the following actions, within 30 calendar days of receiving notice under subparagraph (d)(2), with respect to any employee who is so convicted-

(1) Taking appropriate personnel action against such an employee, up to and including termination, consistent with the requirements of the Rehabilitation Act of 1973, as amended; or

(2) Requiring such employee to participate satisfactorily in a drug abuse assistance or rehabilitation program approved for such purposes by a Federal, State, or local health, law enforcement, or other appropriate agency;

(g) Making a good faith effort to continue to maintain a drug-free workplace through implementation of paragraphs (a), (b), (c), (d), (e), and (f).

B. The grantee may insert in the space provided below the site(s) for the performance of work done in connection with the specific grant:

Place of Performance (Street address. city, county, state, zip code)

_____

_____

_____

Check [ ] if there are workplaces on file that are not identified here.

DRUG-FREE WORKPLACE
(GRANTEES WHO ARE INDIVIDUALS)

As required by the Drug-Free Workplace Act of 1988, and implemented at 34 CFR Part 85, Subpart F, for grantees, as defined at 34 CFR Part 85, Sections 85.605 and 85.610-

A. As a condition of the grant, I certify that I will not engage in the unlawful manufacture, distribution, dispensing, possession, or use of a controlled substance in conducting any activity with the grant; and

B. If convicted of a criminal drug offense resulting from a violation occurring during the conduct of any grant activity, I will report the conviction, in writing, within 10 calendar days of the conviction, to: Director, Grants Policy and Oversight Staff, Department of Education, 600 Independence Avenue, S.W. (Room 3652, GSA Regional Office Building No. 3), Washington, DC 20202-4248. Notice shall include the identification number(s) of each affected grant.

As the duly authorized representative of the applicant, I hereby certify that the applicant will comply with the above certifications.

NAME OF APPLICANT	PR/AWARD NUMBER AND/OR PROJECT NAME
PRINTED NAME AND TITLE OF AUTHORIZED REPRESENTATIVE	
SIGNATURE	DATE

6. IRS Letter of Determination

Exhibit 47. IRS Letter of Determination.

Internal Revenue Service
District Director

Department of the Treasury

521244583
Employer Identification Number:

Date: February 16, 1983

December 31
Accounting Period Ending:

509(a)(2)
Foundation Status Classification:

Dec. 31, 1986
Advance Ruling Period Ends:

▷ College University Resource
Institute, Inc.

Person to Contact: Taxpayer Service
Division
Contact Telephone Number:
488-3100

Dear Applicant:

Based on information supplied, and assuming your operations will be as stated in your application for recognition of exemption, we have determined you are exempt from Federal income tax under section 501(c)(3) of the Internal Revenue Code.

Because you are a newly created organization, we are not now making a final determination of your foundation status under section 509(a) of the Code. However, we have determined that you can reasonably be expected to be a publicly supported organization described in section 509(a)(2)

Accordingly, you will be treated as a publicly supported organization, and not as a private foundation, during an advance ruling period. This advance ruling period begins on the date of your inception and ends on the date shown above.

Within 90 days after the end of your advance ruling period, you must submit to us information needed to determine whether you have met the requirements of the applicable support test during the advance ruling period. If you establish that you have been a publicly supported organization, you will be classified as a section 509(a)(1) or 509(a)(2) organization as long as you continue to meet the requirements of the applicable support test. If you do not meet the public support requirements during the advance ruling period, you will be classified as a private foundation for future periods. Also, if you are classified as a private foundation, you will be treated as a private foundation from the date of your inception for purposes of sections 507(d) and 4940.

Grantors and donors may rely on the determination that you are not a private foundation until 90 days after the end of your advance ruling period. If you submit the required information within the 90 days, grantors and donors may continue to rely on the advance determination until the Service makes a final determination of your foundation status. However, if notice that you will no longer be treated as a section 509(a)(2) organization is published in the Internal Revenue Bulletin, grantors and donors may not rely on this determination after the date of such publication. Also, a grantor or donor may not rely on this determination if he or she was in part responsible for, or was aware of, the act or failure to act that resulted in your loss of section 509(a)(2) status, or acquired knowledge that the Internal Revenue Service had given notice that you would be removed from classification as a section 509(a)(2) organization.

If your gross receipts each year are normally more than $5,000, you are required to file Form 990, Return of Organization Exempt From Income Tax, by the 15th day of the fifth month after the end of your annual accounting period. The law imposes a penalty of $10 a day, up to a maximum of $5,000, for failure to file a return on time.

You are not required to file Federal income tax returns unless you are subject to the tax on unrelated business income under section 511 of the Code. If you are subject to this tax, you must file an income tax return on Form 990-T. In this letter we are not determining whether any of your present or proposed activities are unrelated trade or business as defined in section 513 of the Code.

You need an employer identification number even if you have no employees. If an employer identification number was not entered on your application, a number will be assigned to you and you will be advised of it. Please use that number on all returns you file and in all correspondence with the Internal Revenue Service.

Please keep this determination letter in your permanent records.

Sincerely yours,

Gerald G. Portney
District Director

P.O. Box 13163, Baltimore, MD 21203

Letter 1045(DO) (6—77)

---

7. Request for Taxpayer Identification and Certification Form

Exhibit 48. Request for Taxpayer Identification and Certification Form.

| Form **W-9**
(Rev. January 2003)
Department of the Treasury
Internal Revenue Service | **Request for Taxpayer**
Identification Number and Certification | Give form to the
requester. Do not
send to the IRS. |

Print or type **See Specific Instructions on page 2.**

Name

Business name, if different from above

Check appropriate box: ☐ Individual/ Sole proprietor ☐ Corporation ☐ Partnership ☐ Other ▶ .... ☐ Exempt from backup withholding

Address (number, street, and apt. or suite no.)

Requester's name and address (optional)

City, state, and ZIP code

List account number(s) here (optional)

Part I Taxpayer Identification Number (TIN)

Enter your TIN in the appropriate box. For individuals, this is your social security number (SSN). **However, for a resident alien, sole proprietor, or disregarded entity, see the Part I instructions on page 3.** For other entities, it is your employer identification number (EIN). If you do not have a number, see **How to get a TIN** on page 3.

Social security number

or

Employer identification number

Note: *If the account is in more than one name, see the chart on page 4 for guidelines on whose number to enter.*

Part II Certification

Under penalties of perjury, I certify that:

1. The number shown on this form is my correct taxpayer identification number (or I am waiting for a number to be issued to me), **and**

2. I am not subject to backup withholding because: **(a)** I am exempt from backup withholding, or **(b)** I have not been notified by the Internal Revenue Service (IRS) that I am subject to backup withholding as a result of a failure to report all interest or dividends, or **(c)** the IRS has notified me that I am no longer subject to backup withholding, **and**

3. I am a U.S. person (including a U.S. resident alien).

Certification instructions. You must cross out item **2** above if you have been notified by the IRS that you are currently subject to backup withholding because you have failed to report all interest and dividends on your tax return. For real estate transactions, item **2** does not apply. For mortgage interest paid, acquisition or abandonment of secured property, cancellation of debt, contributions to an individual retirement arrangement (IRA), and generally, payments other than interest and dividends, you are not required to sign the Certification, but you must provide your correct TIN. (See the instructions on page 4.)

Sign Here Signature of U.S. person ▶ Date ▶

Purpose of Form

A person who is required to file an information return with the IRS, must obtain your correct taxpayer identification number (TIN) to report, for example, income paid to you, real estate transactions, mortgage interest you paid, acquisition or abandonment of secured property, cancellation of debt, or contributions you made to an IRA.

U.S. person. Use Form W-9 only if you are a U.S. person (including a resident alien), to provide your correct TIN to the person requesting it (the requester) and, when applicable, to:

  1. Certify that the TIN you are giving is correct (or you are waiting for a number to be issued),

  2. Certify that you are not subject to backup withholding, or

  3. Claim exemption from backup withholding if you are a U.S. exempt payee.

  Note: *If a requester gives you a form other than Form W-9 to request your TIN, you must use the requester's form if it is substantially similar to this Form W-9.*

Foreign person. If you are a foreign person, use the appropriate Form W-8 (see **Pub. 515,** Withholding of Tax on Nonresident Aliens and Foreign Entities).

Nonresident alien who becomes a resident alien. Generally, only a nonresident alien individual may use the terms of a tax treaty to reduce or eliminate U.S. tax on certain types of income. However, most tax treaties contain a provision known as a "saving clause." Exceptions specified in the saving clause may permit an exemption from tax to continue for certain types of income even after the recipient has otherwise become a U.S. resident alien for tax purposes.

If you are a U.S. resident alien who is relying on an exception contained in the saving clause of a tax treaty to claim an exemption from U.S. tax on certain types of income, you must attach a statement that specifies the following five items:

  1. The treaty country. Generally, this must be the same treaty under which you claimed exemption from tax as a nonresident alien.

  2. The treaty article addressing the income.

  3. The article number (or location) in the tax treaty that contains the saving clause and its exceptions.

  4. The type and amount of income that qualifies for the exemption from tax.

  5. Sufficient facts to justify the exemption from tax under the terms of the treaty article.

Cat. No. 10231X   Form **W-9** (Rev. 1-2003)

Exhibit 48. (*Continued*)

Example. Article 20 of the U.S.-China income tax treaty allows an exemption from tax for scholarship income received by a Chinese student temporarily present in the United States. Under U.S. law, this student will become a resident alien for tax purposes if his or her stay in the United States exceeds 5 calendar years. However, paragraph 2 of the first Protocol to the U.S.-China treaty (dated April 30, 1984) allows the provisions of Article 20 to continue to apply even after the Chinese student becomes a resident alien of the United States. A Chinese student who qualifies for this exception (under paragraph 2 of the first protocol) and is relying on this exception to claim an exemption from tax on his or her scholarship or fellowship income would attach to Form W-9 a statement that includes the information described above to support that exemption.

If you are a **nonresident alien or a foreign entity** not subject to backup withholding, give the requester the appropriate completed Form W-8.

What is backup withholding? Persons making certain payments to you must under certain conditions withhold and pay to the IRS 30% of such payments (29% **after** December 31, 2003; 28% **after** December 31, 2005). This is called "backup withholding." Payments that may be subject to backup withholding include interest, dividends, broker and barter exchange transactions, rents, royalties, nonemployee pay, and certain payments from fishing boat operators. Real estate transactions are not subject to backup withholding.

You will **not** be subject to backup withholding on payments you receive if you give the requester your correct TIN, make the proper certifications, and report all your taxable interest and dividends on your tax return.

Payments you receive will be subject to backup withholding if:

1. You do not furnish your TIN to the requester, or

2. You do not certify your TIN when required (see the Part II instructions on page 4 for details), or

3. The IRS tells the requester that you furnished an incorrect TIN, or

4. The IRS tells you that you are subject to backup withholding because you did not report all your interest and dividends on your tax return (for reportable interest and dividends only), or

5. You do not certify to the requester that you are not subject to backup withholding under **4** above (for reportable interest and dividend accounts opened after 1983 only).

Certain payees and payments are exempt from backup withholding. See the instructions below and the separate **Instructions for the Requester of Form W-9.**

Penalties

Failure to furnish TIN. If you fail to furnish your correct TIN to a requester, you are subject to a penalty of $50 for each such failure unless your failure is due to reasonable cause and not to willful neglect.

Civil penalty for false information with respect to withholding. If you make a false statement with no reasonable basis that results in no backup withholding, you are subject to a $500 penalty.

Criminal penalty for falsifying information. Willfully falsifying certifications or affirmations may subject you to criminal penalties including fines and/or imprisonment.

Misuse of TINs. If the requester discloses or uses TINs in violation of Federal law, the requester may be subject to civil and criminal penalties.

Specific Instructions

Name

If you are an individual, you must generally enter the name shown on your social security card. However, if you have changed your last name, for instance, due to marriage without informing the Social Security Administration of the name change, enter your first name, the last name shown on your social security card, and your new last name.

If the account is in joint names, list first, and then circle, the name of the person or entity whose number you entered in Part I of the form.

Sole proprietor. Enter your **individual** name as shown on your social security card on the "Name" line. You may enter your business, trade, or "doing business as (DBA)" name on the "Business name" line.

Limited liability company (LLC). If you are a single-member LLC (including a foreign LLC with a domestic owner) that is disregarded as an entity separate from its owner under Treasury regulations section 301.7701-3, **enter the owner's name on the "Name" line.** Enter the LLC's name on the "Business name" line.

Other entities. Enter your business name as shown on required Federal tax documents on the "Name" line. This name should match the name shown on the charter or other legal document creating the entity. You may enter any business, trade, or DBA name on the "Business name" line.

Note: *You are requested to check the appropriate box for your status (individual/sole proprietor, corporation, etc.).*

Exempt From Backup Withholding

If you are exempt, enter your name as described above and check the appropriate box for your status, then check the "Exempt from backup withholding" box in the line following the business name, sign and date the form.

Generally, individuals (including sole proprietors) are not exempt from backup withholding. Corporations are exempt from backup withholding for certain payments, such as interest and dividends.

Note: *If you are exempt from backup withholding, you should still complete this form to avoid possible erroneous backup withholding.*

Exempt payees. Backup withholding is **not required** on any payments made to the following payees:

1. An organization exempt from tax under section 501(a), any IRA, or a custodial account under section 403(b)(7) if the account satisfies the requirements of section 401(f)(2);

2. The United States or any of its agencies or instrumentalities;

3. A state, the District of Columbia, a possession of the United States, or any of their political subdivisions or instrumentalities;

4. A foreign government or any of its political subdivisions, agencies, or instrumentalities; or

5. An international organization or any of its agencies or instrumentalities.

Other payees that **may be exempt** from backup withholding include:

6. A corporation;

7. A foreign central bank of issue;

8. A dealer in securities or commodities required to register in the United States, the District of Columbia, or a possession of the United States;

Exhibit 48. (*Continued*)

9. A futures commission merchant registered with the Commodity Futures Trading Commission;

10. A real estate investment trust;

11. An entity registered at all times during the tax year under the Investment Company Act of 1940;

12. A common trust fund operated by a bank under section 584(a);

13. A financial institution;

14. A middleman known in the investment community as a nominee or custodian; or

15. A trust exempt from tax under section 664 or described in section 4947.

The chart below shows types of payments that may be exempt from backup withholding. The chart applies to the exempt recipients listed above, **1** through **15.**

If the payment is for . . .	THEN the payment is exempt for . . .
Interest and dividend payments	All exempt recipients except for **9**
Broker transactions	Exempt recipients **1** through **13.** Also, a person registered under the Investment Advisers Act of 1940 who regularly acts as a broker
Barter exchange transactions and patronage dividends	Exempt recipients **1** through **5**
Payments over $600 required to be reported and direct sales over $5,000 [1]	Generally, exempt recipients **1** through **7** [2]

[1] See **Form 1099-MISC**, Miscellaneous Income, and its instructions.

[2] However, the following payments made to a corporation (including gross proceeds paid to an attorney under section 6045(f), even if the attorney is a corporation) and reportable on Form 1099-MISC are **not exempt** from backup withholding: medical and health care payments, attorneys' fees; and payments for services paid by a Federal executive agency.

Part I. Taxpayer Identification Number (TIN)

Enter your TIN in the appropriate box. If you are a **resident alien** and you do not have and are not eligible to get an SSN, your TIN is your IRS individual taxpayer identification number (ITIN). Enter it in the social security number box. If you do not have an ITIN, see **How to get a TIN** below.

If you are a **sole proprietor** and you have an EIN, you may enter either your SSN or EIN. However, the IRS prefers that you use your SSN.

If you are a single-owner **LLC** that is disregarded as an entity separate from its owner (see **Limited liability company (LLC)** on page 2), enter your SSN (or EIN, if you have one). If the LLC is a corporation, partnership, etc., enter the entity's EIN.

Note: *See the chart on page 4 for further clarification of name and TIN combinations.*

How to get a TIN. If you do not have a TIN, apply for one immediately. To apply for an SSN, get **Form SS-5,** Application for a Social Security Card, from your local Social Security Administration office or get this form on-line at **www.ssa.gov/online/ss5.html**. You may also get this form by calling 1-800-772-1213. Use **Form W-7,** Application for IRS Individual Taxpayer Identification Number, to apply for an ITIN, or **Form SS-4,** Application for Employer Identification Number, to apply for an EIN. You can get Forms W-7 and SS-4 from the IRS by calling 1-800-TAX-FORM (1-800-829-3676) or from the IRS Web Site at **www.irs.gov**.

If you are asked to complete Form W-9 but do not have a TIN, write "Applied For" in the space for the TIN, sign and date the form, and give it to the requester. For interest and dividend payments, and certain payments made with respect to readily tradable instruments, generally you will have 60 days to get a TIN and give it to the requester before you are subject to backup withholding on payments. The 60-day rule does not apply to other types of payments. You will be subject to backup withholding on all such payments until you provide your TIN to the requester.

Note: *Writing "Applied For" means that you have already applied for a TIN **or** that you intend to apply for one soon.*

Caution: *A disregarded domestic entity that has a foreign owner must use the appropriate Form W-8.*

Exhibit 48. (*Continued*)

Form W-9 (Rev. 1-2003)

Page **4**

Part II. Certification

To establish to the withholding agent that you are a U.S. person, or resident alien, sign Form W-9. You may be requested to sign by the withholding agent even if items 1, 3, and 5 below indicate otherwise.

For a joint account, only the person whose TIN is shown in Part I should sign (when required). Exempt recipients, see **Exempt from backup withholding** on page 2.

Signature requirements. Complete the certification as indicated in **1** through **5** below.

1. Interest, dividend, and barter exchange accounts opened before 1984 and broker accounts considered active during 1983. You must give your correct TIN, but you do not have to sign the certification.

2. Interest, dividend, broker, and barter exchange accounts opened after 1983 and broker accounts considered inactive during 1983. You must sign the certification or backup withholding will apply. If you are subject to backup withholding and you are merely providing your correct TIN to the requester, you must cross out item **2** in the certification before signing the form.

3. Real estate transactions. You must sign the certification. You may cross out item **2** of the certification.

4. Other payments. You must give your correct TIN, but you do not have to sign the certification unless you have been notified that you have previously given an incorrect TIN. "Other payments" include payments made in the course of the requester's trade or business for rents, royalties, goods (other than bills for merchandise), medical and health care services (including payments to corporations), payments to a nonemployee for services, payments to certain fishing boat crew members and fishermen, and gross proceeds paid to attorneys (including payments to corporations).

5. Mortgage interest paid by you, acquisition or abandonment of secured property, cancellation of debt, qualified tuition program payments (under section 529), IRA or Archer MSA contributions or distributions, and pension distributions. You must give your correct TIN, but you do not have to sign the certification.

What Name and Number To Give the Requester

For this type of account:	Give name and SSN of:
1. Individual	The individual
2. Two or more individuals (joint account)	The actual owner of the account or, if combined funds, the first individual on the account [1]
3. Custodian account of a minor (Uniform Gift to Minors Act)	The minor [2]
4. a. The usual revocable savings trust (grantor is also trustee)	The grantor-trustee [1]
b. So-called trust account that is not a legal or valid trust under state law	The actual owner [1]
5. Sole proprietorship or single-owner LLC	The owner [3]

For this type of account:	Give name and EIN of:
6. Sole proprietorship or single-owner LLC	The owner [3]
7. A valid trust, estate, or pension trust	Legal entity [4]
8. Corporate or LLC electing corporate status on Form 8832	The corporation
9. Association, club, religious, charitable, educational, or other tax-exempt organization	The organization
10. Partnership or multi-member LLC	The partnership
11. A broker or registered nominee	The broker or nominee
12. Account with the Department of Agriculture in the name of a public entity (such as a state or local government, school district, or prison) that receives agricultural program payments	The public entity

[1] List first and circle the name of the person whose number you furnish. If only one person on a joint account has an SSN, that person's number must be furnished.

[2] Circle the minor's name and furnish the minor's SSN.

[3] **You must show your individual name,** but you may also enter your business or "DBA" name. You may use either your SSN or EIN (if you have one).

[4] List first and circle the name of the legal trust, estate, or pension trust. (Do not furnish the TIN of the personal representative or trustee unless the legal entity itself is not designated in the account title.)

Note: *If no name is circled when more than one name is listed, the number will be considered to be that of the first name listed.*

Privacy Act Notice

Section 6109 of the Internal Revenue Code requires you to provide your correct TIN to persons who must file information returns with the IRS to report interest, dividends, and certain other income paid to you, mortgage interest you paid, the acquisition or abandonment of secured property, cancellation of debt, or contributions you made to an IRA or Archer MSA. The IRS uses the numbers for identification purposes and to help verify the accuracy of your tax return. The IRS may also provide this information to the Department of Justice for civil and criminal litigation, and to cities, states, and the District of Columbia to carry out their tax laws. We may also disclose this information to other countries under a tax treaty, or to Federal and state agencies to enforce Federal nontax criminal laws and to combat terrorism.

You must provide your TIN whether or not you are required to file a tax return. Payers must generally withhold 30% of taxable interest, dividend, and certain other payments to a payee who does not give a TIN to a payer. Certain penalties may also apply.

Section V. Annotated Bibliography

The following annotated bibliography is not intended to be comprehensive. It is an attempt to provide a sampling of sources of information regarding the process of grant seeking and grant administration. The prices and addresses are always subject to change. We have included only those publications we are familiar with and realize that there are undoubtedly other sources of comparable value that you may want to add to the list.

The search for support possibilities has changed dramatically since the earlier edition of *Ideas* was published. There has been major improvement in the Web sites containing information on Foundation Corporate and government grants. Details on how to apply, suggestions on proposal writing, even detailed requirements for style, typing size, and content appear in grantor's Web site. Do your homework on cost and value of your needs before spending a fortune on expensive publications. Remember most government information is free online. We reviewed a couple of publications, we tested an offer selling for $100 for "important" government phone numbers and found they were a photocopy of the listing in the DC phone book.

Considerable attention has been given to the Foundation Center publications because this nonprofit organization offers the most comprehensive information and service on private foundations. The Foundation Center (http://foundationcenter.org/) operates public reference libraries and ongoing workshops in New York City, with field offices in Atlanta, Cleveland, San Francisco, and Washington, DC. These Foundation Center Libraries have "free" orientation to teach you how to use their library and online resources. It maintains collections in numerous libraries throughout the United States and maintains a catalog of nonprofit literature online. The national offices will gladly give you information on the location of these collections. The staff at the Foundation Center are highly professional and very helpful. E-mail, write, or fax your request to one of the following Foundation Center locations.

Monthly cost for subscription to the Foundation Centers *online* directory begin at $19.95 for a basic directory to $179.95 for the professional directory.

The Foundation Center
79 Fifth Avenue/16th Street
New York, NY 10003-3076
Tel: 212-620-4230
foundationcenter.org/newyork

Field Offices:
Atlanta
50 Hurt Plaza, Suite 150
Atlanta, GA 30303-2914
404-880-0094
foundationcenter.org/atlanta

Cleveland
1422 Euclid Avenue, Suite 1600
Cleveland, OH 44115-2001
216-861-1934
foundationcenter.org/cleveland

San Francisco
312 Sutter Street, Suite 606
San Francisco, CA 94108-4314
415-397-0902
foundationcenter.org/sanfrancisco

Washington, DC
1627 K Street, NW, Third Floor
Washington, DC 20006-1708
202-331-1400
foundationcenter.org/washington

Annual Register of Grant Support $224.00–249.00
http://infotoday.stores.yahoo.net/anregofgrans4.html
Information Today, Inc.
1-609-654-6266

This exhaustive guide to more than 3,500 grant-giving organizations offering nonrepayable support shows you how to tap the immense funding potential of these sources.

American Council on Education
http://www.acenet.edu//AM/Template.cfm?Section=
Home

ACE, the major coordinating body for all the nation's higher education institutions, seeks to provide leadership and a unifying voice on key higher-education issues and to influence public policy through advocacy, research, and program initiatives.

Catalog of Federal Domestic Assistance   Online
http://12.46.245.173/cfda/cfda.html

This is the most essential and basic publication for federal sources of support and grant administration requirements. When secured directly from an agency or the Government Printing Office (GPO), it costs little or is free in many cases, such as over the Internet. The compilations and analyses of grant opportunities by independent organizations and experts are costly. Learn all you can from the direct federal sources such as www.grants.gov/, then test and choose other publications wisely. Examine any costly publication before subscribing to it. The online *Catalog of Federal Domestic Assistance* gives you access to a database of all federal programs available to state and local governments (including the District of Columbia); federally recognized Indian tribal governments; territories (and possessions) of the United States; domestic public, quasi-public, and private profit and nonprofit organizations and institutions; specialized groups; and individuals. After you find the program you want, contact the agency or office that administers the program to find out how to apply. The agency will provide you with more details of the program than the listing in the CFDA.

The Chronicle of Higher	3 years, 147 issues for $203
Education	2 years, 98 issues for $140
	1 year, 49 issues, $82.50

http://chronicle.com/202-466-1000
Fax: 202-452-1033

The Chronicle of Higher Education is academe's number one news resource. A weekly edition prints and mails on Friday, 49 times a year. Subscribers also receive a special *Almanac of Higher Education* once a year and two supplements on forthcoming events in academe. Your print subscription can be registered to receive full access to this Web site and daily news updates by e-mail—all at no extra charge. Or, you may choose to receive a *digital edition* of *The Chronicle*. You still get complete access to the Web site and daily e-mail updates at no extra cost. But rather than have the newspaper mailed to you, a digital equivalent of the newspaper is delivered by e-mail and viewed using your Web browser.

The Chronicle of Philanthropy $72–179 (1–3 years)
http://www.philanthropy.com/

The newspaper of the nonprofit world. It is the number one news source, in print and online, for charity leaders, fund raisers, grant makers, and other people involved in the philanthropic enterprise. In print, *The Chronicle* is published biweekly except the first two weeks in July and the last two weeks in December (a total of 24 issues a year). A subscription includes full access to this Web site and news updates by e-mail—all at no extra charge. An online-only subscription is also available as a *site-license* option, which makes all of *The Chronicle*'s Web site available to everyone at your organization. The *Guide to Grants* is an electronic database of all foundation and corporate grants listed in *The Chronicle* since 1995. *Chronicle* subscribers can search grants from the two most recent issues. Complete access to the *Guide to Grants* requires a separate subscription. *Subscription rates* are available for terms ranging from one week to one year. *Chronicle* subscribers receive a substantial discount. A joint subscription is your best value. A one-year subscription to both services costs less than a subscription to the *Guide to Grants* alone.

Commerce Business Daily (New Name: Online
FedBizOpps, FBO)

http://www.fbodaily.com/archive/2007/02-February/21-
Feb-2007/

FBO is one of the largest sources of governmental bid and award information both online and offline.

For more information call 800-932-7761 or e-mail them at online@cbdweb.com

Congressional Record   Online

http://www.gpoaccess.gov/crecord/index.html

The *Congressional Record* is the official record of the proceedings and debates of the United States Congress. It is published daily when Congress is in session. *GPO Access* contains Congressional Record volumes from 140 (1994) to the present. At the back of each daily issue is the "Daily Digest," which summarizes the day's floor and committee activities. The current year's Congressional Record database is usually updated daily by 11 a.m., except when a late adjournment delays production of the issue. Documents are available as ASCII text and Adobe Portable Document Format (PDF) files.

The Congressional Yellow Book $450/year

http://www.leadershipdirectories.com/products/cyb.htm

The *Congressional Yellow Book* is the nation's leading directory of Congress. Quarterly editions provide subscribers with the most current information available on Members of Congress as well as the key staff members who support them. All of the information listed in the *Congressional Yellow Book* is verified directly with each congressional office listed.

Depository Libraries   Free public access

http://www.gpoaccess.gov/libraries.html

Federal publications and other information products are made available for free public use in Federal depository libraries throughout the United States. In addition to the publications, trained librarians are available to assist in their use.

Educational Resources Informational Center   Online
(ERIC)

http://eric.ed.gov/

Provides free access to more than 1.2 million bibliographic records of journal articles and other education-related materials and, if available, includes links to full text. ERIC is sponsored by the U.S. Department of Education, Institute of Education Sciences (IES). Included on ERIC is CFAE Casebook.

Directory of Educational   Free public access
Associations

http://www.ed.gov/about/contacts/gen/othersites/
associations.html

Education Resource Organizations   Online
Directory

http://wdcrobcolp01.ed.gov/Programs/EROD/

The Education Resource Organizations Directory (EROD) contains information on more than 3,000 national, regional, and state education organizations including many associations that provide information and assistance on a broad range of education-related topics.

Federal Register   Online or hard copy:
                                              $929.00

http://www.gpoaccess.gov/fr/index.html

Published by the Office of the Federal Register, National Archives and Records Administration (NARA), the Federal Register is the official daily publication for rules, proposed rules, and notices of Federal agencies and organizations, as well as executive orders and other presidential documents. Regulations that often translate into

guidelines provide an opportunity for the public to comment and recommend changes on proposed regulations.

The Federal Yellow Book $450/year

http://www.leadershipdirectories.com/products/fyb.htm

The *Federal Yellow Book* is the nation's leading directory of individuals within the executive branch of the federal government located within the Washington, DC, metropolitan area. Quarterly editions provide you with direct contact information for more than 44,000 federal officials. All of the information listed in the *Federal Yellow Book* is verified directly with each organization listed.

Governmental Organizational Manual $52/year

http://www.gpoaccess.gov/gmanual/index.html

Comprehensive information about U.S. government agencies.

Higer Education Directory, 2007 Version	$75/year

http://www.hepinc.com/hed.htm

Successor to the U.S. Department of Education directory. Contains profiles of over 4,000 college and universities. This directory is noted for its accuracy.

Humanities $24/year

http://www.neh.gov/news/humanities.html

The magazine for the National Endowment for the Humanities (NEH).

Association of Fund Raising Professionals

(formerly National Association of Fund Raising Executives)

http://www.afpnet.org/index.cfm

The Association of Fundraising Professionals (AFP) is the professional association of individuals responsible for generating philanthropic support for a wide variety of nonprofit, charitable organizations. Founded in 1960, AFP (formerly the National Society of Fund Raising Executives) advances philanthropy through its nearly 28,000 members in 185 chapters throughout the world.

National Council of University Research Administrators
(NCURA)

http://www.ncura.edu/

A membership organization based in Washington, DC. Excellent training opportunities in person at annual and regional meetings and online. Extensive list of publications and online opportunities related to grant and contract administration. Networking among members provides valuable help for newcomers and specialists. Covers pre- and postaward information and training.

News, Notes and Deadlines	$90/year or $250/year with copyright waived

http://www.acuo.org/N,N&D.htm

Published continuously since 1971, timely deadlines for government and nongovernment grant opportunities. Deadlines are checked immediately before each issue goes to press. Personal consulting services for subscribers and grant seekers at reasonable fees.

National Institute for Health (NIH)

http://www.nih.gov/

Contains information about the National Institutes of Health, research and training opportunities.

Guidelines, forms, and very detailed information on how to apply for NIH grants.

National Science Foundation Bulletin (NSF Bulletin)

http://www.nsf.gov/funding/pgm_list.jsp?org=NSF&ord=date

Active funding opportunities from the National Science Foundation, updated on regular basis.

Public Health Service (PHS)

http://www.hhs.gov/pharmacy/pp/DHHSpresent/ (overview of programs)

PHS is a government agency and one of the seven uniformed services using Navy ranks. PHS has many grant opportunities (search their Web site).

Society of Research Administrators International (SRA)

http://www.srainternational.org/sra03/index.cfm

A membership organization serving research administrators around the world, publishes a journal and a "tool box" of information, articles, resources, and links essentials to successful research management on all levels. Holds annual and regional meetings with training on all levels for seeking and managing grants and contracts. Certification programs course credit is earned and awarded if full SRA membership is in effect at the time the course is taken. Review the SRA Web page for other information relevant to your needs.

Index

About the Authors

JULIA M. JACOBSEN is a retired Research Administrator, Sweet Briar College, Sweet Briar, VA. She has had extensive experience seeking funds and was chair of an organization that sought and made re-grants. She was formerly Director of Government Relations and Sponsored Programs at Sweet Briar College for over twenty years, and prior to that was Special Assistant, Contracts and Grants, at the University of Southern California.

JAN FAY KRESS is Instructor, Department of Occupational Therapy, Howard University.